NIGERIA: CURRENT ISSUES AND HISTORICAL BACKGROUND

NIGERIA: CURRENT ISSUES AND HISTORICAL BACKGROUND

MARTIN P. MATHEWS (EDITOR)

Nigeria/ economic conditions/ 1960 –
Nigeria/ foreign relations / 1960 –
Nigeria/ politics and government /1960–
Nigeria/ social life & customs/ 1960 –

p185-200

Nova Science Publishers, Inc.
New York

Senior Editors: Susan Boriotti and Donna Dennis
Coordinating Editor: Tatiana Shohov
Office Manager: Annette Hellinger
Graphics: Wanda Serrano
Editorial Production: Jennifer Vogt, Matthew Kozlowski, Jonathan Rose and
  Maya Columbus
Circulation: Ave Maria Gonzalez, Raymond Davis and Vladimir Klestov
Communications and Acquisitions: Serge P. Shohov
Marketing: Cathy DeGregory

Library of Congress Cataloging-in-Publication Data
Available Upon Request

ISBN: 1-59033-316-0.

Copyright © 2002 by Nova Science Publishers, Inc.
            400 Oser Ave, Suite 1600
            Hauppauge, New York 11788-3619
            Tele. 631-231-7269   Fax 631-231-8175
            e-mail: Novascience@earthlink.net
            Web Site: http://www.novapublishers.com

Printed in the United States of America

CONTENTS

Preface   vii

Nigeria in Political Transition   1
    Theodros Dagne

Nigeria   17
    Godfrey Mwakikagile

Problems and Prospects of Sustaining Democracy in Nigeria   51
    Bamidele A. Ojo

Curriculum and Administrative Innovations for the
Nigerian Educational System in the Twenty-First Century   57
    Zephyrinus C. Okonkwo

Managing Nigeria's Economic System in the Third Republic   71
    Adepoju Adeleke

Nigeria: A Country Study   81
    Helen Chapin Metz (Editor)

Glossary -- Nigeria   181

Bibliography -- Nigeria   185

Index   201

PREFACE

Nigeria seems in the news all the time for something, be it regime changes, cooperation, internal strife or oil policies. The most populous country In Africa and the largest in area of the West African states, Nigeria was an early twentieth century colony that became an independent nation in 1960. A country of great diversity because of the many ethnic, linguistic, and religious groups that live within its borders, Nigeria is also a country with a long past. This book brings together current issues and a detailed historical background.

NIGERIA IN POLITICAL TRANSITION

Theodros Dagne

SUMMARY

On June 8, 1998, General Sani Abacha, the military leader who took power in Nigeria in 1993, died of a reported heart attack and was replaced by General Abdulsalam Abubakar. On July 7, 1998, Moshood Abiola, the believed winner of the 1993 presidential election, also died of a heart attack during a meeting with U.S. officials. General Abubakar released political prisoners and initiated political, economic, and social reforms. He also established a new independent electoral commission and outlined a schedule for elections and transition to civilian rule, pledging to hand over power to an elected civilian government by May 1999.

In late February 1999, former military leader General Olusegun Obasanjo was elected president and was sworn in on May 29, 1999. Obasanjo won 62.8% of the votes (18.7 million), while his challenger, Chief Olu Falae received 37.2% of the votes (11.1 million). In the Senate elections, the People's Democratic Party (PDP) won 58% of the votes, the All People's Party (APP) 23%, and the Alliance for Democracy (AD) 19%. In the elections for the House of Representatives, PDP received 59% of the votes, AD 22%, and APP 20%.

The international community welcomed the election of Obasanjo as president. The European Union restored full cooperation with Nigeria and lifted sanctions that were imposed to punish the Abacha government. The Commonwealth moved swiftly and readmitted Nigeria as a member, after 3 years of suspension.

Relations between the United States and Nigeria improved with the transfer of power to a civilian government. In late October 1999, President Obasanjo met with President Clinton and other senior officials in Washington. President Clinton pledged substantial increase in U.S. assistance to Nigeria. In August 2000, President Clinton paid a state visit to Nigeria. He met with President Obasanjo in Abuja and addressed the Nigerian parliament. Several new U.S. initiatives were announced, including increased support for AIDS prevention and treatment programs in Nigeria and enhanced trade and commercial development.

In May 2001, President Obasanjo met with President Bush and other senior officials in Washington. The two presidents discussed a wide range of issues, including trade, peacekeeping, and the HIV/AIDS crisis in Africa. President Bush pledged $200 million into a new global fund for HIV/AIDS. In fiscal year 2001, Nigeria received $77.7 million in economic and development assistance. The Bush Administration has requested $66.2 million for FY2003. In early November 2001, President Obasanjo paid a visit to Washington to express his government's support for the U.S.-led anti-terrorism campaign.

Nigeria continues to make progress in strengthening its fragile democracy but faces serious economic challenges. With a population of over 126 million, Nigeria remains relatively stable, although ethnic and religious clashes in some parts of the country have led to massive displacement of civilian populations. Thousands of civilians have been killed over the past several years and many more wounded in religious clashes.

Economic conditions remain poor, despite serious efforts by the Obasanjo government. Revenues from oil account for more than 90% of foreign exchange earnings and 65% of budget revenues. Meanwhile, high unemployment rate continues to pose serious challenge to the government.

Most Recent Developments

Safiya Hussaini, a woman sentenced to be stoned to death for adultery in October 2001 by a Sharia court in Sokoto, Nigeria, has appealed her sentence and is currently awaiting a ruling. The case was adjourned until March 25, 2002. Hussaini's lawyers argued that she was impregnated by her former husband and that the affair took place before Sharia law was enacted. The State prosecutors asserted that Sharia law should be applied retroactively in this particular case.

In early February 2001, an estimated 100 people were killed and several hundred wounded in religious and ethnic violence in Lagos, Nigeria.

Background and Analysis
Current Issues

In late May 1999, General Obasanjo was sworn in as president of a new civilian government. In his inaugural address, President Obasanjo said he is prepared to restore confidence in government, deal with the growing economic crisis, and tackle corruption. In late June, the Nigerian Senate approved 42 of the 49 cabinet members submitted for confirmation by President Obasanjo.

In early June 1999, the Commonwealth readmitted Nigeria as member, after 3 years of suspension. The European Union also restored full economic cooperation with Nigeria. In July, a court in Abuja convicted the Speaker of the House of Representatives after he pleaded guilty to perjury and forgery. The Speaker was forced to resign from Nigeria's 469-member national assembly after admitting that he lied about his age and educational qualifications.

In mid-August 1999, Energy Secretary Bill Richardson visited Nigeria and met with senior government officials. In late September, the Associate Administrator of the Federal Airports Administration (FAA), Admiral Cathal Flynn, visited Nigeria to discuss the status of the Murtala Mohammed International Airport in Lagos. The United States suspended flights to Lagos because of security concerns. On December 22, 1999, the Department of Transportation removed the suspension after Nigeria met all safety requirements.

In mid-October 1999, Secretary of State Albright visited Nigeria and met with senior government officials and civil society groups. At a press briefing following her Africa tour, Secretary Albright stated that the government and people of Nigeria are "engaged in a dramatic and high-stakes struggle to establish a viable democratic system." She said President Obasanjo "appears truly committed to jump-starting the economy, fighting corruption and resolving regional problems that remain a source of unrest within Nigeria."

In late October 1999, President Obasanjo met with President Clinton and other senior government officials in Washington. At a White House press briefing, President Clinton said that "it is very much in America's interests that Nigeria succeed, and therefore we should assist them in their success. We intend to increase our assistance to Nigeria to expand law-enforcement cooperation and to work toward an agreement to stimulate trade and investment between us. We intend to do what we can to help Nigeria recover assets plundered by the previous regime." President Clinton stated that the United States will support "generous debt rescheduling through the Paris Club and encourage other countries to take further steps."

In late October, Nigeria's Zamfara state introduced Islamic *Sharia* law. The introduction of *Sharia* law has triggered sharp reaction from non-Muslims in other parts of Nigeria. In early November, the Cross River state passed a non-binding resolution declaring the area a Christian state in protest of Zamfara state's action.

Between February and May 2000, more than 500 were killed in Kaduna in northern Nigeria in violence triggered by the proposal to introduce *Sharia* by Muslims. The violence was triggered in reaction to a proposal to introduce *Sharia* by Moslems. Following Zamfar State which began implementing *Sharia* in January 2000, the states of Niger and Sokoto adopted *Sharia* in February. As of August 2000, several more states, including Kano, Katsina, Jigawa, Yobe, and Borno have adopted *Sharia*. (Details available on the BBC News Web site at [gttp://news.bbc.co.uk/low/english/world/africa/newsid_924000/924573.stm].) Despite assurances by authorities in these states that *Sharia* would not apply on non-Moslems, Christian groups complain about restrictions as a result of the new law. President Obasanjo vowed to punish the perpetrators of the violence and assured Nigerians that the security services would restore law and order. President Obasanjo stated in late August 2000 that the best way to respond to *Sharia* was to ignore it: "I think *Sharia* will fizzle out. To confront it is to keep it alive."

In late June, Nigeria and the United States established a new organization to promote trade and investment. The U.S. and Nigeria Trade and Investment Council was inaugurated in late June in the Nigerian capital, Abuja. According to U.S. Deputy Trade Representative Susan Esserman, "the Council shall focus on removing impediments to trade, developing and implementing concrete strategies to strengthen reforms and achieve economic diversification and growth." In February 2000, Nigeria and the United States signed a trade and investment agreement in Washington.

In mid-May, the Economic Community of West African States (ECOWAS) decided to send an estimated 3,000 troops to the war-torn west African country of Sierra Leone. Nigeria was expected to contribute the majority of the 3,000 troops and take command of the West African force in Sierra Leone.

Swiss officials said that about 120 accounts in Zurich and Geneva have been frozen In early April 2000, Swiss officials charged a businessman for falsifying documents to open a bank account in Geneva for the Abacha family. According to the New York Times, the unidentified businessman is Dharam Vir of New Delhi, India. In mid-May, 2000, President Obasanjo announced that his government has recovered $200 million public funds looted by former Nigerian dictator Abacha and his associates. In July, Nigerian authorities announced that Swiss officials have transferred $64.36 million of the looted money to the Central Bank of Nigeria.

In early April, Secretary of Defense William Cohen met with President Obasanjo in Abuja and reportedly pledged $10 million to Nigeria in military aid, including an increase in the International Military Education Training (IMET) program.

In a meeting with President Obasanjo in Abuja on August 26, 2000, President Clinton stated that the U.S. is "committed to working with the people of Nigeria to help build stronger institutions, improve education, fight disease, crime and corruption, ease the burden of debt and promote trade and investment in a way that brings more of the benefits of prosperity to people who have embraced democracy." President Clinton also made an unprecedented address before the Nigerian parliament in which he underscored the major issues facing the country today. Among them were democratization and ethnic and religious strife.

In late February 2001, direct flight from Lagos, Nigeria, to New York resumed after several delays. The direct flight to New York is a joint venture between Nigeria Airways and South African Airways. According to Nigerian officials, flight resumption "signifies the further strengthening of relationship between Nigeria, the United States, and South Africa and these relationships have positive political, social, and economic implications.

In its Country Reports on Human Rights Practices for 2000, issued in late February, the State Department stated that Nigeria's "human rights record was poor; although there were some improvements in several areas during the year, serious problems remain. The national police, army, and security forces continued to commit extrajudicial killings and used excessive force to quell civil unrest and ethnic violence, although they did so less frequently than under previous military governments."

On February 27, 2001, President Obasanjo stated that he would remove all subsidies from petroleum products, as part of an overhaul of the energy sector and would increase subsidies for education, health and water services. President Obasanjo gave a major televised address to the nation in late December 2000, marking the first anniversary of his government. Obasanjo gave an overview of his government's achievements of the past 12 months and outlined his agenda for the future. The president acknowledged that serious challenges face the country, including growing ethnic and religious clashes. He stated that Nigeria will continue its peacekeeping role in West Africa.

In late April 2001, 47 African leaders met in Abjua, the capital, to discuss the AIDS crisis in Africa. U.N. Secretary General Kofi Annan called on donor governments to provide at least $7 billion to combat AIDS in Africa. Former President Bill Clinton, who attended the summit, also urged donor countries to assist in combating AIDS. Secretary of State Colin Powell, who was expected to attend the summit, did not go due to conflict in his schedule, according to the State Department.

In May 2001, President Obasanjo met with President Bush and other senior officials in Washington. President Bush stated that the United States is "in the process of helping provide technical assistance to Nigerian troops so that they are better able to keep those peace missions." At a joint White House press conference, President Bush pledged $200 million into a new global fund for HIV/AIDS. President Obasanjo said he discussed a number of issues of mutual interest, including the conflicts in Angola, Democratic Republic of Congo, and Sierra Leone.

In late July 2001, the government of Nigeria announced a major AIDS treatment program. President Obasanjo declared that his government would provide cheap generic drugs to AIDS patients beginning September 1, 2001. Patients are expected to pay about $7 a month. Nigeria's Health Minister negotiated a $350,000 deal with Cipla, an Indian pharmaceutical company.

In early September 2001, clashes broke out between Muslims and Christians in the city of Jos in northern Nigeria. An estimated 500 people were killed in the clashes and thousands more were injured. Meanwhile, tens of thousands of civilians have reportedly fled their homes for other locations. President Obasanjo sent the army to restore order.

In mid-September 2001, President Obasanjo strongly condemned the terrorist attacks on the World Trade Center and the Pentagon and expressed his support in combating terrorism. Obasanjo described the attacks as "callous and dastardly." The Nigerian House of Representatives also condemned the attacks, calling the terrorist action "an act of terrorism against humanity."

In late November 2001, the Obasanjo government announced that Nigeria has 8.7% of the world's AIDS cases. According to government figures, the number of cases has increased from 2.7 million in 1999 to 3.47 million in 2001. In early December 2001, Nigeria began to distribute cheap generic drugs to people with AIDS/HIV. The government plans to distribute anti-retroviral drugs to an estimated 10,000 patients.

In early November 2001, President Obasanjo met with President Bush in Washington to express his government's support for the U.S.-led anti-terrorism campaign. At a press conference, Presidents Bush and Obasanjo pledged to work together. President Bush said that Obasanjo "has been a steadfast friend of the United States government and the United States people, before and after September 11th, and for that we are most grateful." In response, President Obasanjo stated that he came to the United States "to express solidarity, to express support, to express condolences for the terrorist attack on this country, on innocent people of all faiths and of all races on the 11th of September."

In late December 2001, Nigerian Justice Minister Bola Ige was murdered by unknown gunmen. A suspect in the murder of Ige surrendered to Nigerian authorities in mid-January. In early January, a senior aide to Nigeria's Chief Justice was found dead in Abuja. The Chief Justice stated that the killing of his aide appeared to be murder.

In late January 2002, an estimated 500 people were killed after a huge explosion at an army munitions dump in Lagos, Nigeria's largest city with a population of 15 million. According to press reports, most of those killed were civilians. President Obasanjo has ordered a full investigation.

HISTORICAL AND POLITICAL BACKGROUND

Nigeria, the most populous nation in Africa with an estimated 107 million people, has been in political turmoil and economic crisis intermittently since independence in October 1960. The current borders were demarcated by British colonial rulers in 1914, on the eve of World War I, by merging the British dependencies of Northern and Southern Nigeria into a single territory with promising economic prospects. The new Nigeria, as defined by the British, placed over 250 distinct ethnic groups under a single administrative system. Of this large number of groups, ten account for nearly 80% of the total population, and the northern Hausa-Fulani, the southwestern Yoruba, and the southeastern Ibo, have traditionally been the most politically active and dominant. Since gaining independence from Britain in 1960, Nigerian political life has been scarred by conflict along both ethnic and geographic lines, marked most notably by largely northern and Hausa domination of the military and the Biafran secession movement and civil war fought by the Ibo from 1967 to 1970. Questions persist as to whether or not Nigeria and its multitude of ethnic groups can be held together as one nation, particularly in light of the degree to which misrule has undermined the authority and legitimacy of the state apparatus; but many Nigerians feel a significant degree of national pride and belief in Nigeria as a state.

Nigeria's political life has been dominated by military coups and long military-imposed transition programs to civilian rule. The military has ruled Nigeria for approximately 28 of its 41 years since independence. In August 1985, General Ibrahim Babangida ousted another military ruler, General Muhammadu Buhari, and imposed a transition program that lasted until June 1993, when Nigeria held its first election in almost a decade, believed to be won by Chief Moshood K. O. Abiola, a Yoruba businessman from the south. In the same month, General Babangida annulled the presidential election because of what he called "irregularities in the voting" and ordered a new election with conditions that Abiola and his challenger be excluded from participating. Amid confusion and growing political unrest Babangida handed over power to a caretaker government in August 1993, then ousted the caretaker the following November.

General Sani Abacha took power in November 1993. Abacha had been an active participant in several Nigerian military coups and was an authoritarian figure who seemed unmoved by international opinion. Since 1995, Abacha had imprisoned hundreds of critics, including former military leader Olusegun Obasanjo, the only Nigerian military leader to have handed over power voluntarily to an elected civilian government, and Moshood Abiola, who was charged with treason after declaring himself president following the annulled election. The senior wife of Abiola, Kudirat Abiola, was assassinated in June 1996 by unidentified men. Her daughter blamed the military junta.

In October 1995, under pressure to implement political reforms, Abacha announced a 3-year transition program to civilian rule, which he tightly controlled until his death on June 8, 1998. Abacha established the National Electoral Commission of Nigeria (NECON), which published guidelines for party registration, recognized five political parties in September 1996 and officially dissolved opposition groups after refusing to recognize them. The military professed its support for Abacha should he seek reelection as a civilian, and by April 20, 1998, all five parties had nominated Abacha as the single presidential candidate despite pressure by the international community and dissident groups. Major opposition figures, especially those in exile, dismissed the transition program and called for boycotts of the parliamentary and presidential elections. Only candidates from among the five state-sanctioned political parties participated in state assembly elections held in December 1997 and parliamentary elections held on April 25, 1998. The United Nigeria Congress Party (UNCP), considered by many government opponents to be the army's proxy, won widespread victories.

TRANSITION TO CIVILIAN RULE

Abacha died, reportedly of a heart attack, on June 8, 1998. The Provisional Ruling Council quickly nominated Major General Abdulsalam Abubakar to assume the presidency. General Abubakar, a career serviceman from the Northern Hausa-speaking elite, was regarded as a military intellectual. He served as chief of military intelligence under General Ibrahim Babangida and was Abacha's chief of staff. He led the investigations of reported coup attempts by former President Olusegun Obasanjo and Lt. General Oladipo Diya, charges that, critics argue, were fabricated by the government. Following Abacha's death, General Abubakar addressed the nation and expressed his commitment to uphold the October 1998 hand-over date to civilian government established by Abacha. In an effort to prove his commitment, Abubakar released several prominent political prisoners, including General Olusegun Obasanjo.

Nigeria At A Glance

Population: 126.6 million
Independence: October 1960
Comparative Area: Slightly more than twice the size of California
Religions: 50% Muslim, 40% Christian, 10% Indigenous beliefs
Languages: English (official)
GDP: $117 billion (2000)
GDP Per Capita: $950 (2000)
Unemployment rate: 28% (1992)
Exports: $22.2 billion (1999)
Imports: $10.7 billion (1999
External Debt: $32 billion (1999)

Source: The World Fact book, 2001

Immediately following Abacha's death, pro-democracy leaders demanded that Abiola be released from prison and be declared the legitimate ruler of Nigeria. To mark the fifth anniversary of the annulled elections, many dissidents protested and demanded the release of Abiola in spite of a ban on demonstrations by the government. Reports of secret talks between top government officials and Abiola led many observers to believe that the government intended to release Abiola on the condition that he renounce his claim to the presidency. Government officials granted U.N. Secretary-General Kofi Annan an audience with Abiola in which Annan reportedly attempted to persuade Abiola to give up his title in order to earn immediate release. Annan reported that Abiola had agreed to renounce his title and cooperate with the transition program, and the government promised to release all political prisoners, including Abiola. However, a letter reportedly written by Abiola and published after his death called into question the accuracy of Annan's report. According to Abiola, Annan behaved like a "Nigerian diplomat" who wanted him to relinquish the title for which he and his supporters had fought over the past 5 years.

During a meeting with a U.S. delegation led by Undersecretary of State Thomas Pickering on July 7, 1998, Abiola suffered a heart attack and died soon after. Pro-democracy leaders immediately claimed that Abiola was murdered. The autopsy report, monitored by an independent team of Canadian, American, and British doctors, confirmed that Abiola died of natural causes due to a long-standing heart condition and that death as a result of poisoning was highly unlikely. Many observers said, however, that Abiola's care was deliberately neglected, resulting in his early demise. His death crushed the hopes of many democracy supporters and spurred riots for several days.

Abubakar replaced several of Abacha's top advisors in the military hierarchy with men of his own choosing, and began to establish a framework for the transition to civilian rule. On July 20, 1998, General Abubakar admitted that the October 1998 hand-over date established by Abacha was unrealistic in light of the disruption caused by his death. He announced in a public speech a series of political and economic reforms that his government would implement before handing over power to an elected civilian government on the new official date of May 29, 1999. In an early effort to demonstrate his government's commitment to reconciliation, General Abubakar announced the release of all political detainees and decided to "withdraw all charges against political offenders."

Although politicians and leading opposition figures have generally welcomed the transition program, many were disappointed that Abubakar rejected their call for a national unity government. The leader of the National Democratic Coalition of Nigeria (NADECO), a leading opposition group, proposed a sovereign conference to decide how the different ethnic groups should be represented to draft a constitution for the nation as a whole, at which point elections would be held. Abubakar rejected this suggestion, saying that it replaces one unelected government with another, that the process would take too long, and that "such an arrangement is full of pitfalls and dangers, which this administration cannot accept."

In August and September, Abubakar undertook rapid and dramatic reforms to the Nigerian political system and economy. He replaced Abacha's top security staff and cabinet and dissolved the five political parties that Abacha had established. He abolished major decrees banning trade union activity, which had been used by Abacha to put down the political strikes that followed the nullification of the 1993 election results and ended treason charges against Nobel Prize-winning writer Wole Soyinka and 14 others. Abubakar has also made a concerted effort to appeal to Nigerians in exile to return home and assist in the transition process, and many have done so, most notably Nobel-Prize-winning author Wole Soyinka in mid-October. Journalists reported that freedom of the press improved during Abubakar's tenure. On September 7, Abubakar released the draft constitution for the next civilian government, which Abacha had kept secret, but announced on October 1 that he was setting up a committee to organize and collate views from various sections of the country, after which he would finalize changes to the draft document in order to make it "more representative and acceptable." In early May 1999, the government approved an updated version of the 1979 Nigerian constitution instead of the constitution drafted by the Abacha regime.

Abubakar outlined a specific timetable for the transition to civilian rule, with local polls on December 5, 1998, gubernatorial and state polls on January 9, followed by national assembly polls on February 20, 1999, and presidential polls on February 27. The official hand-over date was set for May 29, 1999. He also nullified all of the previous state and gubernatorial elections because they were held under the Abacha system, and dismissed the

National Electoral Commission established by Abacha, replacing it with one of his own, the Independent National Electoral Commission (INEC), in early August. Political party registration for elections ended after an extension on October 12, and the INEC released the names of the nine registered parties on October 19. The three major parties are the People's Democratic Party (PDP), the All People's Party (APP), and the Alliance for Democracy (AD). In order to be registered, a party must be considered "national," defined as having offices in at least two-thirds of the 36 states that make up Nigeria, and furthermore must win at least 10% of votes in two-thirds of the states in the local elections in December in order to qualify a candidate for the national elections in February. Abubakar warned of the dangers of a "proliferation of political parties with parochial orientation, that may lead to disunity and instability," while urging political leadership to represent the will of people of all tribes and ethnicities.

Highlights of Abubakar's Transition Program

Rejected:
National Conference
National Unity Government

Accomplished:
Debt relief talks with World Bank and IMF
Release of all political prisoners
Dissolution of old electoral commission and establishment of new Independent National Electoral Commission
Dissolution of old political parties and registration of new parties
Voter registration
Annulment of elections under Abacha
Most political prisoners freed
Greater freedom of press, human rights better
Publicized and amended 1995 constitution
Dismissed Abacha officials and began investigation into misappropriated funds
Exiled dissidents returned home
Better-paid civil servants to combat corruption
Repairs started on refineries, more oil imported, privatization program started
Hand-over May 29, 1999
Presidential elections February 27, 1999
National assembly elections February 20, 1999
State/Gubernatorial elections January 9, 1999
Local elections December 5, 1998. partial lifting of international sanctions

Abubakar announced in a public speech on October 1 that the election commission had already met delegates from the United Nations and the Commonwealth to discuss ways of ensuring free and fair elections in February. Registration of an expected 60 million voters began in early October and lasted until October 19. Despite television advertisements taken out by the INEC and assurances that the lists of voters were checked and cross-checked in order to prevent any faults or double registration, the process was reportedly marked by fraud and controversy. INEC members cited unconfirmed reports that their officials were being bribed to hand over piles of cards to representatives from political parties, in order to improve their changes in the upcoming elections (BBC, October 14, 1998). These accounts were in addition to complaints of shortages of cards in certain areas and that the registration offices were not open at regular hours in certain states. Although the INEC had denied responsibility, political parties and leaders accused the commission of poor preparation and ineptitude.

The international community cautiously welcomed the transition program. Donor governments in Europe expressed support and urged transparency. French, British, and German delegations met with the Nigerian leadership in Abuja, the capital, in late July, and Abubakar has made numerous trips abroad in an effort to improve relations with African and world leaders. The European Union announced in late October 1998 that, effective November 1, some sanctions would be relaxed. The visa ban was officially removed and some officials indicated that even the military measures might be lifted after the official hand-over date in May. On May 31, 1999, the European Union restored full economic cooperation with Nigeria. In late May, the Commonwealth also readmitted Nigeria as a member, after 3 years of suspension.

Elections

In early December 1998, the PDP won in 389 out of 774 municipalities in local elections, while the All People's Party (APP) came a distant second with 182, followed by Alliance for Democracy. In the governorship elections in early January, the PDP won 21 states out of 36, the APP won in nine states, and the AD won in six states. Shortly after the elections in January, the APP and AD began talks to merge the two political parties. However, the Independent Electoral Commission rejected a merger but agreed that the two parties "can present common candidates" for the presidential elections.

In mid-February, the People Democratic Party nominated General Olusegun Obasanjo as its presidential candidate. Obasanjo won the support of more than two-thirds of the 2,500 delegates and a northerner, Abubakar Atiku, who was elected governor in the January elections, was chosen as his running mate. The APP and AD nominated Chief Olu Falae, a Yoruba, as their joint candidate for president. A former Nigerian security chief and a northerner, Chief Umaru Shinakfi, was chosen as Falae's running mate.

In late February 1999, General Obasanjo was elected president by a wide margin. Obasanjo won 62.8% of the votes (18.7 million), while his challenger, Chief Olu Falae received 37.2% of the votes (11.1 million). In the Senate elections, the PDP won 58% of the votes, APP 23%, and AD 19%. In the elections for the House of Representatives, PDP received 59% of the votes, AD 22%, and APP 20%.

On May 29, 1999, Obasanjo was sworn in president and the Nigerian Senate approved 42 of 49 members of his cabinet. In his inaugural address, President Obasanjo said that "the entire Nigerian scene is very bleak indeed. So bleak people ask me where do we begin? I know what great things you expect of me at this New Dawn. As I have said many times in my extensive travels in the country, I am not a miracle worker. It will be foolish to underrate the task ahead. Alone, I can do little."

CURRENT ECONOMIC AND SOCIAL CONDITIONS

Western officials believe that Sani Abacha may have stolen over $3.5 billion over the course of his 5 years in power. Abacha's former national security adviser, Ismaila Gwarzo, has been connected to the disappearance of $2.45 billion from the Nigerian Central Bank. Due in large part to large-scale theft from the Nigerian Treasury, the education system is collapsing, industry has idled, refineries are in poor conditions, and the sixth-largest oil-producing country in the world suffers from severe fuel shortages. The Nigerian economy depends heavily on oil revenues; about 20% of Nigeria's GDP comes from petroleum and petroleum products, which also represent 95% of its foreign exchange earnings and 65% of its budgetary revenues (*CIA World Factbook, 2001*). The European Union is a major trading partner, and the United States imports more oil from sub-Saharan Africa, primarily Nigeria, than from the Middle East. Oil prices are currently low and expected to drop further, which could lead to even more severe consequences for the Nigerian economy.

The state of the economy has most affected the poorest segments of the population, and has sparked violence around the country, particularly in the oil-producing regions. Several thousand people have been killed in pipeline explosions in southeast Nigeria since July, though the largest single toll from an explosion was approximately 1,000 in October of 1999. These explosions result from the siphoning off of oil from holes punched in the above-ground pipeline. Ethnic clashes over rights to a promising oil prospect in the southwest also killed hundreds of people in September and October 1999. In the Niger Delta, youths from the ethnic Ijaw tribe have stopped the flow of one-third of Nigeria's oil exports of more than two million barrels per day in order to protest sub-standard living conditions in the country's richest oil-producing region. The government established a national task force on surveillance of petroleum pipelines in order to prevent a recurrence of the pipeline explosion tragedy.

As part of his reforms, Abubakar launched a long-promised privatization program and he also implemented measures to ease the fuel shortage, increasing the number of firms importing oil and beginning repairs on state-owned refineries. Money owed to oil companies was paid under Abubakar, and he gave contracts for new oil imports to established firms, not presidential acquaintances. The pay for civil servants was also increased in an effort to lower the high level of corruption present in all levels of government, and Abubakar ordered open bidding for all government contracts. Abubakar also recovered money stolen and misappropriated during the Abacha regime. The Abacha family had reportedly surrendered $750 million to the government and former national security adviser Ismaila Gwarzo turned over more than $250 million. To recover funds, the military junta used quiet pressure rather than the threat of imprisonment. Observers reported that Abubakar was concerned about initiating too broad an inquiry, since an investigation could implicate almost the entire army hierarchy and spark another coup (Associated Press, November 1, 1998).

ISSUES IN U.S.-NIGERIAN RELATIONS

Background

Relations between the United States and Nigeria began to deteriorate with the annulment of the 1993 elections by the military junta. Three issues dominated U.S.-Nigerian relations: the absence of democracy, human rights abuses, and drug trafficking. Washington took a series of measures against the military junta shortly after the 1993 election results were annulled. These included suspending development assistance, terminating joint military training with Nigeria, and imposing visa restrictions of Nigeria's military leaders and their family members, but did not affect trade between U.S. companies and Nigeria. Washington was also engaged in diplomatic efforts, albeit unsuccessful, to break the political impasse in the West African nation. The Clinton Administration sent civil rights leader Jesse Jackson, then-U.N. Ambassador Bill Richardson, and former Ambassador Donald McHenry as envoys to convince Abacha to implement reforms.

In response to the execution of nine Ogoni activists in 1995, the Clinton Administration recalled its ambassador and pushed a resolution at the U.N. General Assembly that condemned Nigeria's action. The imprisonment of Moshood Abiola and many others was a contentious issue in U.S.-Nigerian relations. In its Country Report on Human Rights Practices for 1997, the Department of State wrote: "The human rights record remained dismal. Throughout the year, Abacha's Government relied regularly on arbitrary detention and harassment to silence its most outspoken critics." The report further stated that security forces "continued to commit extrajudicial killings and use excessive force to quell anti-government protests as well as to combat crime, resulting in the death or injury of many individuals, including innocent civilians." Human rights groups reported the torture of prisoners and constant harassment of journalists under the Abacha regime.

Washington's concern was not limited to human rights abuse allegations. Drug trafficking by Nigeria has emerged as a major issue in U.S.-Nigerian relations since the mid-1980s. Although Nigeria is not a drug-producing country, it has become a major transit point. An estimated 35-40% of all the heroin coming into the United States is brought by Nigerian couriers. In 1989, the United States and Nigeria established a joint Counter-Narcotics Task Force. Lack of cooperation by Nigerian authorities in combating the drug trafficking problem led to a decision by the Clinton Administration in March 1998, as in 1994 and 1996, to put Nigeria on the State Department's list of non-cooperative drug trafficking nations, which includes Burma and Iran. As a consequence, the U.S. had to vote "no" on all loans to Nigeria being considered by the World Bank and the African Development Bank, and Nigeria was ineligible for any Export-Import Bank financing of U.S. exports.

In March 2000, however, President Clinton provided a waiver, a Vital National Interests Certification, for Nigeria in order to allow support for the democratic transition program. According to the U.S. Drug Enforcement Agency (DEA), Nigeria's anti narcotic efforts remain "unfocused and lacking in material support." According to the DEA (Lagos), despite the new government's efforts in dealing with the problem, "Nigerian law enforcement agencies did not significantly improve their counter-drug performance in 1999" [http://www.usembassy.state.gov/ nigeria/]. Nigerian authorities point to the government's active cooperation with U.S. officials and increased funds appropriated by the Nigerian government to fight drug trafficking. In March 2001, however, the Bush Administration certified that Nigeria was fully cooperating with U.S. officials. According to a U.S. embassy (Lagos) press release, "in spite of continued problems with corruption and a weak judicial system, the Nigerian government has shown a commitment to improving its efforts in fighting organized crime and drug trafficking [http://usembassy.state. gov/nigeria]."

Through legislative action, Members of Congress were active concerning Nigeria. In 1994, the House of Representatives passed H.Con.Res. 151, which called for additional measures against the military junta by the Clinton Administration. A bill calling for the imposition of sanctions and freezing of assets was introduced in 1996 by then-Senator Nancy Kassebaum and Representative Donald Payne. Although the bill enjoyed significant bipartisan support, it did not move out of committees, in part because of opposition by Members of Congress who favor dialogue with the Nigerian government. Pro-Nigerian groups and some American business interests actively opposed the bill (*The Washington Post*, November 24, 1996). The Nigerian Democracy Act, introduced by Representative Donald Payne and Representative Amo Houghton in 1997 (to be discussed below), contained similar provisions, including a ban on new U.S. corporate investment in Nigeria. In May 1998 House International Relations Committee Chairman Benjamin A. Gilman and Representative Donald M. Payne introduced the Nigerian Democracy and Civil Society Empowerment Act (H.R. 3890), calling for additional sanctions and increased U.S. aid to democratic opposition groups. The bill was also introduced in the Senate in May 1998 by Senators Feingold, Jeffords, Leahy, and Wellstone. The bill was sent to committees in both houses, but the 105th Congress did not act further on either piece of legislation.

Conflicts within the Clinton Administration regarding the appropriate strategy toward Nigeria while under the control of Abacha surfaced in speeches given by senior Administration officials and President Clinton in early 1998. Assistant Secretary of State for African Affairs Dr. Susan Rice stated in a speech on March 17, 1998, that the United States would hold "General Abacha to his 3-year-old promise to undertake a genuine transition to civilian rule this year and to establish a level playing field by allowing free political activity, providing for an open press, and ending political detention. Let me state clearly and unequivocally to you today that an election victory by any military candidate in the forthcoming presidential elections would be unacceptable." In late March, President Clinton stated that U.S. policy toward Nigeria was "to do all that we can to persuade General Abacha to move toward general democracy and respect for human rights, release of political prisoners, and the holding of elections." Referring to General Abacha's rumored candidacy, however, President Clinton seemed to contradict Rice by suggesting that "if [Abacha] stands for election we hope he will stand as a civilian." President Clinton's March statement led some critics to question the Administration's policy toward Abacha and the military junta.

The Administration came to a final decision on May 28, saying that the proposed transition was clearly "unacceptable" as long as Abacha remained the single candidate and that current sanctions would remain (*The Washington Post*, May 29, 1998). Following Abacha's death, State Department spokesman James P. Rubin stated that Abubakar had "a historic opportunity to open the political process and institute a swift and credible transition to civilian democratic rule." Rubin said that Washington would "accept" only a transition that included "three things: first, freeing political prisoners; second, ensuring respect for the basic freedoms of speech, press, and assembly; and third, returning the Nigerian army to its rightful position as a professional armed force committed to defending the constitution and civilian rule." U.S. officials had anticipated that Abubakar would be more cooperative with the United States because he received military training here. On June 14, 1998, President Clinton called Abubakar and "underscored our desire for improved bilateral relations in the context of Nigeria taking swift and significant steps toward a successful transition to a democratically-elected government" (Associated Press, June 14, 1998).

The U.S. officials who met with Abubakar in July 1998 reported that he appeared very receptive to implementing the transition to democracy, although he would continue consultations before releasing the final details of the transition. Critics asserted that the United States should have pushed harder for Abiola's unconditional release in order for him to consult with advisers rather than consent to renouncing his title under political pressure. Critics also warned that a hands-off policy could enable the regime to proceed slowly with reforms that may escalate civil conflict to the point of war in which ethnic rivalries could erupt on a massive scale. The Clinton Administration, nonetheless, welcomed Abubakar's transition program, and on October 30, 1998, the U.S. State Department announced that the Secretary, after consulting with Members of Congress, has terminated a Presidential Proclamation that restricted entry into the United States by high-ranking Nigerian officials and their family members.

The United States and the Abasanjo Government

Relations between Washington and Abuja began to improve shortly after General Abubakar assumed power. In September 1998, Abubakar visited the United States for the U.N. General Assembly meeting, and also came to Washington to meet with President Clinton at the White House. After the meeting, Abubakar said President Clinton told him that if Nigeria stayed on its democratic course, the United States was prepared to help win some debt relief from international lending institutions and might also allow the resumption of direct air links between the U.S. and Nigeria. U.S. Secretary of State Madeleine Albright also praised Abubakar for "taking steps to bring Nigeria back into the world community."[1] U.S. officials applauded Abubakar's transition program and warmly welcomed the transfer of power to an elected civilian government and promised to work closely with the Obasanjo government.'

In mid-October 1999, then Secretary of State Albright visited Nigeria and met with senior government officials and civil society groups. At a press briefing following her Africa tour, Secretary Albright stated that the government and people of Nigeria are "engaged in a dramatic and high-stakes struggle to establish a viable democratic system." She said President Obasanjo "appears truly committed to jump-starting the economy, fighting corruption and resolving regional problems that remain a source of unrest within Nigeria." In late October 1999, President Obasanjo met with President Clinton and other senior government officials in Washington. At a White House press briefing, President Clinton said that "it is very much in America's interests that Nigeria succeed, and therefore we should assist them in their success. We intend to increase our assistance to Nigeria to expand law-enforcement cooperation and to work toward an agreement to stimulate trade and investment between us. We intend to do what we can to help Nigeria recover assets plundered by the previous regime." President

---

[1] The *New York Times*, September 25, 1998.

Clinton stated that the United States will support "generous debt rescheduling through the Paris Club and encourage other countries to take further steps."

In a meeting with President Obasanjo in Abuja on August 26, 2000, President Clinton stated that the United States is "committed to working with the people of Nigeria to help build stronger institutions, improve education, fight disease, crime and corruption, ease the burden of debt and promote trade and investment in a way that brings more of the benefits of prosperity to people who have embraced democracy." Clinton also made an unprecedented address before the Nigerian parliament in which he underscored the major issues facing Nigeria today, including democratization and ethnic and religious strife. President Clinton announced a number of new initiatives during his Nigeria visit. He pledged $60 million for AIDS vaccine research and more than $20 million for Obasanjo's campaigns against malaria, polio, and HIV/AIDS. He also praised Nigeria's regional leadership and promised continued U.S. support for the West African peacekeeping mission in Sierra Leone. He pledged continued U.S. support for education, including the provision of Internet access through the work of NGOs and universities.

In May 2001, President Obasanjo met with President Bush and other senior officials in Washington. President Bush stated that the United States is "in the process of helping provide technical assistance to Nigerian troops so that they are better able to keep those peace missions." At a joint White House press conference, President Bush pledged $200 million into a new global fund for HIV/AIDS. President Obasanjo said he discussed a number of issues of mutual interest, including the conflicts in Angola, Democratic Republic of Congo, and Sierra Leone.

Table 1. U.S. Assistance to Nigeria
($ millions, fiscal years)

Program	1994	1995	1996	1997	1998	1999	2000	2001	2002*	2003**
DA	5.893	6.520	1.670	4.100	3.500	10	10.500	30.9	18.5	66.2
CSD	--	--	--	--	3.500	6.8	17.000	23.3	37.0	
ESF	--	--	--	--	--	6.9	20.000	23.4		
FMF Grants	--	--	--	--	--	--	10.000			
P. Corps	1.047	.429	--	--	--	--	--			
IMET	--	--	--	--	--	.090	.600			
Total	6.940	6.949	1.670	4.100	7.000	23.80	58.100	77.7	55.6	66.2

Table Abbreviations:
DA = Development Assistance
CSD = Child Survival and Disease Programs Fund
ESF = Economic Support Fund
P. Corps = Peace Corps
IMET = International Military Education and Training
* Estimate
** Request

CONGRESSIONAL HEARINGS, REPORTS, AND DOCUMENTS

Testimony by Assistant Secretary of State for African Affairs Susan Rice before the House
Committee on International Relations. "Prospects for Democracy in Nigeria." June 25,
1998.

U.S. Congress. House. Committee on International Relations. Subcommittee on Africa.
United States Policy Toward Nigeria. Hearing, 105th Congress, 1st session. September 18,
1997. Washington, U.S. Government Printing Office, 1997. 35 pp.

FOR ADDITIONAL READING

For an extensive list of Internet resources on Nigeria, including news on politics, the
economy, and the culture, see [http://www-sul.stanford.edu/depts/ssrg/africa/nigeria.html].

Boustany, Nora. "Quiet Confidence in Nigeria's Future." *The Washington Post*. November
11, 1998, A30 p.

Onishi, Norimitsu. "Hopeful but Skeptical, Nigerians Await Democracy." *The New York
Times*. November 9, 1998. A3 p.

Rupert, James. "Denied Wealth, Nigeria's Poor Take Dire Steps." *The Washington Post*.
November 6, 1998. A17 p.

U.S. Department of State Press Statement. "End to Special Visa Restrictions on Certain
Nigerian Nationals." October 30, 1998.

NIGERIA[*]

Godfrey Mwakikagile

Nigeria stands out in several respects more than any other African country. It is the most populous country on the continent, and one of the richest and most powerful. It is also the largest black nation in the world. Before the end of apartheid in South Africa, Nigeria was unquestionably the richest and most powerful black country on Earth.

And besides the former Belgian Congo, Nigeria also has had the most turbulent history on the continent since the sixties, due to its sheer size, ethnic diversity unequaled anywhere else in Africa, a succession of military coups, and a devastating civil war which until then was the bloodiest in Africa's post-colonial history. Nigeria also has had the largest number of military coups, seven by 1993, followed by Benin which has had six; although Benin, when it was called Dahomey, breaks the record in one respect, with all its six coups having taken place in less than 10 years during the sixties. And with a population of more than 120 million people, Nigeria is also one of the fastest growing nations in the world. It is estimated that in 2025, Nigeria will have a population of 246 million people,[1] and will be the sixth most populous country in the world after China, India, the United States, Indonesia, and Pakistan, in that in that descending order.[2]

Only four other African countries are expected to experience such phenomenal growth during the next 25 years, which will place them among the 20 most populous nations in the world by 2025: Ethiopia, which is expected to have 133.2 million people by then, and will rank 12th; Congo-Kinshasa, 104.5 million and ranked 16th; Egypt with 97.9 million as the 18th most populous; and Tanzania with 74.2 million, which is expected to be the 20th most populous country.[3] Yet they will all be far surpassed by Nigeria whose population even today dwarfs that of every other major African country.

The people of Nigeria are divided into more than 250 ethnic groups, the largest of which are the Hausa-Fulani in the north; the Yoruba in the southwest, and the Ibo in the southeast.

---

[*] Excerpted from *Military Coups in West Africa since the 1960's,* Mwakikagile, Godfrey. © Nova Science Publishers, Inc. 2001.

[1] "World's 20 Most Populous Contries: 1994 and 2025," in "Almanac: 1995" (New York: Houghton Mifflin, 1994), p. 133.

[2] Ibid.

[3] Tanzania, ibid.

Other large groups include the Ijaw in the Niger Delta who are the fourth largest; the Ibibio-Efik in the southeast; the Kanuri, Nupe, and Tiv in the north; the Edo in the southwest; and several other smaller ones, but no less important, which constitute the other half the population.   About half of all Nigerians live in the north and are mostly Moslem. Southerners, who constitute the other half, are mainly Christian.   It is dichotomy, and an imbalance, which has proved to be disastrous in much of Nigeria's post-colonial period.

Nigeria won independence from Britain on October 1, 1960, under a federal constitution. But the federation was not proportionally structured to reflect ethnic and regional balance in the allocation of power and resources.   Ominous signs of what was yet to come were clearly seen in the last few months of colonial rule.   Yet the desire for independence seems to have overshadowed these warnings.

During the elections of 1959 shortly before independence, none of Nigeria's three major political parties won majority support across the nation because they were all regionally entrenched, with a strong ethnic base.   Therefore in order to form a federal government when independence came, two parties, in effect two regions, formed an alliance: the National Council of Nigeria and Cameroons (NCNC) - changed to National Convention of Nigerian Citizens in 1960 - of Eastern Nigeria, supported mostly by Ibos, and the Northern People's Congress (NPC), with overwhelming Hausa-Fulani ethnic group of Northern Nigeria.

Abubakar Tafawa Balewa, a northerner, became the federal prime minister, and Dr. Nnamdi Azikiwe, an Ibo from Eastern Nigeria, became Nigeria's governor-general (later president).   The Action Group, led by Chief Obafemi Awolowo and supported mostly by Yorubas of Western Nigeria, was excluded from power.   Awolowo felt frustrated by his exclusion, and there was a riotous split between his supporters and those of Chief Samuel Akintola whose local faction of the Action Group controlled the government and the Regional Assembly of the Western Region with him as the premier.

The federal Government intervened and took control of the region, and a big scandal involving misappropriation of regional revenues which were diverted into political factions and individual pockets was revealed, involving several leaders.   Awolowo was tried for treason and convicted, along with Chief Anthony Enahoro, the celebrated fugitive offender who also wrote a book with the same title, "The Fugitive Offender."   Awolowo's rival, Chief Samuel Akintola, was restored to power in 1962 with the help of the Northern People's Congress which manipulated him as a puppet to perpetuate domination of the federation by the Hausa-Fulani.   All those troubles broke out only two years after independence; and they were only the beginning of what was yet to come.

The first five years of independence were characterized by bitter conflicts within and between the three regions.   It was also a period of political intrigue involving formation of alliances cutting across regional lines for sheer expediency, coalitions most Nigerians would not have thought possible only a few months before.   The liberal NCNC under Azikiwe teamed up with the feudalistic ultra-conservative NPC of Northern Nigeria at independence in 1960 to form the federal government.   In the Western Region, a bloc of the Action Group broke away in 1962 from the main party led by Awolowo and formed the Nigerian National Democratic Party (NNDP) under the leadership of Akintola who was still prime minister of the region.   Shortly before the 1964 general election, the NNDP joined forces with the Northern People's Congress (NPC) to form a new party, the Nigerian National Alliance (NNA).   The rest of the Action Group Yoruba members led by Awolowo teamed up with the predominantly Ibo NCNC under Azikiwe (also known as Zik) to form the United Progressive Grand Alliance (UPGA).

The 1962 census further inflamed passions. It not only recorded a population of 55.6 mill ion - a quantum leap from the 30.4 million counted in 1953 - but declared that 29.8 million of them were northerners; thus automatically giving Northern Nigerians (that is, the Jausa-Fulani) an absolute majority over the combined.

The government of Eastern Nigeria immediately rejected the census figures. And in 1963, a new region, the Mid-West, was carved out the Western Region, fueling demands among different ethnic groups in other parts of the country for their own regional governmnts. The agitation led to the imprisonment of a large number of people in the North in an area called the Middle Belt, which is in the southern part of the Northern Region, bordering the northern part of Eastern Nigeria. Many of them were imprisoned arbitrarily. The crackdown was prompted by fear among the Hausa-Fulani, dominant in the North, who felt that creating a new region out of Northern Nigeria would end their domination of the federation.

The demand for new regions and regional governments were forcefully articulated along ethnic lines; hence the creation of the Mid-West which was mostly Edo, not Yoruba. And that is why there was bitter conflict over the 1962 census because it had to do with allocation of power and national resources controlled by the federal government. Therefore like the Eastern Region, the Mid-West also rejected the census results. Both argued that the census overestimated the population of Northern Nigerians, giving them over-representation in the federal parliament and a far larger share of the federal budget than they deserved.

The debate over the 1962 census continued, and political parties tried to maneuver their way through the treacherous waters of turbulent politics which got worse as the country inched towards a general election scheduled for 1964. As the date for the election approached there was intimidation and fraud of every kind in all the parties and regions, but especially in the North. Members of the United Progressive Grand Alliance (UPGA) - a coalition of the Action group and the NCNC - almost boycotted the election, especially in the Eastern Region. But they were persuaded to change their position and reluctantly entered the electoral contest in early 1965, in which they won about half the number of seats in the federal legislature dominated by their opponents: a coalition of the Northern People's Congress (NPC) and Chief Akintola's break-away Action Group (the Nigerian National Democratic Party - NNDP) known as the Nigerian National Alliance (NNA).

Yet another crisis developed, serious enough by itself to threaten the whole country. In October 1965, the Western region held an election which led to chaos and bloodshed that amounted to a virtual civil war. Fighting out between Akintola's group, NNDP, which was backed by Northerners and the UPGA. Thousands died, and the Nigerian Federation seemed to be caught between two contending forces: the Hausa of the North and the Ibo of the East, with the Yoruba of the West split into two between them. There was another factor to the equation. The Ibos had no allies among the Hausa while the Hausa had allies among the Yoruba - and were the only group among the big three (Hausa, Yoruba, and Ibo) without allies in both the North and South.

Because northerners already dominated the federal government, and were allied with Akintola's Yoruba group in Western Nigeria which was no more than a junior partner in the Nigerian National Alliance (NNA) controlled by northerners, Northern Nigerians were on their way to taking full control of the federation, permanently. It was in the midst of all this that a cataclysmic event took place, and changed Nigeria forever. In the early hours of

January 15, 1966, just three months after the rigged election in Western Nigeria which was manipulated by northern politicians to their advantage, a group of young Ibo army officers executed a military coup. They had reached the conclusion that nothing could save Nigeria from total domination by northerners but a military coup, and political assassination. It was the first military coup in Nigerian history.

Although the fraudulent election of October 1965 in Western Nigeria manipulated by northerners - contributed to the coup, the main reason for the violent takeover was fear of perpetual domination of the federation by northerners, and oppression of other ethnic groups by the Hausa-Fulani. And there were other factors involved. As Odumegwu Ojukwu, who led the secession of Eastern Nigeria as the Republic of Biafra, stated in his address to the conference of the Organization of African Unity (OAU) in Addis Ababa, Ethiopia, in August 1968, while the Nigerian civil was going on:

> "The five years immediately after (independence) were marred by successive crises; notably the Tiv Riots of 1960 – 66, the Western Nigeria Emergency of 1962, the National Census controversy 1962 - 63, the Federal election Crisis of 1964 - 65 and the Western Election 1965 - 66.
>
> By January 1966 it had become clear that, unless the situation was arrested, the successive crises experienced by the country before and since independence would certainly lead to unutterable disaster. The existing Independence Constitution gave Northern Nigeria a built-in 50 per cent representation in the Federal Parliament, an arrangement which assured the Region a permanent control of the Federal Government.
>
> A great number of the politicians and others in public life were known to be corrupt, ostentatious and selfish. Bribery and nepotism were rife. There was widespread inordinate ambition for power, an evil mirrored in the prevalence of thuggery, hooliganism and lawlessness...public men had sown unhealthy rivalry, suspicion and mistrust amount the various communities of the country.
>
> Thus the unabashed rigging of the Western Election of October 1965 came to be the last straw. The widespread violence which it precipitated took thousands of lives. Law and order broke down in the Western Region.
>
> Since each of the other Regions had an interest in the election, it was obvious that the country was on the brink of civil war. And yet the Northern Nigeria-controlled Federal Government, the last hope of the people, would not discharge its responsibility. Indeed many an objective observer interpreted its inaction in the face of the impending national collapse as virtual abdication. These were the circumstances in which some young Army Officers and men decided to act."[4]

All those reasons, cited by Ojukwu, undoubtedly contributed to the military coup of January 1966. But probably the overriding factor was the failure of the former colonial power, Britain, to form a federation which would have taken into account the interests and diversity of the 250 different ethnic groups that make up Nigeria - even if that meant creating a weaker federation or a confederation from which the members would have the right to

---

[4] Odumegwu Ojukwu, in his address to the Organization of African Unity (OAU) conference on the Nigerian civil war, Addis, Ababa, Ethopia, August 5, 1968, in "Africa Contemporary Record: 1968-1969" (London: Africa Research Ltd., 1969), p. 655. See also "The Nationalist," Dar es salaam, tanzania, August 1968.

secede after conducting a plebiscite among those who wanted to pull out; instead of dumping them together into three massive regions dominated by only three major ethnic groups under a federal government perpetually controlled by only one such group: the Hausa-Fulani of Northern Nigeria. And there would have been nothing wrong with secession if a plebscite were conducted to ascertain the wishes of those who wanted to secede. Every group of people, let alone those who are oppressed, has the right to self-determination.

It would, of course, be tragic if African countries break up. But oppression of some ethnic groups inevitably leads to such disintegration or chaos. The junior army officers who launched the coup in Nigeria in January 1966 wanted to avert this catastrophe by getting rid of a tribalistic federal government dominated by the Hausa-Fulani at the expense of other Nigerians. It was an undemocratic government which could eventually have destroyed the federation. Even the composition of the coup makers reflected the dissatisfaction of such domination by Northern Nigerians, although Ojukwu disagrees with this assessement, of the ethnic composition of the coup makers, that they were mostly Ibo:

"They originated from all parts of Nigeria - the North, West, Mid-West and East. It was a revolt against injustice and oppression. From available information, their aims were threefold: to put an end to the suffering of Nigerian citizens in Tiv land and Western Nigeria, to dethrone the corrupt and dishonest politicians, and to restore public faith at home and retrieve Nigeria's reputation abroad. They attempted to overthrow the Federal and Regional Governments. In desperation the Federal Government handed over power to General Officer Commanding the Nigerian Armed Forces under the Army, Major-General J. T. U. Aguiyi-Ironsi, who happened to originate from the then Eastern Nigeria (now the independent Republic of Biafra), and had in no way been connected with the Revolution."[5]

From all available evidence after the coup, and confirmation of the identity and ethnic origin of the coup makers, it is obvious that young Ibo officers conspired with Yoruba army officers and others to overthrow the government; although Ibos constituted the majority of the conspirators. The pattern of killings alone - who was killed and who was spared - reflects (despite Ojukwu's denial) an unmistakable ethnic bias; which only confirms what could be called an Ibo "conspiracy" among the young army officers who carried out the coup together with non-Ibo officers and enlisted men. It is the nature of the conspiracy - why they overthrew the government - which exonerates them from the charge of tribalism, that the Ibo army officers wanted Ibos to dominate the federation. That was not the case. But that does not mean that the young lbo army officers did not play the most important role in overthrowing the government - they planned and led the coup. It simply means that their motive was not to establish Ibo domination of the federation the way the Hausa-Fulani and their northern allies did.

The Ibo army officers played a critical role in the 1966 coup because Iboa in general had legitimate grievances against Northern Nigerians, going as far back as 1945 and 1953 when hundreds of their tribesmen were massacred in the North; prompting the junior Ibo army officers to make a move against the federal government dominated by northerners who deliberately discriminated against Ibos and other Eastern Nigerians, especially those who had settled in Northern Nigeria. As late as 1964, just two years before the coup, members of the Northern Regional Assembly openly called for the expulsion of all Ibos from Northern Nigeria, simply because they were Ibos. As Ibrahim Musa Gashash, Minister of Land and

---

[5] Ojukwu, Ibid.

Survey in the regional government of Northern Nigeria, stated in the February-March 1964 session of the Northern Regional Assembly:

"I would like to assure Members that having heard their demands about Ibos holding land in Northern Nigeria, my Ministry will do all it can to see that the demands of members are met. How to do this, when to do it, all this should not be disclosed. In due course, you will all see what will happen (Applause)."[6]

What happened was a massacre of more than 30,000 Ibos and other Eastern Nigerians (but mostly Ibos) in Northern Nigeria in 1966 by the northerners; a continuation of the genocidal rampage that took place in the 1940s and 1950s when hundreds of Ibos were killed in the North. As Ojukwu stated:

In May 1953, ... Northern Nigerian leaders organized and carried out violent demonstrations during which they slaughtered and wounded hundreds of our people in Kano, Northern Nigeria - acts of genocide which had perpetrated at Jos in Northern Nigeria earlier in 1945."[7]

Yet while they were calling for the expulsion of Ibos from the North – "Fire the Southerners, as they shouted in the Northern Regional Assembly in February-March 1964 - they were at the same time working to neutralize them in the South by forming an alliance with Chief Samuel Akintola and his Yoruba faction, the Nigerian National Democratic Party (NNDP), was no more than a junior partner in the Nigerian National Alliance dominated by the Northern People's Congress (NPC) that controlled the federal government. The NNDP was formed to further Akintola's partisan political ambitions - not to promote a national agenda - and was virtually taken over by Northern Nigerians to perpetuate their domination of the federation, while pretending that they had formed an alliance with some Southerners (Akintola's Yoruba faction) to advance national interest.

But many Nigerians, including those who overthrew the government, knew better than that. And there seems to have been a consensus, at least initially on the fact that the coup was a positive development in the history of Nigeria because it had ousted a rotten leadership. It is an observation that was also shared by Federal Nigerian and Diafran leaders, one of the very few things the two sides agreed on. As Chief Anthony Enahoro, leader of the Nigerian delegation to the OAU conference on the civil war, held in Addis Ababa, Ethiopia, in August 1968, stated in his speech:

"Nigeria was plagued with a deep-seated imbalance in its political structure, stemming from the inequality of its component units which placed one of the regions in a dominant position in the Federation ... By the end of 1965, five years after independence, (several) factors - agitation in certain areas for self-determination, suspension of the Western Region government and parliament in 1962 by Federal action, disputes over the 1962 census, banning of public meetings and the press, the much disputed federal election of December 1964, then another hotly disputed election in the former Western Region (split into two in 1967, one of which became the Mid-West Region) in October 1965 that resulted in widespread rioting, arson and lawlessness - all those factors had combined to produce an explosive situation little short of a breakdown of law and order.

It became increasingly clear that sooner or later there would be a fundamental, and probably violent, change. That change came on 15th January, 1966...In assessing the motives

---

[6] Ibrahim Musa Gashash, in "Africa Contemporary record," op. cit., p. 665.
[7] Ojukwu, ibid.

as well as the consequences of the military coup of 15th January, 1966, attention should be drawn to the various interpretations and excuses offered. Firstly, some people saw in it an attempt to end Northern domination. Secondly, some regarded it as an attempt to remove corruption in Government. Thirdly, others hoped that it would introduce an honest and just program of political and administrative reform to correct the structural imbalance in the Federation. No one quarreled with these aims. Consequently there was an atmosphere of general relief immediately after the coup."[8]

Enahoro himself, a prominent Yoruba politician, was imprisoned in 1962 by the Nigerian Federal Government dominated by northerners. He was not released until Colonel Yakubu Gowon came to power after the second military coup at the end of July 1966 when he freed him, together with Awolowo, for the sake of national reconciliation. Otherwise the two prominent Yoruba politicians would have remained in prison, had the Northern People's Congress remained in control of the federal government. Therefore Enahoro also probably felt that it was good that the government which had put him behind bars was gone, since he believed that he had been wrongly convicted and even went into hiding until he was caught.

There was no doubt that many Nigerians - if not the majority - were relieved when they learned that the goverment had been overthrown. They saw the change as a new beginning which could lead to a better future without northern domination and widespread corruption; and without the old federation which was seriously flawed and guaranteed only one thing: perpetual conflict among Nigeria's ethnic groups. Ojukwu's assessment of the general reaction to the coup, across the country, was no different from Enahoro's. As he put it: "The Revolution was spontaneously acclaimed in and outside Nigeria. Nigerians basked in the general relief that a corrupt, unpopular and unstable regime had been deposed."[9]

And in the words of Margery Perham who knew about Nigeria and its people for more than 30 years before the coup, living and working in the country at different times, and was an official guest of the new federal government at the 1960 independence celebrations:

"A group of Ibo army officers decided that nothing could save Nigeria from a complete northern take-over but political assassination. So, in a well-organized plot, in the early hours of January 15th, 1966, the northern prime minister Abubakar Tafawa Balewa and the finance minister were abducted in Lagos and murdered. The same treatment was meted out to Akintola, the western premier, in Ibadan and to the premier of the north, the Sardauna of Sokoto (Ahmadu Bello), at his home in Kaduna. A number of northern army officers were also murdered the same night.

The murders brought constitutional government to an end. The remaining Federal ministers handed their powers over to the senior soldier, the Ibo General Ironsi, and a military administration took over the headless federation. Ironsi appointed four military governors, who included Colonel Hassan Katsina, of the royal family, for the Northern Region, and the Oxford graduate soldier, Colonel Ojukwu, for the Eastern Region...

There was at first a general sense of relief at the murders of the two premiers, whose alliance had led to such disorder in the west and which threatened complete northern domination. The Prime Minister (Balewa's death), however, was regretted: his honourable character and difficult position in relation to the dominant premier of the north were

---

[8] Anthony Enahoro, leader of the federal Nigerian delegation to the OAU conference on the Nigerian-Biafran war, Addis Ababa, Ethiopia, August 1968, in "Africa Contemporary Record," op. cit., pp. 673, and 674.
[9] Ojukwu, ibid., pp. 655 – 656.

understood. There was a hope that the corruption and violence of recent years would come to an end."[10]

But in spite of this consensus on the fact that most Nigerians were to hear that domination of the federation by northerners had ended, and a corrupt government had been overthrown, there is one aspect of the coup which many people could not fail to notice only a few days after the violent take-over. No Ibo politicians or officials in the ousted federal government were killed by the coup makers, most of whom were Ibos themselves. And no Ibo military officers were killed, except one junior officer who refused to surrender the key to an armory in Lagos, the nation's capital.

And no reason was given by the coup makers why all those people (Ibo federal and regional government officials and military officers) were spared, while others weren't, when one of the purposes of the coup was to get rid of corrupt officials by assassination. Were they not corrupt? If they weren't, what were they doing - especially as high-ranked officials - in a corrupt government? And if they were corrupt like the rest who were killed, why were they spared, then? Was the purpose of the coup to eliminate only members of particular ethnic groups? As Enahoro stated:

"Historians will continue to debate whether what happened in Nigeria on 15th January, 1966, was a rebellion, a coup or a mutiny. Whatever it was, there was a change of Government. The civilian administration was removed from office.

In the morning of that date, the Prime Minister of the Federation, Sir Abubakar Tafawa Balewa; the Federal Minister of Finance, Chief Okotie-Eboh; the Premier of the Northern Region, Sir Ahmadu Bello; the Premier of the Western Region, Chief Samuel L. Akintola; the second and third ranking officers in the Nigerian Army, Brigadier Maimalari and Brigadier Ademulegun; other senior officers - Colonel Sodeinde, Colonel Pam and others - were seized and murdered. All of them had one thing in common - they were not Ibos.

The Premier of the Eastern Region, Dr. Michael Okpara; the Premier of the Mid-West Region, Chief Dennis Osadebe; the Head of the Army, Major-General Aguiyi Ironsi; the Federal Minister of Trade, Dr. K.O. Mbadiwe and others in like position were not killed. They had one thing in common - they were Ibos...

The pattern of killings which emerged revealed that this was a coup organized by young Ibo officers in the Army. Whatever they may claim was their basic plan, its effect was that civilian leaders and senior military officers from other areas and ethnic groups were killed while those from Ibo areas were spared. All non-Ibo senior military officers above the rank of Major who were accessible were killed in the January 15 coup. There was only one exception to this when a junior Ibo officer half-awake through his midnight sleep, was killed in Apapa for refusing to hand over the key to the armory. Therefore, to most Nigerians, the incidents of 15th January were a clumsily camouflaged attempt to secure Ibo domination of the Government of the country."[11]

Yet Enahoro's claim that the coup was the work of Ibo army fficers is contradicted by his own admission that officers from his own ethnic group, the Yoruba, also participated in the coup for the same reason he says the Ibos did, tribalism, and inadvertently gives credibility to

[10] Margery Perham, "Nigeria's Civil War, in "Africa Contemporary Record," op. cit., p. 6. See also "West African" January, 1966.
[11] Enahoro, ibid., pp. 674-675.

Ojukwu's contention that that it was not just the Ibos who carried out the coup but members of other tribes as well. As Enahoro himself concedes:

"The leaders of the Opposition (Enahoro himself, together with Awolowo and other Yorubas) remained in prison, whereas it was freely said that some Yoruba Army officers had participated in the coup expressly for the purpose of securing their release."[12]

If Yoruba army officers also participated in the coup, as Etahoro himself concedes, what made the coup, as he put it, "an Ibo Master Plan to dominate the country"?[13] Why would Yoruba army officers, who themselves participated in the coup for the benefit of fellow Yorubas, allow that to happen or help Ibos achieve such a goal? Were they so stupid that they helped the Ibo army officers to overthrow the government in order for them and other Yorubas to be dominated by Ibos?

And since they took part in the coup to help fellow Yorubas, were they not just as guilty of tribalism, the Ibos were accused of, by Enahoro and others? What made Ibo tribalism worse, and Yoruba tribalism benign - if not entirely harmless? Obviously, according to Enahoro, Ibo tribalism was worse because Ibos wanted to dominate the government after the coup. Yet facts do not bear him out.

He contends that Ibos dominated the Federal Military Government formed after the coup because it was under the leadership of General Ironsi, an Ibo. Yet a look at the composition of the ruling military council, the supreme decision-making body for the whole country which was therefore the government, clearly shows that the majority of the members were not Ibos or Easterners but members of other ethnic groups. And they came from other regions of Nigeria – North, West, and Mid-West - other than the Eastern Region. Even the three Easterners on the ruling military council were not all Ibos; further reducing the number of Ibos among Nigeria's military rulers.

It is impossible for Enahoro and other Nigerians not to have noticed that. The military rulers were known publicly, and everybody, including Enahoro himself, knew that most of those military rulers were not Ibos. And they all together, not just General Ironsi, approved or rejected appointments of officials to all senior government positions including ambassadorial and civil service, as well as other posts such as mid-level. Nor was Ironsi the only author of Decree No. 34, as his critics claimed, which abolished Nigeria's three massive regions in favor of a unitary state, triggering a violent reaction from northerners who wanted their region to maintain its numerical preponderance (it claimed to have half of the entire Nigerian population) and supremacy over the rest of the country. Northerners were guaranteed perpetual domination of the country because they constituted an absolute majority in the federal parliament, controlled the federal government, and the army. They had all levers of power in their hands, almost to the total exclusion of their follow countrymen. The military coup sought to correct that imbalance, and was relatively successful, but never secured Ibo domination of the government. As Ojukwu pointed out:

"The main orgins of the Central Government - the Supreme Military Council and the Federal Executive Council – were representative of all the Regions of the country ... On May 24, 1966, Major-General Aguiyi-Ironsi promulgated Decree No. 34. That decree was the implementation of a decision of the Federal Military Council in which all the Regional Military Governors were represented. The Decree was intended to establish a National

---

[12] Ibid., p. 675.
[13] Ibid.

Executive Council for the whole country with the Regional Military Governors as members to unify the top cadres of the Civil Service to ensure the efficient administration of the country for the duration of the Military Regime.

Ironically enough, it was this Decree - popularly known as the Unification Decree - that sparked off wide-spread rioting and violence directed against the lives and property of Eastern Nigerians in Northern Nigeria! It did not seem to matter to the leaders who planned the riots that Eastern Nigerians were in a terrible minority - 3 out of 9 members - in the Supreme Military Council that took the collective decision.

The death-toll of our people in the massacres of that month stood at 3,000. A high-powered commission was appointed by the Supreme Military Council to investigate the causes and the conduct of the May riots in Northern Nigeria. Northern Nigeria leaders never allowed that commission to meet."[14]

Much has been said about the killing of non-Ibo military officers and others. And there is a lot of evidence which proves that, as the list of victims shows. Relatives and friends knew whom they had lost; soldiers also knew their officers and which ones had been killed. And many Nigerians knew which leaders had been assassinated during the January 1966 coup.

But the death toll among the Ibos after the coup and several months thereafter, was just as appalling, if not more so, in terms of numbers. And they were targeted for no other reason than that they were Ibos, starting with General Ironsi himself when their enemies started to eliminate Ibo leaders. The conflict was clearly defined along ethnic and regional lines: Ibo versus Hausa, East versus North, as northerners saw it.

When General Ironsi announced the abolition of the regions in his promulgation of Decree No. 34 as the leader of the Supreme Military Council, he inadvertently signed his own death warrant. Not only would a unitary government have ended northern domination of the federation; it would also have seriously affected northerners by requiring them to apply for jobs on competitive basis - in a streamlined and unified civil service demanding merit - along with the more educated Southerners (especialy Ibos and way they could avoid that was by doing two things: force General Ironsi to rescind the order (Decree No. 34) and return the country to the status quo ante – the good old days when Nigeria was a fedreration (not a unitary state) dominated by northerners; and massacre the Ibos who had "swamped" the North, "taking jobs away" from northerners, and expel them from the region.

Thus, one of the tragedies of the January 1966 military coup was that Ibos were massacred by their fellow countrymen in Northern Nigeria because of what they had achieved. In other words, they were being punished for being successful. Instead of being an asset, their education and entrepreneurship became a liability, and it cost them thousands of lives in only a few weeks after the coup; had Yorubas also settled in the North, they would have met the same fate as their southern counterparts, the Ibos; not only are Yorubas probably the most educated ethnic group in Nigeria, they are also the most successful in business. But unlike the Ibos, they have traditionally remained and prospered in their home region, although a substantial number of them also live outside the southwest, their homeland.

As Northern Nigerians went on a genocidal rampage against the Ibos, they tried to justify the killing frenzy by invoking images of a complete take - over of the defenseless, country by these southerners. Isolated in the North, and they became even more vulnerable to attack by marauding bands of thugs full of hate. As the death-toll continued, Northern authorities

---

[14] Ojukwu, ibid., p. 656.

simply looked the other way and in many cases even encouraged the ethnic cleansing. Many saw in this the end of Nigeria itself as a country. As Margeru Perham states:

> "The northerners in some of the towns, suspecting a complete Ibo take-over (after the coup), fell upom the scattered minorities and massacred some hundreds of them...(after) Ironsi, in Edict No. 34, announced (in May 1966) the abolition of the regions and therefore of the Federation, in favor of a unitary government and also a unification of the civil service which would have very adversely affected the prospects of the northerners, more backward in modern education than their southern competitors. Ironsi retracted his policy of unification but too late for his own safety. On July 29th, 1966, he and the military governor of the Western Region were murdered along with a number of Ibo (army) officers by northern soldiers.
> This time there was no valid constitutional power left to act and after some confusion the young Chief of Staff, Colonel Gowon, took over. He had the advantage not only of a good reputation, but, as a northerner who yet came from a Middle Belt small tribe, and was also a Christian, he seemed to bridge the fissures which had split Nigeria."[15]

Gowon introduced his own measures to avert an even worse catastrophe involving more massacres and outright civil war. But nothing seemed to work, although some prisoners, including two prominent ones (Awolowo and Enahoro), benefited from his -Policy of clemency:

> "Colonel, later General, Gowon began by releasing prisoners, including the two eminent ones, Awolowo and Enahoro, who from this point played a major role. He repealed the obnoxious Edict No. 34 and in September called a meeting of notables from all regions to discuss the future of Nigeria. All possible solutions were considered (including dissolution of the Federation and secession).

But even while the conference was sitting there was a new wave of massacres in the northern towns in which Ibos and other Easterners were killed, often in the most revolting manner. Estimates of the number killed vary from three to thirty thousand and the survivors fled back to the east to inflame their families and clansmen with hatred for their oppressors and a desire to cut all links with the Federation. It was, therefore, not surprising that in the confusion of the moment, with the army and the civil service tending to break up into their regional parts, and the east alienated by the successive massacres, progress could be made in rebuilding the Federation."[16]

There is the question of what could have been done immediately after coup. The records of course, shows that events unfolded in rapid succession thereafter. Could Ironsi, as the new head of state, have averted further tragedy - the massacre of Ibos and other Easterners in Northern Nigeria by forming a truly national government instead "dominated" by Ibos, as Chief Enahoro and others claimed?

The answer is, he probably could not have been able to prevent such tragedy. The supreme ruling organ of the state during that time, which was the Supreme Military Council, was already, as we have shown and as the record shows, a nationally representative body and

---

[15] M. Perham, ibid., p. 656.
[16] Ibid., pp. 6 – 7.

was not dominated by Ibos. Easterners on the ruling council were far outnumbered 3 to 9; and the three Eastern representatives were not all Ibos.

And the measures Ironsi tried to implement, ruling Supreme Military Council in pursuit of national reconciliation, achieved nothing of the sort. Even his retraction of the policy to abolish regions did not avert the catastrophe. Things had already been set in motion, thanks to Northern hostility towards the Ibos, and the events that unfolded had their own momentum, fueled from within. That is because the distrust and hatred of Ibos by many northerners was nothing new. Nor did Ironsi's national tour when he met with different traditional rulers and other leaders to discuss the country's future achieve anything.

There was nothing that could constrain the fury of northerners against Ibos and other Easterners living in Northern Nigeria. Instead, more massacres took place, including Ironsi's assassination. Although Ironsi was an Ibo and the highest-ranked military officer, Ibos did not control the Nigerian army as some people claimed. As Chief Anthony Enahoro himself conceded:

> "It became clear after a few months, that the country had no satisfaction from the events of January 15, 1966. Once again, conditions were ripe for a change. In the last week of July 1966, the change came ... Some of the senior army officers of non-Ibo origin were now holding some key positions in the Army and still prevented an all-Ibo command at the top of the Nigerian Military Administration.
>
> There were also rumours of a counter-coup to reverse the effects of the January 15 coup ... A mutiny started at the Army Barracks in Abeokuta in the former Western Region in the morning of July 29...An officer of Northern origin ... asked all soldiers from other (non-Ibo) ethnic groups to take up their arms ... Disorders spread to other barracks in the rest of the country and continued through that weekend.
>
> Major-General Aguiyi-Ironsi, who was then visiting Ibadan (capital of the Western Region), and his host, the Military Governor of the West, Lieutenant-Colonel Adenkale Fajuyi, were kidnapped at the Government House in Ibadan. The net result of this was another coup. Following the coup, Major-General Yakubu Gowon - then Lieutenant-Colonel - succeeded Major-General Aguiyi-Ironsi on 1st August (1966) as Head of the Federal Military Government."[17]

With the assassination of Ironsi on July 29, 1966, Nigeria had experienced its second coup, in only about six months after the first. And there is no doubt that it was northerners who were behind the second coup. It was led by Hausa army officers in retaliation against the Ibos for launching the first one and killing Northern Nigerian leaders and army officers.

Enahoro does not go into details about the second coup, but the pace of events accelerated from there. And Ironsi's fate - including the national tour which cost him his life - as well as that of the Ibos in general was determined by what turned out to be a conspiracy by northerners, not only to retaliate against the Ibos and avenge the murder of northern leaders mainly to regain control of the federation they had lost in the first coup.

There is no doubt that further catastrophe could have been avoided had exercised restraint, instead of trying to impose their will on the rest of the Nigerians which, as the rest of the history of Nigeria shows, is exactly what happened.

Northerners regained control of the federation and retained their dominant position for decades. All of Nigeria's military heads of state since the assassination of Ironsi were northerners, except Olusegun Obaganio, a Yoruba from the southwest. And both civilian leaders, one prime minister and one president, the only ones the country had since independence, were also northerners; until 1999 when Obasanjo, a retired general, was elected as a civilian president soon after he came out of prison where he was locked up by the military head of state Sani Abacha on false charges of treason. But even he was elected - on February 27, 1999, and assumed office on May 29 – with the support fof northern generals, active and retired, and other powerful northern politicians and businessmen; thus ensuring their continued domination of the federation even from behind the scenes.

And even though during that turbulent period in Nigerian history the majority of the military officers were southerners mostly Ibos and Yorubas - since they are ones who were more educated than their northern counterparts; they still did not dominate the Nigerian armed forces. Most of the enlisted men were northerners, as they still are today; and they, along with northern civilians, had always resented what they considered to be the "privileged" status of educated Southerners, although that status is not inherited but earned by going to school. Unfortunately, for historical and cultural reasons, northerners lagged behind their fellow countrymen in the south in pursuit of education. As Thomas Sowel states in his book "Race and Culture: A World View":

> "The less modernized of the indigenous peoples have supplied a disproportionate share of the ordinary soldiers ... When colonial peoples were eventually allowed into commissioned different ethnic groups supplied officers officer corps, often very than the enlisted soldiers. This was especially those which supplied so when becoming a commissioned officer required education at military academies, rather than promotion from the ranks.
> An educated officer corps has tended to draw upon the more modernized indigenous ethnic groups, whereas the enlisted men have come from more traditional ethnic or tribal regions. Thus, while the enlisted ranks of the Nigerian colonial army had a substantial majority of Jausa riflemen, more than half of its first African commissioned officers were Ibos...
> Genocidal levels of violence have been unleashed not only against the Jews but also against such groups as the Ibos of Nigeria...Frictions that are all too familiar in intergroup relations tend to become extreme in the case of hostility toward middlemen minorities ... During intergroup violence in Nigeria in 1966, tens of thousands of Ibos were slaughtered indiscriminately by their fellow Nigerians."[18]

The magnitude of the tragedy itself - tens of thousands of Iboa massacred - was determined by the nature of the nation's leadership: the ethnic group which dominated the federation the Hausa-Fulani. Because of the numerical preponderance of northerners both in the federation as a whole and in the military among enlisted men, there is nothing Southerners could have done on their own to redress the imbalance or stop northerners from re-asserting their control of the Nigerian federation the way it was then structured; virtually guaranteeing

---

[17] Enahoro, ibid., ibid., p. 676.
[18] Thomas Sowell, "Race and Culture: A World View" (New York: Basic Books, 1994), pp. 132-133; T. Sowell, "Migrations and Cultures: A World View" (New York: Basic Books, 1996), p. 28. See also David Lamb, "The Africans" (New York: Random House, 1982), p. 308.

the North veto power over national affairs. The first coup was only a brief interruption of the hegemonic rule secured for northerners by the independence constitution which did nothing to correct structural flaws in the power-structures of the vast federation.

Ibos had undoubtedly incurred the wrath of northerners because of what happened in the first coup. They masterminded it. But they had never won endearment either, from northerners in the past, as the massacres of hundreds of Ibos in Jos in 1945 and again in Kano in 1953 in Northern Nigeria, and other murdersof Ibos through the years by northerners clearly shows. And the virtual absolute power northerners had over the federation - because of their vastly superior numbers - even when Ironsi was head of state; and especially their dominant position in the military where they flexed muscles In defense of Northern Nigeria's hegemonic control of the country, meant that the course of events during those tragic years would hardly have been any different, even if all Ibos were saints. And that is why Ironsi's tour of the nation to try and discuss the future of the federation turned out to be so fruitless, and tragic. As Ojukwu stated:

"Firm assurances of personal safety for our people in Northern Nigeria had been given by the Supreme Military Council itself (in which Easterners were outnumbered 3 to 9), and by the Sultan of Sokoto and the Emirs of the North. On the strength of these assurances, we appealed to our people who had their stations to return to Northern Nigeria. They did.

At this point Major-General Aguiyi-Ironsi unertook an extensive tour of Northern and Mid-Western Nigeria, and arranged to round off his tour at Ibadan in Westrn Nigeria with a meeting of traditional rulers and chief s from all over Nigeria to seek advice on matters affecting the future of the country. The meeting was scheduled for July 29, 1966.

But in the morning of that day, a well-organized group of Northern soldiers kidnapped the Supreme commander and his host, Lieutenant-Colonel Adenkule fajuyi, the Military Governor of Western Nigeria, and subsequently murdered them in very gruesome circumstances. The cruel massacre of over 200 of Eastern Nigerian Army Officers and men also took place."[19]

Perhaps what happened in Nigeria during the sixties - the massacres, the secession of the Eastern Region, the clamor for self-determination from different ethnic groups across the country - might have been avoided if the Nigerial leaders themselves had decided to delay independence for a few years; may be for five or even for seven years, until they had restructured the federation to reflect the ethnic composition of the country in the allocation of power and resources, instead of having it dominated by the three major ethnic groups: Hausa-Fulani, Ibo, and Yoruba. And that would have entailed breaking down the three massive regions into several, probably even autonomous or semi-autonomous, states to accommodate the interests of all ethnic groups, especially the smaller ones which were dominated by the three major ones; guaranteeing each limited autonomy or even self-determination should they choose to secede. But that would be only after a plebiscite had been conducted the people of the state or region that was demanding total separation from the rest of the federation, in order to make sure that the demand for secession was not just the work of a few agitators and opportunists seeking power for personal glory.

And there seems to have been a consensus among Nigerian leaders during the tragedy of the sixties that they probably had demanded independence too soon; much sooner than they should have, given the volatile ethnic mix and numerical disparity of these groups in the

---

[19] Ojukwu, in "Africa Contemporary Record," op. cit., p. 656.

structurally flawed federation. As Chief Enahoro stated during that time as the civil war was going on:

"Unfortunately, during the years of British occupation, Nigeria did not produce one nationalist movement in the classic sense, as was the case in India and Ghana, to mention only two former British colonial territories. Instead, Nigeria produced three nationalist movements which, unfortunately, were based on the three major tribal groupings. The major political parties grew out of these movements, and political developments during the compromises struggle for independence therefore took the shape of between these political parties which were different in their outlook and programmes and which were regionally entrenched.

The only common factor among them was the struggle for independence. In their common desire to win independence, many vital problems were left unsolved. One of these outstanding problems was the creation of more states which would have provided a more lasting foundation for stability of the Federation of Nigeria. The British Government pointed out at the time that if new states were to be created, the new states must be given at least two years to settle down before independence could be granted. On reflection, Nigerian leaders have admitted that the British were right and they were wrong on this vital issue in hurrying to independence without solving the problem of the Federation."[20]

Despite the flawed structure of the federation which threatened the very existence of Nigeria as a single political entity, as the attempted secession of Eastern Nigeria tragically demonstrated, the composition of the country's diverse ethnic groups was, by itself, enough of a threat to the survival of Nigeria as much as it is to the rest of the African countries all of which, without a single exception, are plagued by ethnic and regional tensions only in varying degrees. The only difference is that in the case of Nigeria much more complex because her population is much bigger – the largest of any African country – crowded in an area smaller than that of Angola, Mali, Niger, or Tanzania; and her ethnic composition is also the most diverse on the continent: 250 different ethnic groups, several of which - such as the Hausa, Fulani, Yoruba, Ibo, and Ijaw - have millions of people per group. There are, for example, more than 30 million Yorubas, enough to constitute a viable independent nation, like Tanzania which has the same number of people. And the Ijaws - the fourth largest, are more than 4 million strong.

And that alone - the ethnic diversity and different historical and cultural background for each of the 250 groups, large or small - fueled demands for secession through the years. Even Northern Nigerians who dominated federation wanted to secede. So did Eastern and and Western Nigerians, although to a smaller degree compared to Northerners, until Eastern Nigerians made the most determined attempt - more than anybody else - to pull out of the federation during the sixties. But Northern Nigerians had a much longer history of secessionist demands.

Even during the 1950s when Southern politicians (in Eastern and Western Nigeria) were making a concerted effort to win independence for Nigeria as a single secession. As Professor Ali their Northern Mazrui states in "Black Africa and the Arabs":

"Whereas the spread of Islam through East and West Africa provides a cultural bond, it also, in some cases serves to reinforce separatist tendencies. In Nigeria in

---

[20] Enahoro, ibid, p. 673.

the last decade before independence, Muslim Northerners, fearful of the political militancy of Christian Southerners - talked seriously of secession ...

Ironically, separatism moved southward militancy of Christian after independence, into Azikiwe's community, for it was Ibo Christians rather than Hausa Muslims who eventually sought to break up Nigeria. And many Christian missionary organizations moved to the support of Biafra, almost seeming to regard the Nigerian Civil War as a re-enactment of the crusades - a religious was rather than an ethnic confrontation. In reality the religious factor in the Civil fundamental."[21]

Religion did play a role, probably more than the subsidiary one Mazrui assigns it. But it is true, as he says, that it was not fundamental. However, the magnitude of its significance and impact was evident in the denunciations in religious terms that went back and forth between the Northerners and the Easterners during the civil war. Many Ibos denounced the Hausa-Fulani as "Muslim hordes" bent on the elimination of the "Christian Ibo," and Ojukwu, in one midnight broadcast from Biafra's radio station in Enugu, the secessionists' capital, pleaded: "Holy Archangel Michael, defend us in battle."[22] It was an invocation reminiscent of the crusades.

And from Northerners came denunciations of Southern "infidels." But despite the fact that the Nigerian head of state during the civil war, General Yakubu Gowon, was a Christian although a northerner yet not a northern Muslim; there is enough evidence to show that regional ties transcended religious bonds. The majority of Northern Nigerians, including many Christians most of whom come from smaller tribes (in what was then known as the Middle Belt and other parts) as opposed to the Hausa-Fulani who are predominantly Muslim, supported the expulsion of Ibos from the North. And the vast majority of them also supported the war against Biafra.

Northern Muslim leaders were also emphatic in their determination to embrace northern Christians at all costs, for no other reason than that they were fellow northerners; even if that meant giving them money from the Northern Nigerian Government to help them start businesses to replace the Ibos and other Southerners (most of them easterners) who were being expelled. As long as they were Southerners, and Christian, they had to go. As one representative in the Northern Regional Assembly, A.A. Abogede representing Igala East, stated during the February-March 1964 session:

"I am very glad that we are in Moslem country, and the Government of Northern Nigeria allowed some few Christians in the Region to enjoy themselves according to the belief of their Religion, but building of hotels should be taken away from the Ibos and even if we find some (northern) Christians who are interested in building hotels and have no money to do so, the Government should aid them, instead of allowing Ibos to continue with the hotels."[23]

Another member of the Northern Regional Assembly, Alhaji Usman Liman representing the Sarkin Musawa constituency, won sustained applause from the other representatives in the same session when he said:

---

[21] Ali A. Mazuri, "Black Africa and the Arabs," in "Foreign Affairs," July 1975, p. 737.
[22] Ojukwu, in "Africa Contemporary record," ibid., p. 553.
[23] A. A. Abogede, ibid., p. 664.

"What brought the Ibos into this Region? They were here (sic) since the Colonial days. Had it not been for the Colonial Rule there would hardly have been any Ibo in this Region. Now that there is no Colonial Rule the Ibos should go back to their Region. There should be no hesitation about this matter. Mr. Chairman, North is for Northerners, East for Easterners, West is for Westerners and the Federation is for us all (Applause),"[24]

Even the powerful Northern Premier who virtually controlled the Nigerian Federation, Sir Ahmadu Bello who was also known as the Sardauna of Sokoto, was openly hostile to the Ibos. As he bluntly stated during the same February-March 1964 session in the Northern House of Assembly:

"It is my most earnest desire that every post in the Region, however small it is, be filled by a Northerner (Applause).[25]

He was also roundly applauded. And from members of the Government Bench in the same Regional Assembly came shouts of "Good talk," and "Fire the Southerners."[26] They obviously included southern Moslems in this expulsion order – "Fire the Southerners" - in spite of the fact that the members of the Northern Regional Assembly were all Moslems themselves, without a single exception, just as the vast majority of northerners are. And almost all the regional representatives were Hausa-Fulani.

The strength of ethnic bonds superseding religious ties was also demonstrated in 1993 when Moshood Abiola, a Yoruba and southern Moslem, was blocked by the military rulers - who were northern Moslems - from becoming Nigeria's president, although he won the election held in June that year. Yet his Moslem identity he shared with the military rulers from Northern Nigeria who said they would hand over power to a democratically elected president, did not help him. He was, instead, locked up and languished in prison until northerner.

In African politics, ethnic and regional ties are like family ties. And religion cannot dissolve family ties. It is clear that the Nigerian military rulers wanted a fellow northerner to win the presidential election; and if he didn't, they would stay in power themselves in order to perpetuate northern domination of the federation. As Barbara Croosette states: "Chief Abiolal a wealthy businessman ... entered politics against the advice of his family ... He is a Muslim Yoruba from the south whose decision to enter politics was seen as a provocation to northerners who had dominated the political scene. But he won, by most accounts, democratic election ever in the country."[27]

The person they really wanted to win was an obscure candidate from the North who was also a Moslem, Bashir Tofa, with neither the national stature nor the ability to attract nationwide support like Abiola did. Wole Soyinka, in his book "The Open Sore of A

---

[24] Alhai Usman Liman, ibid., p. 665.
[25] Ahmadu Bello, ibid.
[26] Government Bench, quoted ibid., p. 664.
[27] Barbara Crossette, "Nigeria Prisoners: Forgotten by World, Democracy Fighters Languish" in the "International Herald Tribune," December 27, 1996, p. 10.

Continent: A Personal Narrative of the Nigerian Crisis," dismisses Tofa as "a straw figure specifically set up by the perpetuation machinery of (military head of state)."[28]

By denying Abiola the presidency he had rightfully won, the military rulers acted as if Nigeria was hardly out of the sixties when the country almost fell apart because of ethnic conflicts. As Chinua Achebe poignantly states in his book "The Trouble with Nigeria":

> "The trouble with Nigeria is simply and squarely a failure of leadership. There is nothing basically wrong with the Nigerian character. There is nothing wrong with the Nigerian land or climate or water or anything else. The Nigerian problem is the unwillingness or inability of its leaders to rise to the responsibility, to the challenge of personal example which are the hallmarks of true leadership ... We have lost the twentieth century; are we bent on seeing that our children also lose the twenty-first?"[29]

It is a question that applies to the rest of the African countries as well. But in the case of Nigeria, that loss was probably best dramatized during the 1960s, with the secession of Eastern Nigeria and subsequent civil war being the most tragic chapter in the nation's history. Yet, there had been warnings through the years that a catastrophe was in the making, even if not imminent. Right from the beginning when Nigeria was established as one colony in 1914, uniting North and South, northerners openly contended that the amalgamation was "a mistake."[30]

In 1947, Chief Obafemi Awolowo, leader of the Yoruba of Western Nigeria, argued just as vehemently, contending in his book, "Path to Nigerian Freedom," that "there are no Nigerians. Nigeria is a mere geographical expression."[31] Instead, he suggested that the country should be divided into 40 states on cultural and linguistic basis, and did not rule out secession. As George Padmore states in his book "Pan-Africanism or Communism?: The Coming Struggle for Africa":

Mr. Awolowo is definitely committed to tribal separatism ... advocates self-government and separatism not only for each of the existing regions, but claims autonomy for the dozen or more tribes which, he maintains are 'nations,' with nothing in common except their color.

Mr. Awolowo's organization began as a political off-shoot of the Egbe Omo Oduduwa, a Yoruba religious and cultural society whose patron is the Oni of Ife, a wealthy Ibadan chief. It came into being in 1951 under the auspices of Mr. Awolowo and other Yoruba intellectuals who formerly belonged to the Nigeria Youth Movement, the pioneer nationalist organization in Lagos, as an opposition to 'Ibo domination' in the West...

(At the) constitutional conference in London in August 1953...Northern and Western delegates (were) both committed to regionalism upon the basis of tribal separatism ... Since the emergence of Yoruba tribalism as a virile force in Nigerian politics, the Action Group leaders have been demanding that Lagos be incorporated into the Western Region...

---

[28] Wole Soyinka, "The Open Sore of A Continent: A Personal Narrative of the Nigerian Crisis" (New York: Oxfrd University Press, 1996); Makau wa Mutua, "Can Nigeria be One?," in "The Wilson Quarterly," Summer 1996, p. 92.

[29] Chinua Achebe, "The Trouble with Nigeria" (Engu, Nigeria: Fourthdimension Publishing, 1985), p. 3.

[30] Northern Nigeria, in its opposition to the continued existence of the Nigerian federation, qoted in "African Contemporary Record," op. cit., p. 654.

(When the Colonial Secretary) Mr. Lyttleton decided that Lagos should remain the federal capital, ... the decision so annoyed the Westerners that their leader, Mr. Awolowo, walked out of the Conference and threatened secession of the Western Region from the rest of Nigeria."[32]

The Eastern Region also had its own ethnocentric tendencies. In 1948, Nnamdi Azikiwe and his party, the National Council of Nigerian Citizens (later changed to the National Council of Nigeria and the Cameroons – NCNC) promulgated the Freedom Charter calling for the establishment of states based on ethnic and linguistic basis. And in the same year, Azikiwe also inflamed passions across the nation by claiming manifest destiny for the Ibos, stating that the God of Africa had specially created Ibos to lead Africa out of bondage; a highly inflammatory statement which meant only one thing: Ibos are better than other Nigerians and the rest of the Africans across the continent; hardly a basis for national and continental solidarity.

About two years later after Azikiwe's arrogant and inflammatory statement, Northern Nigerians at the constitutional conference held at Ibadan, Western Nigeria, in January 1950, said they would pull out of the federation and re-establish the borders that existed in 1914, when Northern and Southern Nigeria were separate colonies (before amalgamation) - unless they were given half of the seats in Nigeria's f ederal parliament. They also insisted at the same conference that only northerners should be eligible for seats in Nigeria's federal parliament. They also insisted at the same conference that only northerners should be eligible for election to the Northern Regional Assembly; a euphemism for "only those of Hausa-Fulani stock" who have always dominated the region. In May 1953, northerners again demanded secession from the rest of Nigeria, and continued to make the same threat through the decade.

In 1954, Western Nigeria again threatened to pull out of the federation. But it was Northern Nigerians who made the biggest threat through the 1950s to secede. In 1964, almost two years before the first military coup and the massacre of the Iboa in Northern Nigeria, the Northern premier himself, Sir Ahmadu Bello, ridiculed those who talked about Nigerian unity and existence of Nigeria as one political entity:

"Politicians always delight in talking loosely about the unity of Nigeria. Sixty years ago there was no country called Nigeria. What is now Nigeria consisted of a number of a number of large and small communities all of which were different in their outlooks and beliefs. The advent of the British and of Western education has not materially altered the situation and these many and varied communities have not knit themselves into a complete unit."[33]

Soon after the assassination of Ironsi on July 29, 1966, in the second military coup staged by Northern Nigerian soldiers, the northern military officers and their kinsmen demanded dissolution of the Nigerian federation and total independence for each of the three massive regions. They got a lot of support from fellow northerners including politicians. In fact, before May 1966, Northern Nigerian leaders were contemplating secession within months.

---

[31] Obafemi Awolowo, "Path to Nigerian Freedom" (London: Faber & Faber, 1947), see especially chapter 5, in which he forcefully articulates his view that Nigeria as an entity is a fiction, except as a mere geographical term.

[32] George Padmore, "Pan_Africanism or Communism?: The Coming Struggle for Africa" (London: Dobson, 1956), pp. 276, 278, 279, and 285. See also chapter "XV: Constitutional Development and Tribalism in Nigeria," pp. 266-288.

[33] Ahmadu Bello, quoted in "Africa Contemporary Record," op. cit., p. 670.

"It was well known before May, 1966 that there were very powerful moves in Northern Nigeria for secession from the Federation... (Northern) traditional rulers, politicians, civil servants and intellectuals were known to have planned and led the riots of May (in which thousands of Ibos were massacred in the North) and the rebellion of July (in which Ironsi was overthrown and killed by Northern Nigerian soldiers). Their July putsch was given the code name of *araba* or secession."[34]

Even the Nigerian military head of state, General Gowon, who was a northerner himself, expressed serious doubt about the existence of the federation, especially as it was then structured. He stated in his first broadcast to the nation as head of state on August 10, 1966: "The base for unity is not there."[35]

And in a memorandum submitted to the ad hoec conference on the Nigerian constitution in Lagos in September 1966, the Northern Nigerian delegation hardly expressed any confidence in the viability of the Nigerian federation stating unequivocally:

"We have pretended for too long that there are no differences between the peoples (of Nigeria). The hard fact which we must honestly accept as of paramount importance in the Nigerian experiment especially for the future is that we are different peoples brought together by recent accidents of history. To pretend otherwise will be folly."[36]

At the same constitutional conference, Northern Nigeria again threatened to secede. It was a thinly veiled threat contained in the memorandum Northern Nigerians submitted to the conference, arguing that Nigeria should be broken up into:

"A number of autonomous states ... that is to say, Northern Nigeria, Eastern Nigeria, Western Nigeria, or by whatever name they choose to be called ... (under) a Central Authority (whose powers are to be) delegated by the component states except that powers connected external or foreign affairs and immigration can be unilaterally withdrawn by the State Government...Nigarian citizenship (should be replaced by) Associate citizenship ... Any Member State of the Union should reserve the right to secede completely and unilaterally from the Union and to make arrangements for cooperation with the other members of the Union in such a manner as they may severally or individually deem fit."[37] This struck at the very core of the union, threatening to dissolve some of the very ties which made its existence possible. Any territorial unit which controls its own foreign affairs and immigration policy is, at the very least even without international recognition, a sovereign entity short of diplomatic representation. Those are some of the key areas - besides - which fell under the jurisdiction of the national goverment; not of the component units of a unitary state a union or federation. Even in a confederation, member states or provinces or regions don't conduct their own foreign affairs or formulate their own immigration policy. Quebec, for example, with all its separatist tendencies, does not have its own foreign or immigration policy separate from what is carried out by the

---

[34] Northern Nigerian secessionish plan in 1966, cited ibid., p. 657.
[35] Yakubu Gowon, quoted ibid. See also Crawford Young, "The Impossible Necessityof Nigeria: A struggle for Nationhood," in "Foreign Affairs," November/December 1996, p. 139.
[36] Northern Nigerian delegation, in its memorandum to the constitutioal conference, Lagos, Septmber 1966, quoted in "Africa Contemporary Record," ibid., p. 670.
[37] Ibid., p. 658.

Canadian government; nor do the states of India or the territories of Australia or the cantons of Switzerland.

What Northern Nigerians presented to the constitutional conference in Lagos in 1966 was a specific agenda for dissolution of the Nigerian federation. Had any of the major items in their memorandum been adopted by the national delegates, or been incorporated into the conference's final resolutions, that would have been the end of the Nigerian federation. Even a confederation, of whatever configuration, would not have been consummated, given the concerted effort by northerners to separate from the rest of Nigeria or remain an integral part of this sovereign entity only if they could dominate it perpetually.

Western Nigerians also communicated an implied threat to secede, forcefully articulated in their memorandum to the constitutional conference in Lagos, the nation's capital. They proposed a "Commonwealth of Nigeria," if the other regions did not accept federalism: "The Commonwealth of Nigeria (shall comprise) the existing Regions and such other Regions as may be subsequently created. The Government of each state within the Commonwealth shall be completely sovereign in all matters excepting those with respect to which responsiblity is delegated to the Council of State."[38]

No one would seriously argue that the British Commonwealth, now simply known as the Commonwealth - comprising former British colonies round the globe, except for a few such as Cameroon and Mozambique, which are former French and Portuguese colonies, respectively - is a single political entity like Brazilp Ghana, China, Iran, Tanzania, Argentina, South Africa or any other sovereign state. If the member states in the proposed Commonwealth of Nigeria were to be sovereign as proposed by the Western Nigerian delegation to the 1966 constitutional conference, Nigeria would cease to exist as a single sovereign nation; if this proposal was implemented.

And probably that is exactly what Western Nigerians had in mind, dissolution of the federation, when they presented their memorandum proposing the establishment of a Nigerian Commonwealth. They were already frustrated with their inability to end northern domination of the federation; and were bitter for being excluded from the central government when easterners and northerners formed an alliance to establish the first African government at independence in 1960. It seemed as if the two regions - Northern and Eastern Nigeria - had conspired against them to exclude them from power. And they never forgot that. Therefore ending the federation would not be much of a loss to them.

Therefore as this record shows, Northern and Western Nigerians threatened to break up the Nigerian federation far more often, and for a much longer period - decades - than their Eastern counterparts did, whose secessionist threat and attempt was made only once, and at a much later date, in 1967. And while Northerners and Westerners were making all those secessionist threats in 1966, massacres of the Ibos in Northern Nigeria continued. By October the same year, more than 30,000 Eastern Nigerians, mostly Ibos, had been massacred in Northern Nigeria over a five-month period. And the pogroms continued. Seven months later, on May 27, 1967, Ojukwu, in his capacity as the Military Governor of Eastern Nigeria, was given the mandate to declare independence for the region:

---

[38] Western Nigerian delegation, in its memorandum to the ad hoc constitutional conference, lagos, September 1966, quoted ibid.

"We, the chiefs, elders, and representatives of all the 20 Provinces of Eastern Nigeria assembled in this joint meeting of the Advisory Committee of Chiefs and Elders, and the Consultative Assembly at Enugu this 27th day of May, 1967, do hereby solemnly mandate His Excellency Lieutenant-Colonel Chukwuemeka Odumegwu Ojukwu, the Military Governor of Eastern Nigeria, to declare at an early practicable date Eastern Nigeria as a free, sovereign, and independent State by the name and title of the Republic of Biafra....(and) recommend the adoption of a federal constitution based on the new provincial units.[39]

On May 30, 1967, Ojukwu declared Biafra independent. On the same day, Goiwon ordered mobilization of federal troops. On June 3, Ojukwu declared a state of emergency. In the early hours of July 6, fighting broke out between the Nigerian Federal Army and Biafra's secessionist forces in the three Eastern states (in the new 12-state Nigerian federation) on the border between Benue-Plateau State and the East-Central State. The civil war had officially begun.

It went on for the next two-and-half years. On January 15, 1970, Biafra surrendered. It is estimated that up to 2 million Eastern Nigerians, mostly Ibos, perished in the civil war. Most died of starvation, which the federal military government also used as a weapon to force the secessionist forces to surrender.

General Gowon remained Nigeria's head of state for the next five-and- a-half years until July 29, 1975, when he was overthrown by Brigadier-General Murtala Muhammed in a bloodless coup. Muhammed, a fellow northerner, overthrew Gowon because the previous year, in October 1974, he had reneged on promise to restore civilian rule. The new military head of state promised to restore democracy. But less than a year later, on February 13, 1976, General Muhammed was assassinated in an arbotive coup attempt. 37 persons were executed in 1976 for being involved in Mluhammed's assassination. His successor, Lieutenant-General Olusegun Obasanjo, commander of the armed forces, promised to restore civilian rule, as Muhammed had also promised to, and took steps to return the country to constitutional order; something rare among military rulers. As President Nyerere, in a compliment to military government of Nigeria for the steps it had taken towards restoration of democratic rule, told Obasanjo at the OAU summit in 1977: "No government has worked so hard to get itself out of p."[40]

The first nationwide elections since 1964 - 65 were held on August 31, 1977, to choose members of the assembly to write a new constitution. In a series of elections in July and August 1979, Nigerians elected a president, members of the federal legislature , 19 state governors, and state legislators. Five parties qualified for the contest: the National Party of Nigeria (NPN), whose presidential candidate was Alhaji Shehu Shagari; the United Party of Nigeria (UPN), led by Chief Obafemi Awolowo; the Nigerian People's Party (NPP), led by Dr. Nnamdi Azikiwe (Zik); the People's Redemption Party (PRP), led by Dr Aminu Kano; and the Great Nigeria People 's Party (GNPP), led by Waziri Ibrahim. The NPN won and Shagari became president on October 1, 1979.

---

[39] Eastern Nigeria,mandating Chukuemeka Odumegwu Ojukwu to declare independence for the entire region as the Republic of Biafra, quoted ibid., p. 649.

[40] Julius Nyerere, quoted by Jean Herskovits, "Democracy in Nigeria," in "Foreign Affairs," Winter 1979/80, p. 316.

However, the perennial problem of African politics wouldn't go away even though the Federal Election Commission (FEDECO), which ruled on legitimacy of the parties, had stiff requirements to ensure that parties would not appeal to tribal, regional or religious sentiments. All the five parties met those stringent guidelines before running for election. But that is not what happened in the field; ethnoregional biases were evident throughout the election, although the contest also transcended such loyalties in a significant way to produce a presidential winner who drew support from all parts of the country. This does not, however, diminish the impact of ethnoregional loyalties on the outcome of the election. As Jean Herskovits stated after observing the electoral contest:

> "The results of the senatorial election brought some answers about how voters would behave. Awolowo's party, UPN, won overwhelmingly in five states - all part of the old West Region and four solidly Yoruba - and came in second in one other, also with a large Yoruba population. Zik's party, the NPP, won almost as massively in two Ibo states, but also had more than 50 percent of the vote in Plateau, a northern state located in an area at the mid-section of the country know as the Middle Belt.

> The northern-based parties led by Aminu Kano and Waziri Ibrahim (PRP and GNPP, respectively) each led in one or two northern states, and GNPP came in second in a number of others. The NPN, however, had clearly the greatest and widest support, having received the most votes in eight states, and the second-largest number in ten others; only in Lagos was it a low third.

> The results provoked general distress over the tenacity of old political ties - which translates as 'tribalism.' The solid Ibo support for Zik showed the persistence of ethnically based interest groups. This was even clearer in the case of the Yoruba, whose support for UPN scarcely fell below 80 percent, and in some states was over 90.

> The Yoruba have since the war gained an ascendancy that they want to preserve in many areas: in the private sector of the economy, civil service the foreign services even the army. Perhaps the more importantlyo the Yoruba remember vividly the politics of the First Republic, when they were excluded from power and their part of the country was made the literal battleground during the elections of 1964 and 1965. In Nigeria people do not forget their own past traumas - but as one of them said, 'We will tryly have a nation when we also remember each other's.'

> In other parts of the country (the North), voting was far less consistent perhaps because the northern counterpart of Zik and Awolowo, the Sardauna (the late Northern Premier Sir Ahmadu Bello), was not there to become a historical focal point, perhaps because there were three presidential candidates from the far north."[41]

Shagari, a northerner and member of the Fulani ethnic group, became Nigeria's second leader thirteen years after his predecessor, Federal Prime minister Tafawa Balewa, another northerner, was assassinated in the military coup of January 1966. In elections from August 6 to September 3, 1983, Shagari was re-elected to a second four-year presidential term. But only about three months later, on December 31, he was overthrown by Major-General Mohammed Buhari in a bloodless coup. Buhari, another northerner, became Nigeria's seventh leader since independence in 1960. He said he took the action to save the country from economic collapse. The coup came only two days after Shagari had announced a government budget reflecting a 50-pereent drop in Nigeria's oil revenues since 1981.

---

[41] Jean Herskovits, ibid., pp. 322-324.

Shagari's government was, up to that time, the most corrupt and inefficient in Nigeria's post-colonial history; and the people had openly called for military intervention to halt the country's descent into total economic chaos. Corruption and mismanagement under Shagari was perhaps only surpassed by Abachals almost total destruction of the economy from 1993 until his sudden death in June 1998.

But military intervention and the ouster of Shagari should have been immediately followed by another general election to re-establish democracy accountability, which is impossible without electoral mandate and press freedom to expose wrong doing. Buhari's military regime suffocated both in April 1984, the military rulers imposed press censorship, forbidding the criticism of the government.

There was also a crackdown on officials of the ousted government. More than 500 former government officials, including President Shagari, were jailed awaiting trials by military tribunals on charges of stealing millions of dollars from the government. One of those sought was Umaru Diko, Minister of Transport and Shagari's fellow northerner, who was accused of stealing $3 billion but was beyond the reach of the law since he escaped to Britain. In July 1984 the Nigerian secret police were caught by Scotland Yard at Heathrow airport, London, when they made a daring attempt to try and kidnap Umaru Diko whom they had drugged and put in a sealed box bound for Nigeria aboard Nigerian Airways under diplomatic cover. The story made international headlines.

Yet in spite of some positive measures taken by Buhari's military junta, his regime still did not have the mandate to rule. Popular demand for ouster of a corrupt democratically elected government, as happened in the case of Shagari, should not be equated with an endorsement of military dictatorship. In fact, Nigeria's overall economic performance did not get any much better under Buhari's autocratic rule.

Nigeria's booming economy slackened in the 1980s as the worldwide oil glut reduced petroleum exports. The lower oil revenues forced the government to cut back on many of its projects, including a drastically reduced budget Shagari announced in 1981. Transfer of Nigeria's capital also cut into the budget: in 1982 the government began moving its departments from Lagos to Abuja, the new capital in the interior of the country, built at a cost of $3 billion. Because of worsening economic conditions, the government in January and February 1983 expelled about 1.2 million illegal aliens who had gone to Nigeria mostly from Ghana, and other West African countries, seeking a better life; many of them had lived in Nigria for decades. The exodus was one of the largest forced migrations in history, and caused a major humanitarian crisis especially for Ghana.

In October 1984, Nigeria broke with other OPEC members and reduced the price of its petroleum by $2 a barrel to earn more revenues faster and shore up its economy. As the economy continued to decline in 1985, the government ordered the second mass expulsion of aliens in two years. It gave 700,000 aliens from neighboring countries three weeks to pack their belongings and leave by May 10, 1985. Three months later, on August 27, 1985, Major-General Ibrahim Babangida, another northerner, overthrew Buhari in a bloodless coup.

Babangida also promised elections, like all soldiers do when they seize power. But five years later in 1990, he postponed elections schedule for that year. And when Abiola won the June 1993 presidential election, he was denied office. The annulment of the 1993 presidential election triggered riots in which many people were killed. Babangida was forced to resign and appointed a civilian to head an interim governments on August 26, 1993. But that government was overthrown on November 17 in a military coup led by Defense Minister General Sani

Abacha, another northerner. He became the ninth Nigerian head of state since independence in 1960 and the seventh military ruler in 27 years of military government since Nigeria's first coup on January 15, 1966.

Abacha himself had no use for democracy. When Abiola declared himself president of Nigeria on June 11, 1994, he was arrested and jailed on June 23. Yet he was the only Nigerian who had the mandate to rule, having won the presidential election on June 12, 1993, almost exactly one year before he was locked up. The new Nigerian military ruler benefited enormously from both Babangida's coup against Buhari, after which he became defense minister, and Babangida's downfall, after which he became president. Yet he brought Nigeria to the brink of collapse because of his kleptocracy and oppression of Southerners. As Professor Peter Lewis states in "Nigeria: From Despair to Expectation":

"General Abacha's palace coup in November 1993 provided the endgame to an abortive democratic transition begun by the military regime of General Ibrahim Babangida ... Under intense domestic and international pressure (because of the annulment of the 1993 presidential election and subsequent riots), Babangida hastily existedj office, handing power to an appointed civilian caretaker committee. Within weeks the civilians were shouldered aside by Abacha, the government's putative defense minister.

The depredations of Abacha's four and one-half years of dictatorship were extraordinary; few aspects of political, economic, and social life were left unscathed ... The regime also jeopardized national unity and stability. The control of Nigeria's central state by northern Muslim elites has fostered long-standing disaffection among southern ethnic and regional groups, notably the Yoruba. When Abacha an ethnic Kanuri from the predominantly Hausa city of Kano - seized power, he provoked further resentment toward the oligarchic domination of northern officers."[42]

Northern domination of the federation is so thorough, and has been going on for so long - since independence in 1960 that many Northerners automatically assume that it is their natural right to rule Nigeria. This hegemonic control is also justified on the grounds that as long as most of the country's wealth (mostly oil and other minerals) is in the South, the North must retain political control in perpetuity, as a counterweight.

But that is a recipe for catastrophe. And it has provoked a strong reaction from many Southerners. As Wole Soyinka described the northern military power-structure imposed on the rest of Nigeria:

> "(It is an) infinitesimal but well-positioned minority ... In denouncing the activities of this minority, described variously as the Kaduna Mafia, the oligarchy, the Sardauna Legacy, the Dan Fodio Jihadists, et cetera, what is largely lost in the passion and outrage is that they do constitute a minority - a dangerous, conspiratorial, and reactionary clique, but a minority just the same. Their tentacles reach deep, however, and their fantaicism is the secular face of religious fundamentalism."[43]

---

[42] Peter Lewis, "Nigeria: From Despair to Expectation, in "Current History: A Journal of Contemporary World Affairs," May 1999, pp. 223, and 224. See also Peter Lewis, Barnett Rubin, and Pearl Robinson, "Stabilizing Nigeria: Sanctions, Incentives and Support for Civil Society" (New York: Council on Foreign Relations Press, 1998).

[43] Soyinka, "The Open Sore of A Continent," op. cit., p. 8.

Nigeria has been dominated by northern military rulers since July 29, 1996. The only military rulers from the South were General Ironsi, who was assassinated in Nigeria's second military coup on July 29, 1966; and Obasanjo, who came to power after Murtala Muhammed was assassinated in an abortive coup attempt on February 13, 1976, and stepped down and out of politics and the army in 1979 when he handed over power to democratically elected President Shagari on October 1 the same year.

In 1966 alone, Nigeria had three different governments: under Prime Minister Tafawa Balewa, a northerner and civilian, who was assassinated on January 15, 1966;

General Ironis, a southerner, from January 15, - July 29, 1966; and colonel, later General, Gowon, a northerner, from July 29, 1966 to July 29. Gowon ruled for nine years, and earned distinction - as the longest-ruling military head of state in Nigerian history.

Next was Brigadier-General Murtala Muhammed, another northerner, who ruled from July 29, 1975 to February 13, 1976. He was succeeded by Lieutenant- General Obasanjo, a Southerner, who handed power to Shagari, yet another northerner. Shagari ruled until December 13, 1983, when he was overthrown by Major-General Mohammed Buhari, a fellow northerner.

Buhari ruled from December 13, 1983 - August 27, 1985. Next was Major- General Babangida, another northerner, from August 27, 1985, to August 26, 1993, who also became Nigeria's second longest ruling military head of state - he was in power for eight years - after Gowon. And he was replaced by another northerner, General Sani Abacha, who dominated the interim civilian government appointed by Babangida on his departure, but did not officially become president until November 17, 1993, when he ousted it. Abacha ruled until June 8, 1998, when he suddenly died of a heart attack after drinking a glass of orange juice poisoned by a prostitute at the residence of one of his cabinet officers.

Abacha was succeeded by General Abdulsalami Abubakar, the chief of defense staff and another northerner, who managed a transition to democratic rule and won accolades as the only other Nigerian military ruler - besides General Obasanjo - who handed over power to a democratically elected president. The elected leader in this case, happened to be Obasanjo, who won the presidential election on February 27, 1999, and assumed office on May 29, 1999; becoming Nigeria's first democratically elected leader in 16 years, since President Shagari was overthrown in 1983.

Therefore, simply put, out of 10 Nigerian rulers (11 if you count Obasanjo as two, military then next as civilian ruler) since independence in 1960, eight have been northerners - six soldiers and two civilians; and two have been Southerners - one soldier (General Ironsi), and the other one, both a soldier and civilian (Obasanjo). Dr. Nnamdi Azikiwe, Nigeria's first governor-general and president although a southerner, was not the head of government during the early sixties; Prime Minister Tafawa Balewa was. Azikiwe's position was largely ceremonial, although highly symbolic of power when he became president. But real power over the Nigerian federation was exercised by the Powerful Northern Premier, the Sardauna of Sokoto Sir Ahmadu Bello, through his protege, Federal Prime Minister Balewa; a stranglehold that was abruptly ended by the Ibo-led military coup of January 1966.

But tragically, northern domination continues even today, fueling bitter resentment among southerners against such hegemonic control. Northerners control both political and economic power. They also control the military, the most powerful institution in the country. If they allow southern politicians to be elected to federal office - as they did Obasanjo in 1999 - it is only with the intention of manipulating them to protect northern interests and perpetuate northern domination of the federation, however indirectly. But most of the time, it has been by direct control. As George Ayitteh, a Ghanaian professor of economics who has written extensively about Africa's economic and political problems and possible solutions, states in his book "Africa in Chaos":

> "In Nigeria, this insidious tribalism has retrogressively evolved what Nigerian columnist Igonikon Jack called a 'full-blown tribal-apartheid,' in which people of particular tribal , regional, or religious origin enjoy more privileges than their fellow indigenous compatriots, the Christian Ibos of the Southeast. The Ibos, who lost the Biafran War, are the most disadvantaged and discriminated against. The Northerners, who are the Hausa-Fulani ethnic group and predominantly Muslim, have ruled for 31 military, years."[44]

> Ayittey's book was published in 1998 before Abacha died and another military ruler and fellow northerner, General Abdulsalami Abubakar, succeeded him; thus extending military rule by northern army officers who have held the entire nation hostage for decades.

Nothing poses greater danger to Nigeria's national existence than this kind of ethnic domination by the Hausa-Fulani and their northern allies. And the potential for such a catastrophe - national collapse - cannot be underestimated if the northern elite continues to operate from the crackpot assumption that the stability and prosperity of Nigeria is somehow predicated on inequity of power. Nigeria came perilously close to disintegration during Abacha's reign; and the country would probably have fallen apart had this brutal dictator rigged the presidential election - as he was in the process of doing - to perpetuate himself and his northern cronies in office. Northerners have played with the fate of Nigeria as a nation for decades as if it were a toy, pushing the nation to the brink of catastrophe with dire consequences if it were to go over the edge. As Pini Jason, a Nigerian journalist, stated in the "New African," April 1994:

"Since the North controlled political power, it also controlled, decided and manipulated the allocation of posts, resources and values. And with this power it kept the competition for the crumbs alive in the South and the cleavages and political disunity very wide. The fact that North, like the Tutsis of Burundi, controls the military and uses its military might to monopolize political power, and is not willing to part with the privileges power has brought the North over the years, make many Nigerians fear a possible blood-bath *a la* Burundi," Burundi."[45]

The collapse Nigerians of Nigeria a possible blood-bath would be entirely their fault, justifying secession by southerners who would probably opt for such a course instead of trying to rebuild a federation in which they are not treated fairly by their fellow countrymen from the North. And secessionist sentiments are still simmering in the South, especially among the Yoruba, who feel that their candidate Olu Falae and not Obasanjo (whom they believe is controlled by northern generals, politicians and businessmen) should have been the winner of the 1999 presidential election; and the Ibos, who feel that their leader Alex

---

[44] George B. N. Ayittey, "Africa in Chaos" (New York: St. Martin's Press, 1998), pp. 170 –171.
[45] Pini Jason, in the "New African," April 1994, p. 8.

Ekwuema, and not Obasanjo, should have been the candidate of the People's Democratic Party (PDP) which won the election with Obasanjo as its standard-bearer.

Ekwuema served as Nigeria's vice-president under Shagari, and was a major driving force behind the creation of the People's Democratic Party which - with behind-the-scenes manipulation and financial clout by former military ruler General Babangida to tip scales in favor of Obasanjo - did not choose him as its presidential candidate, despite his formidable political credentials. And his identity as an Ibo probably did not sit well with many delegates at the national convention. As Ayittey says, "the Ibos are ... the most disadvantaged and discriminated against." And that is not very good the future of the federation, power, unless there is extensive devolution of power.

But probably at no other time in the nation's history since the 1960s when the Ibos tried to secede has Nigeria come so close to breaking up as it did in 1993 – 1998, because of northern domination and disgust among the Yoruba for having been excluded from power for so long since independence in 1960. As Norimitsu Onishi reported from Ibadan (in Yoruba heartland), Nigeria, in "The New York Times," April 24, 1999:

> "After a Yoruba leader, Moahood K.O. Abiola, was denied an apparent victory in he 1993 presidential elections by Nigeria's northen military rulers, many Yoruba called for secession. Not since the Biafran civil war three decades ago, when the Ibo tried to break away, had Nigeria's survival been so strongly put into doubt...

> 'The nationality question is the most important one facing not only Nigeria, but many other places in the world,' said Bola Ige, a leading Yoruba politician and former governor of the southern Oyo state. 'That's why you have Kosovo, Indonesia, and, nearer home, Zaire, Rwanda and Burundi'...

> Can General Obasanjo, serving as President in a civilian government (and who is) distrusted by many of his own people..., win over the Yoruba without alienating the country's 250 other ethnic groups?... 'If General Obasanjo succeeds in settling this (nationality) question, his name will be written in gold,' Mr. Ige, 68, said. 'His place in Nigerian history will be assured. So the ball is in his court.'

It is also in the court of the Yoruba leaders (who don't trust him, yet) without whom the President-elect will not be able to begin creating unity.

What role the Yoruba should play in a Nigeria led by one of their own is being debated passionately here in the quintessentially Yoruba city of Ibadan. It is home to the nation's first university, built in 1948 by the British, the county's former colonial rulers, a lasting testament to the Yoruba's position as Nigeria's best educated ethnic group."[46]

Obasanjo alienated fellow Yorubas for a number of reasons. They saw him as a traitor. They also considered him to be a northern stooge. And when he was military head of state, he infuriated many Yorubas, including younger ones more interested in music than politics, when soldiers burned down the residential compound of Fela Kuti, a Yoruba and Nigeria's - and one of Africa's music giants - most famous musician; and tossed out his elderly mother - who was in her late 70s and lived on her son's premises - out of a second-floor window at her house. She was badly injured and died several days later from the injuries she sustained.

---

[46] Normitsu Onishi, "A Nigerian Region Warms to an Unfavorite Son," in "The New York Times," April 24, 1999, p. A-3.

The soldiers did all this because Fela wrote and sang songs critical of the government, as he had always done. But they accomplished exactly the opposite. Fela never stopped criticizing the government, continued to sing those songs, and saw his popularity soar even higher. Yet in spite of all this and other acts of "betrayal" against his people, there are those who were ready to embrace Obasanjo as a prodigal son after he won the 1999 presidential election:

> "On February 27, General Obasanjo won decisively nationwide, but he lost here in Oyo state (where Ibadan is located), as well as in his home state, Ogun - in fact, he lost in all six Yoruba states. His loss was rooted in his first presidency (when he was the military of head state and handed over power to an elected civilian, a northerner, Shehu Shagari)...
> In a close presidential race between a northerner (Shagari) and a revered Yoruba politician (Chief Obafemi Awolowo), General Obasanjo was seen by the Yoruba as having favored the northerner. The discovery that he had cast his own ballot for the Northerner fueled the Yoruba's anger and betrayal. General Obasanjo's close ties to a military dominated by northerners added to the Yoruba's lasting mistrust, which deepened in recent years when he was quoted as saying that 'Abiola is not the messiah'... Once held in suspicion by the Yoruba for his own close ties to northerners, Mr. Abiola became in prison the living embodiment of the Yoruba's political disenfranchisement."[47]

When he joined the People's Democratic Party (PDP), which was strongly supported by highly influential retired northern generals, Obasanjo engraved his name in stone as a traitor in the eyes of many of his fellow Yorubas. And they made that clear during the 1999 presidential election. As Layi Balogun, a prominent Yoruba architect and businessman in Ibadan stated: "They campaigned against Obasanjo on the fear of marginalization and extermination of the Yoruba race. Under those circumstances, Obasanjo had no chance in Yorubaland."[48] Yet after Obasanjo's victory at victory at the polls, a number of Yoruba leaders invoked their culture and Yoruba philosophical underpinnings to justify their gradual shift towards embracing Obasanjo as a prodigal son. As Lam Adesina, the governor-elect of Oyo state, explained:

"We believe in Yorubaland that you do not send a bad child to be eaten by a lion. The Yoruba leaders have put our heads together with our obas, our kings, to see how we could help him. We should not be seen as a race fighting against each other. Whether Obasanjo is good or bad, he is part of the Yoruba race. He is part of us."[49]

Invocation of such images and distinct identity which is virtually seen as fundamentally different from that of other groups, hence the use of the term "Yoruba race," is at the very heart of Nigeria's problem as a highly volatile polyethnic society. It has been used by the Hausa-Fulani to justify their domination of the federation; and has propelled many Yorubas towards secession, even if they may not be able to realize this objective. One of the most vocal exponents of this "racial" separation, and critic of Obasanjo, is Ola Oni, a former professor of economics at the University of Ibadan.

---

[47] Ibid.
[48] Layi Balogun, quoted ibid.
[49] Lam Adesina, ibid.

He once believed in Pan-Africanism and nonethnic politics, but gave up on the idea of a united Nigeria after northern generals annulled the 1993 presidential election won by a fellow Yoruba, Chief Abiola. As he bluntly put it:

> "Obasanjo still hangs on to the old idea of one Nigeria. I no longer believe in one Nigeria. We are calling on the Yoruba people not to accept his government and to regard it as no more than a transitional government (towards dissolution of the nigerial federation). He has been chosen by the north to assist in realizing the northern agenda of domination."[50]

The critical role Babangida and other retired - and active - northern generals, businessmen, and politicians played in securing nomination for Obasanjo as the presidential candidate of Nigeria's main political party, left no doubt about their intention to perpetuate and consolidate northern control of the federation, even when the presidency of the country shifted to the South. They also did that, support Obasanjo, to insulate themselves criminal investigations and possible prosecutions by the incoming Administration f or their abuse of power - corruption and other criminal acts - when they were in office. A government they put in power would hardly go after them.

It was all part of a grand design by northerners to keep Nigeria united probably until the oil wells dry up in the South - to benefit the North, which hardly has any natural resources, let alone oil which earns more than 90 percent of the country's foreign exchange; amount of which is siphoned off by the military-dominated Northern plutocracy.

They have stolen billions of dollars from oil revenues every year, while tens of millions of their fellow countrymen – including those in the oil-producing regions of the Niger Delta – remain paupers. Under Abacha, the people of this oil-rich nation, one of the world's ten leading oil exporters, became some of the poorest in the world; bled to death by northern military officers and their cronies, all of whom became instant multimillionaires, and some of them billionaires.

And while General Abdulsalami Abubakar conducted himself well and facilitated the transition to civilian rule, he ominously warned about a possible military comeback in one of his last speeches before he handed over power to Obasanjo. According to a report from Abuja, Nigeria's capital, in "The New York Times," May 10, 1999:

> "Nigeria's military ruer, General Abdulsalami Abubakar, today (May 9) urged politicians due to take power on May 29 to stick to 'the rules" if they want the military to stay in barracks. The general, who has promised to hand over to Nigeria's first elected President in 15 years, issued the warning at a meeting today with newly elected legislators ...

Generals returned power to the civilians in 1979 only to take over again in December 1983 because they were exasperated by the behavior of irresponsible civilian politicians 'carried away by the glamour of office,' General Abubakar said.

---

[50] Ola Oni, ibid.

The general has said repeatedly that he intends to play no part in political life after the President-elect, Olusegun Obasanjo, takes office on May 29, but plans to retire to him home in northern Nigeria."[51]

But while General Abubakar made an honorable exit from the Nigerian political scene on which he had unexpectedly emerged after the sudden death of Sani Abacha, it is clear from all available evidence - as we have presented here - that northerners don't seriously intend to share, let alone give up, power to southerners. But the real problem is not with all northerners but northern military officers who through the years have staged coups and counter-coups to perpetuate northern domination of the federation. And that is extremely dangerous. Such domination could lead to civil war, as it did in the 1960s when the Ibos seceded; or to total disintegration of Nigeria several independent states, each with its own national flag, army and government, as southerners desperately seek to end northern control. And it can be ended. The question is how.

Elections will not do the trick. Northern military rulers are not going to hand over power to civilian leadership permanently no matter who wins the presidential election, unless it is a northern candidate of their choices or someone else they can manipulate at will once in office. They even overthrew Shagari, a fellow northerner. Yet he won the presidency twice in democratic elections. That did not stop the soldiers from tossing him out of office; his government was, of course, extremely corrupt, but the people of Nigeria were still not given the chance shortly thereafter to elect another leader - or even Shagari himself if they wanted him back in office. And, as is well-known, the military rulers blocked Abiola from taking office he had rightfully won in what was considered to be the most democratic election in Nigerian history. Northern soldiers even overthrow each other; that they make sure it is a fellow Northerner who takes over.

So what can be done? Power sharing between the military and elected civilian leaders comes to mind as one possible solution. Re-writing the Nigerian constitution under which the military is guaranteed a permanent in the national government by reserving some cabinet posts such as defense, internal security, and other powerful government posts for high-ranking military officers backed up by a team of civilian advisers is one option; but not very democratic, even under a democratically elected president who should have the freedom to choose his own cabinet members subject to parliamentary approval.

But civilian-military government as the lesser of two evils - better than full military control - should not be entirely ruled out as a pre-emptive measure against military coups, not only in Nigeria, but in other African countries as well. It will not stop military coups completely - soldiers overthrow soldiers all the time; and they also overthrow all kinds of governments, including those which have both military officers and civilians in the cabinet, for the same reason: personal glory and power. But it may help, at least by assuring the military leadership that it has a say on how the country is run.

But there is an even better alternative especially for a vast and complex country such as Nigeria which can, not only prevent coups, but keep Nigeria as a federation of 36 states as presently constituted. Some people, of course, including many Nigerians themselves (some Yorubas, for example) and not just outsiders, see the disintegration of Nigeria as a virtual certainty - if northern domination continues. Wole Soyinka sees that as a very strong

---

[51] Abdulsalami abubakar, cited in "Exiting General Warns New Nigeria Leaders," in "The New York Times," May 10, 1999, p. A-3.

possibility, as he bluntly states in his book, "The Open Sore of A Continent: A Personal Narrative of the Nigerian Crisis."[52] And as Maku wa Muta, a Kenyan professor at Harvard Law School, states:

> "Few accounts of (the) brutal acts by the military are as poignant as persecution of Ken Saro-Wiwa, the writer and defender of one of Nigeria's many minority ethnic groups, the Ogoni. Together, minority groups comprise 33 percent of the total population.
>
> The Ogoni, who occupy one of the richest oil-producing regions have suffered the consequences of ecological devastation, seeing their once-lush farmlands turned into an inferno of burning oil swamps. Hence the Movement for the Salvation of the Ogoni People, a civic organization seeking better conditions or, failing that, secession.

In 1994, Saro-Wiwa and several other Ogonis were arrested and charged with the murder of four pro-government Ogoni leaders...In November 1995, they were hanged. In the case of Saro-Wiwa, a man in his fifties, it took five attempts to kill him ... What the death of Saro-Wiwa demonstrated was the determination of the Abacha regime to crush any credible threat to its control of the country's main industry (oil).

The incident further proves that the northern military clique is not about to share power with non-northerners.

What, then are the Yoruba, Igbo, and other minorities (like the Ogoni) supposed to do? How long are they supposed to wait before they receive their due as fellow Nigerians? It seems only a matter of time before a three-state partition becomes the sole option. But will the north ever allow separation? For now, Nigeria seems headed toward the apocalypse."[53]

---

[52] Soyinka, "The Open Sore of A Continent," op. cit.
[53] Makau wa Mutua, "can Nigeria be One?," op. cit.

Democratization, devolution of power to the states orregions, and decentralization of the military: that is what can ensure the survival and stability of the Nigerian federartion. Centralization of power and suffocation of dissent does exactly the opposite.

The collapse of several African states, and civil wars which have devestated many countries acoss the continent since independence, are the result of such abuse of powe. Tyranny, corruption, and tribalism; that is what is destroying Africa. Rigged elections, which are a product of those triple evils, have tirggered some of the bloodiest wars on the continent. The Liberian civil war which lasted for seven years, is just one such tragic example, thanks to miltiray dictator Samuel Doe, who rigged the 1985 presidential election.

For comparative anlaysis, see, for example, "Guinea-Bissau: One War Ends," in "The Economist," May 15, 1999, p. 48:

"It was not a huge war, but for the 1 million people of the West African state of Guinea-Bissau, it was devestating...Hundreds of people were killed, the city (Bissau, the captial) was destroyed and hundreds of thousands fled into the countryside. It lasted 11 months, but much of the killing was in the final assault on Bissau on May 6th.

Unlike the wars that drag endlessly on in Sierra Leone and Liberia, Guinea-Bissau's came to an end when the rebels stormed the presidential palace and the commander of the president's forces ordered his men to surrender. Mr. Vieira...was in power for 19 years and, although the people of Guinea-Bissau voted for him in the 1994 multiparty election, today they seem glad to be rid of him...

Mutiny broke out last June when Mr. Veira tried to arrest Brigadier Mane (the army chief), accusing him of smuggling arms to rebels in the (separatist) southern Casmance region of Senegal...For years, Senegal has fretted that its neighbor (Guinea-Bissau) was backing th rebels in Casamance...Guinea-Bissau's new prime minister has suggested that Senegal should hold a referendum on independence for Casamance."

One way to rob separatist movements of momentum is to grant their regions or provices greater autonomy – short of full independence. If that dosen't neutralize them, the alternative is full-scale war (whiCh is not worth

The election of Obasanjo in 1999 as president seems to have averted such a catastrophe. But if the military intervenes again, by overthrowing Obasanjo or the next democratically elected government, that could be the end of Nigeria as one country. But it can still survive, and thrive, as one nation if some measures are taken by Obasarijo or his successor, to prevent a military coup.

The three-state partition Professor Matua sees as inevitable doesn't, have to be that extreme, at least not initially; a six-state partition could be even better – North, Central, East, West, Southeast, Southwest, to give smaller groups more freedom.

But Nigeria can still remain one country, under one government, if its most powerful institution, the military, is effectively contained. It is the military (the northern military elite) which, by overthrowing goverenments to perpetuate northern domination, is responsible for stirring up and fueling secessionist setiments among Yorubas, Ibos and other Nigerians who resent being dominated by the Hausa-Fulani who control the armed forces, hence virtually the entire federation. Otherwise there would be no need for such agitation, for secession; and the Ibos would not have tried to secede in 1960s, had there been no such northern domination.

What needs to be done, and it is a herculean task given the track record of northern military officers - of whom there is no shortage - to block the move or launch coups and counter-coups, is decentralize the military; instead of having it under one central command as presently constituted. There is a need for regional armies to prevent military coups. Each of

---

the cost) or a plebiscite to determine whether or not the majority of the people in contested regions want to separate.

Such referendums should be seriously considereed by africancoountires as a way of ending civil wars across the continent. Presidnt Moi of Kenya is one African leader who, in a spech in 1997, openly advocated the separation of the Hutu and the Tutsi in Rwanda and Burundi into independent states to end ethnic conflict between the two enemies. He bluntly stated that each ethnic group should have its own independent country.

In Nigeria, Biafran leader Ojukwu proposed the same solution to end the civil war. As he stated in his speech to the OAU summit in Addis Ababa, Ethiopia, on August 5, 1968:

"The Nigerian Army has occupied some non-Ibo areas of Biafra. But this cannot be regarded as a settlement of the'minority question.' This is why we have suggested a plebiscite. Under adequate international supervision, the people of these areas should be given a chance to choose whether they want to belong to Nigeria or to Biafra. Plebiscites have been use in southern Cameroons, in Togo, in Mid-Western Nigeria – and by the British recently in Gibraltar – to determine what grouping is most acceptable to the people of disputed areas. If Nigeria believes that she is really defending the true wishes of the minorities (non-Ibo tribes in the East), she should accept our proposal for a plebiscite in the disputed areas of Nigeria and Biafra,"

Nigeria never accepted this proposal. For the full text of Ojukwu's speech, see "Africa Contemporary Record," op. cit., pp. 652 – 672. For a contrasting view, see Enahoro, ibid., pp. 672 – 689.

The idea of plebiscites as an integral part of conflict resolution in Africa may, in the long run, be accepted as an inescapable necessity in countries mired in perpetual civil wars and other conflicts. Ethopia used it to end its 30-year civil war when it allowed the people of Eritea to decide in a referendum if they wanted full independence. They did, and in May 1993, Eritrea became the 53rd independent African state.

Southern Sudan could become the 54th independent African state, any time, if the people in the region, almost all of whom are black, vote for independence from the Northern Arab-dominated government of Sudan.

African countries will tehn, out of necessity, be compelled to cooperate with their neighbors and form some kind of association – which may eventually lead to federationor confederation – because most of them cannot survive and thrive on their own aas viable economic entities. That may propably be the most realistic approach towards African unity, about which so much is said, but so little done, as Africa remains powerless in the global arena.

The existence of Nigeria as a federation, and the role it plays as a major Third World country, clearly demonstrates the imperative for African unity. If some African countries break up, or give more power to the regions, it should be with the intentionof forming a large federation or confederation with their neighbors, and preferably on a sub-continental –West, North, East, Central, and South – or even on a continental scale. Without such unity, Africa is doomed, and will continue to mark time, till kingdom come.

Nigeria's three geographical regions (North, East, and West) - they are no longer political units, of course - should have its own full-fledged army, and its own supreme command.

That is one way to prevent military coups, since the national army will then not be under one central command, which makes it easy for military officers to plan coups and overthrow governments. The only supreme organ those three regional armies should be the council of the three top military officers from each region who are equal in rank and power, each in full command of his own army. And the final decision of what is to be done with those joint armies in discharging national responsiblity must be made by all three commanders. Where there is dissent, they should work towards a consensus, until a stalemate is broken. Two of them simply won't have the capability to impose their will on their dissenting colleague. He has his own full-fledged army, and any attempt to sway him by force will amount to a declaration of war in which even a Pyrrhic victory by the other two armies will not be worth the cost.

Should any of the regions attempt to impose its will on one or the other or the other – or on both – as the north has done to the rest of the country for years, that is ground for secession; and even when two regions team up against one. With a decentralized military, the targeted region will at least have its own full-fledged army for self-defense and the capacity to wage full-scale war against the aggressor (or aggressors); and will even have the right to seek help from outside if it declares independence, if the residents of the region choose to do so, but only after their wish has been determined in a plebiscite conducted under international supervision.

Will the north ever allow such decentralization of the military they have dominated for so long, and the disintegration of the federation on which they depend so much for survival? They probably will not allow any of that; because of all that oil in the South, and access to the sea, also in the South, they are determined to control permanently; although Northerners themselves have sought secession through the years since 1914 when the North and South were amalgamated to form one colony of Nigeria. They openly talked about secession until as late as the sixties.

And because northern military officers will probably block the move to decentralize the military, which would mean an end to their domination of the federation, it is then for southern military officers to exert pressure collectively, within the military, on the top northern leadership to decentralize and regionalize the armed forces before it's too late; warning northerners in no uncertain terms that the alternative is massive civil unrest inexorably leading to civil war and total disintegration of Nigeria into 250 independent ethnostates as they were before the partition of Africa which united them into what they are today as the multiethnic nation of Nigeria. The North, which is both poor and landlocked, will then not even have access to the sea - let alone oil - and would wish it had agreed to decentralization of the armed forces while remaining in the same federation under elected civilian government. Therefore southern military officers could be Nigeria's last hope for democracy after years of northern militocracy.

PROBLEMS AND PROSPECTS OF SUSTAINING DEMOCRACY IN NIGERIA[*]

Bamidele A. Ojo

PREFACE

The past few years have been very traumatic for many Nigerians. With the exception of those in power or close to the seat of power, the changes of 1998 were a welcome relief given the tyranny and repression that the country has suffered under General Abacha. With many people in prison and more in exile, the death of Abacha was received with a sigh of relief. The situation got even worse with the death of Chief M.K.O Abiola on the eve of his release from prison but as always the country must go on. Many observers saw in Nigeria, the resilience that has come to signify the strength and potential of this once "giant of Africa". Many have seen the destruction and the socio-political and economic decay of the past decades and as the whole world prepare for the new millennium, things could only get better in Nigeria. That is why the administration of President Obasanjo, even in the absence of anything significant, would still be preferable than the previous military administrations. Many Nigerians have seen the way the leadership has mishandled the Nigerian economy and abuse the rights of the people while exploiting and politicizing the ethnic diversity to satisfy their own individual agenda. It is with this in mind, and the renewed desire to begin to cultivate a Nigerian culture that appreciates the rule of law and sustains democratic governance as a means toward providing the best for all its people, that the aspiration and goals of a representative generation of Nigerians are put together in this volume. The call for Nigerians who want to make a difference received many responses and out of which the following has been selected to address some critical issues facing the new Nigerian political experiment. These opinions, sometimes academic and sometime less so, is considered a preliminary attempt to initiate a dialogue among Nigerians, in an attempt to foster better understanding of our need and identify what could bring us all together. This book is divided into four main parts: Constitutionalism and political reconstruction, social and economic

---

[*] Excerpted from *Problems and Prospects of Sustaining Democracy in Nigeria,* Ojo, Bamidele A., © Nova Science Publishers, Inc. 2001.

issues, foreign policy issues and wither Nigeria? There are fourteen chapters in all and each representing the view of the authors as so noted. Many others responded to the call for contributions and due to inability to meet the deadline, set and extended several times, their essays cannot be included in this volume. The voice of a generation on democracy in Nigeria, I hope will constitute a renaissance of a more active role in the Nigerian political process by all Nigerians home and abroad.

INTRODUCTION : A MISSION WITH A VISION

I was in the office that morning preparing for an 11 o'clock class when the telephone rang and a colleague informed me about the death of General Sanni Abacha. I immediately contacted the Nigeria Consulate in New York City and the news was confirmed. My feeling was that of amazement at the recent turn of event and as a political scientist and out of instinct, began to ponder possible political scenario, including whither Nigeria?, who takes over, what will happen to Chief Abiola and whether this is the turning point in Nigeria history. The following days confirmed my fears and raised many questions, many of which remain unanswered even almost two years to the day.

The assumption of power of General Abubakar and the death of Chief Abiola and the transition program followed by the election of Olusegun Obasanjo, were trend that will continue to baffle Nigerian historians and political scientist alike. With the transition and the democratic election of Olusegun Obasanjo, albeit a former military leader, came another opportunity for socio-political and economic rebirth in the life of a people. The task of nation building as well as state building therefore became the most important agenda for the leadership in Nigeria. I therefore put together a collection of issues that need to be addressed by the new leaders in an open letter to the newly elected president, calling for a responsible and accountable leadership in the country because one of the most important problem facing this country since independence and probably since its existence is the lack of effective and responsible leadership. The letter was also published by the Guardian Newspaper (Lagos) on the 22nd. of April 1999 as New Leadership In Nigeria. This piece is presented below as a forward to this collection of essays by a generation of Nigerians, who have been observing the Nigerian dilemma for decades now.

NEW LEADERSHIP IN NIGERIA

As a student of politics and democratic process, I have no doubt that we as a people are capable of reaching greater heights with the right leadership capable of promoting the human rights, the welfare and the prosperity of its people. While we celebrate this renewed opportunity to do something positive by our people since independence, we must understand that no domestic peace can exist and no prosperity will be attainable without social justice and the commitment to the promotion of and the defense of human rights. This is very much within our reach if we as a people are committed to it especially if we can eliminate the indifference on the part of the entire leadership. Yours is an opportunity to set a good example and I hope you will take this second chance to do just that. I also hope your government will endeavor to exploit to its limits the tremendous human assets that the country is endowed. We also need to bridge the gap between the government and the governed, between the elite and the mass, between the north and the south, within the north and within the south and within the groups and among our people.

A POPULAR CONSTITUTION

The first step toward achieving a viable democratic governance revolves around a legitimate and popularly accepted constitution. Your government must find a way to put in place a constitution but which is embraced by all Nigerians. There is a need to remove the military fingerprints that seems to soil all democratic experiments since independence.

The new constitution(the 1979 constitution was the best we have ever had) should be ratified by the states and approved through a referendum because a legitimate constitution is imperative for both socio-political and economic development. It will reinforce the institutionalization of our democratic experiment and the future of our polity. We must find a way to prevent the suspension of our constitution. Every Nigerian must be able to rise up and resist any attempt to violate a popularly accepted constitution. There is the need to end ruling Nigeria through decrees. This may dissuade future coup attempts.

AN IDENTIFIABLE CITIZENRY

One important step toward achieving any growth and prosperity in Nigeria is for our government to know and be able to respond to every Nigerian through an effective identification process. We need an identification card or social security card that would help the government in directly focusing its policy initiatives on the citizenry. This would help in monitoring social and economic welfare of Nigerians and facilitate effective taxation.

STATE AUTONOMY

To strengthen our federal system and sustain the process of nation building, there is a need for state autonomy. Additional resources need to be allocated to the states and they should have more control over education, health, transportation and other significant aspects of governance with direct and immediate impact on our people. The states should be allowed to define their respective agenda and to embody in their respective state constitutions and legitimate administrative structures from which to promote their domestic agenda and aspirations. It is at this level that I think we should involve our traditional institutions in this democratic experiment. Our traditional leaders/rulers because of their continued pseudo-political and spiritual role and as a link to our pre-colonial past should be allowed to provide a far reaching legitimacy for our new institutions and democratic engagements. We can no longer ignore their gradual irrelevance in our societal structure when they remain the only viable remnant of our authentic but forgotten traditions and identity.

Domestic Agenda

Obviously, you will be preoccupied with problems such as food and fuel shortages, unemployment, unpaid salaries, hyperinflation, sluggish economic growth and foreign debts but these are the problems that our leaders must resolve and many more. The mark of a good leader is not in the amount in foreign accounts nor is it in the disdain shown towards criticism nor the imprisonment of those who dare challenge their position or the desire to cater to ones personal needs. But a great leader is known for his courage and efforts to resolve the variants ills that befalls his nation. All that Nigerians ask for, is for you to do your best. Give it all and you shall be remembered as one of the few if any we have seen in our country. Many before you if not all have failed the nation and you have the unique opportunity of a second chance. The new leadership, you must end the endemic nature of the fuel shortages that suffocates our nation by privatizing oil refineries while taking firm control of foreign monopolies and at the same time ridden this sector of its paralyzing corruption.

Our tax system needs to be overhauled. We are a nation in need of an equitable tax system. We need all, not the civil servants alone, to pay their taxes. We call for a system capable of generating revenue necessary for our social and economic growth. It is time, to improve government ability to collect internal revenue effectively. To encourage investment and small business as well as to promote entrepreneurial spirit, our banking system need to be liberalized. A renewed life need to be injected into our economy.

The Military

This country must find a way to end military intervention in politics. A commission should be set up including both civilians and military personnel (retired and active) to find a way to restructure the military and provide them a more viable and constructive role to play in our society especially when we are not in dare need of them to defend our country. A civilian control of the military is indispensable in a democratic society and an effort should made to de-politicized the entire armed forces. The Nigerian police need to be retrained and provided necessary hardware in order to perform effectively. They remain a far more important agent in sustaining stability in a society riddled with corruption and criminal activities. I implore you to do all that is necessary to turn this around. Our law enforcement institutions need to be reformed and our prisons updated, equipped and reoriented towards rehabilitation and positively impacting on those that it serves.

Ethical Leadership

An ethical and accountable leadership is a means toward establishing the public trust in government and in this spirit, I hope your government and the entire elected representatives should declare their assets within three months of assuming office. The public must be brought along to realize that public office is not a means to accumulate wealth but an avenue to provide public service in the interest of all Nigerians. We must begin to change our public persona and the prevailing culture of corruption through a systematic and radical purging of our entire governmental structures and service system, of dishonesty, inefficiency and ineptitude. All contracts involving over a million naira should be made public and all information regarding the award and contractors should be disclosed and in pubic domain. We need good communication and adequately funded and equipped medical facilities in Nigeria. It is about time the government focus on the epidemic and the destructive impact of AIDS and HIV. It is time to provide effective preventive and quality health care for people. A healthy population is a productive population. Your government should respond with vigor and focus in addressing these issues. The mark of your leadership should be felt in the rural as well as in the urban Nigeria. Considering that, agriculture accounts for 40% of our gross domestic product but employs over 65% of our people, I think its about time to do something about this. We need to redistribute our wealth and provide capital to our farmers in order to engage in large scale agriculture. The farmers should be helped as well as protected so that we can be able to feed ourselves again. I call on you to privatize all agencies providing basic social services in order to generate competition and better services for our people.

We do not need our government spending our hard earn revenues in supporting unprofitable ventures and ineffective services such as NEPA, NITEL, Nigeria Airways, to mention a few. Privatization should not mean preserving the domination of these agencies, it must include choices and the opportunity for other capable entrepreneur to establish competition and as such provide better services for our people. It is time to revamp our economy and make it work for all Nigerians.

VISIONARY LEADERSHIP

We need a visionary leadership with an agenda. You government needs to develop a **national agenda** which should include a plan to reduce our dependence on oil and compulsory savings from revenues generated from it. The people in those areas where these resources are extracted should be protected and guaranteed a healthy and save environment. A domestic agenda should center on the promotion of socio-political and economic well being of all Nigerians. It should seek to exploit to the maximum our industrial capacity. Your government should undertake the review of budgetary allocation to ministries and parastatals and the reduction of our defense spending in order to reallocate funds towards those areas in needs such as education, health, communication, to mention just a few. We need to prepare our country to compete in the next millennium because a self-critical leadership with a viable domestic agenda will promote a stable foreign policy. We also need an immediate and structured payment plan that will eliminate our foreign debts within a period of time and there should be a moratorium on any loan or other form of indebtedness. Nigeria has lost her place in the region and on the world stage. You can reclaim our moral and political leadership in Africa and beyond. Our embassies abroad should be responsive to our citizens and engage in promoting the image and well being of Nigeria. We need a strong Nigeria capable of leading Africa through its present woes. Not only do we all as Africans need to work together on such problems as AIDS and the prevailing wars in many parts of the continent but also to generate enough market and economic interdependence that would make this continent the envy of the world. We are lagging behind in technology and the computer age is already passing us by.

What we need is an action plan champion by a group of countries already making necessary strides within their own society. If you lead Nigeria well, Africa will respect your leadership.

Finally, I call on the President and the new leadership, to promote a culture of accommodation in our country. Your leadership should transcend regions and parties. The interests of all Nigerians should be the main stay of your administration. Appointments to federal positions and offices should equitably reflect the diversity of our nation. Your administration must support an independent labor system. To help your administration to focus on this agenda, you need a free press. The freedom of the press is indispensable to the sustenance of our political life and this political experiment. Your government must also promote a free and independent judiciary without which a domestic agenda will fail. A disciplined leadership must provide the much needed direction through bipartisan governmental appointments which should lay the foundation for a stronger and united Nigeria because our nation is in need of all that are capable of making a difference.

This is not the time for some to be prevented from or some to refuse to participate in our political experiment. We are all Nigerians whose birthright is to participate in promoting a common agenda for the best of all Nigerians. I am happy to be a Nigerian, the fact that I was born a Yoruba or Christian is nothing but an accident at birth and removes nothing from the fact that I am a human being whose interests like others should be protected and whose well being should be assured in a polity like ours. We all should be proud of being a Nigerian. The experience of the past years is nothing to write home about but we are encouraged that here is a renewed opportunity to attain our God given potential as all Nigerians have dreamt in those dark days. It is about time to begin to develop within all Nigerians the sense of nationhood. This is our future and this is our road toward bringing together a committed people embarking on a journey to building a great nation- Nigeria.

CURRICULUM AND ADMINISTRATIVE INNOVATIONS FOR THE NIGERIAN EDUCATIONAL SYSTEM IN THE TWENTY-FIRST CENTURY[*]

Zephyrinus C. Okonkwo

This chapter deals essentially with two ideas: Curriculum Innovations for the Nigerian Educational System, and Administrative Innovations for the Nigerian Educational System with emphasis on the tertiary level. Although these two ideas seen to be independent, they have a region of intersection which will be discussed in the sequel. In this chapter, we will discuss in some details the needed curriculum innovations at all levels of the educational system. We will also deal with administrative innovations required at the colleges and universities in order to lay a strong foundation for a stable environment where students, professors, non-academic staff, and administrators can thrive as a community whose objective encompass teaching, research, and service. Like every educational system, the Nigerian Educational System must provide:

(i) An adequate, safe and secure environment for teaching and learning where the educated must imbibe adequate skills and knowledge to seek gainful employment within the society;

(ii) College level education, which must not only provide the student with enough basic skills but must also prepare the student for graduate education within and outside the country;

(iii) Responsive dynamic curriculum at all levels of education. Such curriculum must respond to societal needs, and must include innovative methods of teaching and learning, innovative method of seeking knowledge, computer skills and information technology, strong emphasis on communication both in written and oral forms, reading and public speaking.

---

[*] Excerpted from *Problems and Prospects of Sustaining Democracy in Nigeria,* Ojo, Bamidele A., © Nova Science Publishers, Inc. 2001.

The curriculum at all levels must be reviewed from time to time expunging irrelevant topics and courses and including new ones.

Administrative innovations at the tertiary level must include:

(i)   Tenure system at all tertiary institutions;
(ii) A method of checking the excesses of some professors and administrators through legislation and enforcement of the laws;
(iii) Provision of adequate funding for salaries and research for colleges and universities by the establishment of a stable method of funding including land-grant, Educational Tax, Luxury Tax, and Property Tax;
(iv) Streamlining teaching and research resources and reducing waste by eliminating redundancy and duplications in neighboring colleges and universities.

1. INTRODUCTION

The next millennium presents an extraordinary challenge to the people and government of the federal republic of Nigeria on all facets of life. The development of a strong educational system is very essential for the development of a strong economy, educated and skilled workforce, peace, and stability. Considering the nose dive Nigeria has suffered in the last sixteen years (from 1984- 1999) encompassing very weak economy, high unemployment, dilapidated and neglected educational system, high poverty rate, extraordinary level of corruption and fraudulent practices in both the public and private sectors, armed and pen robbery, international condemnation and sanctions, as a result of bad management of national resources, it has become a matter of urgency that our educational system must be revamped and innovated.

Nigeria is a great country and all Nigerians must have the confidence that the new leadership at both the national level and state levels has the capacity to improved the welfare and living conditions of all Nigerians by fighting the above mentioned vices. This they can do by standing on higher ground than their predecessors. Nigeria has abundance of natural and human resources. The mere population size of Nigeria is an asset as a big market for agricultural goods, manufactured goods, and other services. Nigerians need a strong collective will for the common good. It is essential to mention here that there is a strong relationship between the quality of the educational system of a nation and its technological development. It is clear that if one considers the state of education at the present time, one finds that Nigerian educational system must undergo very radical changes in terms of administration and curriculum. This is the crux of this chapter. Even though this chapter will emphasize innovations in tertiary level education, the importance of primary and secondary education cannot be overlooked. This work will also deal with primary and secondary education adequately.

Section 2 of this chapter outlines the present situation of education in Nigeria. Section 3 deals with anticipated innovations in administration and curriculum at the primary and secondary levels of education while in Section 4, we deal with administrative innovations at the tertiary level. Section 5 deals with curriculum innovations at the tertiary level. Funding of education in Nigeria is discussed in Section 6. The chapter is concluded in section 7.

2. THE PRESENT STATE OF EDUCATION IN NIGERIA

It is difficult to separate the present condition of the Nigerian Education System from the present status of the economy and Nigeria's political stability. An executive summary report on the review of undergraduate education in the United States 1996 (by the National Science Foundation) has this to say "in an increasing technical and competitive world with information as its common currency, a society without a properly educated citizenry will be at great risk and its people denied the opportunity for a fulfilling life". The Nigerian educational system has suffered unprecedented neglect since the unwelcome military intervention of December 1983. For the past fifteen years, education has become one of the main casualties of military dictatorship and misrule despite all the leap service paid to education by subsequent governments.

However, some superficial changes have been introduced since 1984 especially during the regime of Ibrahim Babaginda. One of the main changes was the creation of two tier High-School program, the Junior Secondary School (JSS)- 3 years, and the Senior Secondary School-3 years. The junior secondary school education was to give the student a general education from an adopted national curriculum while at the senior secondary level, students would be placed on career tracts after the junior secondary school education. The senior secondary school education, for example, would create suitable conditions in high schools where students interested in the sciences, technology, engineering, medicine, and the arts can enhance their knowledge in the high school subjects leading them to their chosen careers. Senior secondary schools were to be equipped with science instruments, libraries, and expert teachers employed to teach the respective subjects.

This was not to be. The senior secondary school education was also supposed to eliminate Higher School Education. The primary school education has not undergone any significant changes since the time of the British in the fifties. Neither administrative nor curricular changes or innovations have taken place. In fact, despite the fact that primary school teachers are more qualified now than their counterparts of the sixties, very few students with the First School Leaving Certificate can communicate effectively in English both in oral or written forms. The reasons are obvious. The funding for education is inadequate according to Hope Eghagha, (1999),During the period of the second republic, primary school teachers went on protracted strike, which the government ignored, apparently to underscore the perceived insignificance of teachers in the scheme of things. When the military returned in December 1983, education did not receive better attention. In many local governments of the federation, teachers do not get paid regularly. In fact, in some states, teachers sometimes go without pay for five months. This has adversely affected the morale and discipline in the teaching profession. There are tales of teachers abandoning their jobs and becoming petty traders, shopkeepers, and bricklayers. In many parts of the federation, most primary school buildings look like animal barns.

3. ADMINISTRATIVE AND CURRICULUM INNOVATIONS FOR PRIMARY AND SECONDARY EDUCATION

Since state take over of primary and secondary education from the missionaries in the late sixties and early seventies, community input and local participation in education at the primary and secondary levels have diminished if not entirely evaporated. The consequence of this is the fact that local government supervisors control the hiring of primary school teachers while the secondary school teachers are hired at the state level without community input. National, state, and the local government's education policy markers have ignored the role of communities, which are served by these schools. In order for the schools to return to their Old Glory, the importance of community involvement must be addressed. The community can play a vital role not only in the building of the schools, but also in the hiring and firing of teachers and principals. Every community should elect a governing board for each school. The governing board should participate in fund raising (may be in the form of a small education levy on all tax payers), enhancing enrollment, school security, seeking and hiring of excellent teachers, conducting workshops for the teachers on community expectation. The board should also oversee the principal to make sure that the curriculum is taught. The board should play a vital role in the hiring of school principals. The board should have regular meetings to evaluate school performance. It will make sure that all school age children are in schools. Sometimes, the board should conduct town hall meetings in order to solicit community input. Every school should also have a Parents-Teachers Association whose role should be exclusively advisory. The state should continue to play a leading role in primary and secondary education. The role of the state governments should include provision of funding from line-item budget to cover salaries, administrative, instructional, and maintenance cost for schools. The state will be responsible for in-service and retraining of teachers, as well as keeping records of evaluation of teachers for tenure at the primary and secondary levels. Curriculum innovation is not existent at the primary and secondary levels. This is not surprising since the colleges and universities, which train the teachers do not have the facilities and amenities to embark on innovation of their curriculum.

One significant change that has taken place at the tertiary level education is the discussion of the importance of computers and information technology. However, the number of computers in these institutions is insignificant to impact on a tangible number of students. Most colleges and universities do not have Internet connections and hence the importance of the World Wide Web cannot be explored. Even most instructors do not know how to use the computer.

There is an urgent need to initiate a national debate on the end product of our secondary education. There is no doubt that with the downward trend in the economy, the average Nigerian secondary school graduate is not well prepared for the workforce as well as for higher education. Every high school graduate should be able to communicate strongly (in English) both in oral and written forms. There is also a need to teach basic computer science and information technology at the secondary level. This will enable high school graduates to acquire extra skills to become employable. The federal and state governments must delineate the specific objectives of high school education based on outcomes. It is essential to mention here that select high schools such as Federal Government Colleges and private high schools, which charge exorbitant tuition and fees, which are not within reach of the average Nigerian family, are meeting such capabilities.

Most Nigeria students of high school age attend state high schools, which are located in big cities and local communities. Some of these local schools do not have teachers who hold college degrees in the subjects they teach. There are hundreds of rural high schools, which do not have qualified chemistry, physics, biology and mathematics teachers. A nation, which cannot take care of the young ones, cannot be a great nation. In order for Nigeria to transform to a strong nation with a growing technological base, it must make huge investment in education, science, and technology. There must be a national goal to train and adequately compensate all teachers. Extra compensation should be made to science, mathematics, and technology teachers. In fact, in order to initiate the growth in capacity at the primary and secondary levels of our educational system, the following issues must be considered for implementation.

(i)   Federal and state curriculum standards and regulations.
(ii)   Outcome based National Standards in science, mathematics, technology, communications, and social studies.

These regulations must be brought about by legislation or an act of national and state assemblies and must include:

(i)   Teacher standards,
(ii)   Certification and continuing education,
(iii)   Technology in schools,
(iv)   An outcome driven curriculum,
(v)   Implementation of national standards for tenure and promotion,
(vi)   Ethical standards for all individuals working in the education sector,
(vii)   A method of compensation based on merit and experience
(viii) Exit examinations at the state and national levels based on standardized tests.

If Nigerian children have to be competitive at the international level, they should be able to take standardized culturally unbiased examinations.

Administrative needs include:

(i)   A national standard for hiring teachers and administrators.
(ii)   Professional standards and ethics. There must be a well spelt out relationship between the teacher and the student.
(iii)   Zero tolerance for discrimination based on ethnicity and state of origin.
(iv)   A complete and unambiguous delineation of what constitutes sexual harassment and exploitation. There should be no tolerance for sexual harassment at the workplace or school.

There should be the law to compensate hard working teachers, and remove the lazy and unproductive teachers and administrators. Decadent teachers and administrators who embark on sexual exploitation of students or those who knowingly steal public money or property should be prosecuted and if found guilty sent to jail.

4. ADMINISTRATIVE INNOVATIONS AT THE TERTIARY LEVEL

Essential administrative changes must be made if the tertiary education level in Nigerian is to give optimal educational service to the Nation.

The roles of the Presidency, Federal Ministry of Education, the Ministry of Science and Technology, the Federal Ministry of Industries, the National Universities Commission, the Universities and Colleges, and other stakeholders are very important. The goal of this section is to delineate these anticipated administrative innovations and discuss ways in which they should be implemented.

Classification of Tertiary Institutions: As mentioned earlier on this chapter, it is important that while the present Nigerian Universities continue their role as comprehensive universities, all the nation's universities do not have equal capabilities to be designated as research universities.

It is important therefore that the Federal Ministry of Education and the National Universities Commission backed by an act of the legislature should classify our tertiary institutions as follows:

(a) Research 1 Universities,
(b) Research 2 Universities,
(c) Regional Universities,
(d) 4-year Colleges, and
(e) Two-year Colleges.

This classification has even become more important at this period of scarce financial and human resources.

Research 1 Universities. Our oldest flag-ship universities namely the University of Ibadan, University of Nigeria Nsukka, Ahmadu-Bello University Zaria, The University of Ife (Now Obafemi Awolowo University, and the University of Lagos should be designated Research 1 Universities. Each of these universities has a long history of strong curriculum. They have produced a majority of older generation of Nigerian professionals in the public and private sectors of the country as well as in the academia. These universities have comprehensive curriculum ranging from the liberal arts to medicine. The faculties at these universities have the reputation of producing research results and have published such works in international journals. They have also presented their work at national and international conferences. These universities have world class reputation. They offer a wide range of undergraduate and graduate programs. They should be permitted to continue to do so. These universities should be the host centers for

National Laboratories where advanced research and study should be taking place. Since Nigeria does not have the resources to support doctoral programs in all disciplines, only these universities should be allowed to run doctoral programs in disciplines like mathematics and physics.

The teaching load at these institutions should be 2-three hour courses a semester. Full Professors must be encouraged to make contact with young undergraduates. Assigning first and second year level courses to experienced professors to teach every year can achieve this goal. Research I Universities should be the center for excellence in teaching, research, and service. Other universities should serve as feeders to these universities.

The graduates of other universities should be encouraged to proceed to these universities for their graduate degrees especially the Doctoral programs. The Federal Government and other funding agencies should invest research money at these institutions.

Research 2 Universities: Nigeria's research 2 universities should include:

The Universities of Benin, Port Harcourt, Calabar, Jos, Ilorin, and Bayero University Kano. These universities should continue to offer comprehensive programs in most disciplines as well as Masters Programs. They should be permitted to run Ph.D. programs in select disciplines. They can however offer Ph.D. programs in Mathematics, Physics, Chemistry, Biology, and Engineering provided they can demonstrate that such programs are viable.

Viability should be measured in terms of the number of graduate students in that particular discipline. Any graduate program, which does not graduate 15 Ph.D.s in five years, should be canceled. The resources to run such programs, which include the number of qualified faculty and financial resources should be examined.

The faculty teaching load at these universities should be 9 hours (3-3 hour courses) a semester, two of which must be undergraduate courses. Senior faculty must not be allowed to delegate their teaching to Masters degree holders or graduate assistants in order to run Ph.D. programs. It is therefore the responsibility of the administration to make sure that every faculty member heeds to his or her responsibilities.

Comprehensive Regional Universities: The following universities should be designated as comprehensive regional universities: The Universities of Sokoto, Maidugiri, Abuja, and Uyo. Others are the Federal Universities of Technology at Owerri, Akure, Yola, Minna, Bauchi, and the Federal Universities of Agriculture Markudi, Abeokuta, and Umuahia. These universities should concentrate on the provision of quality undergraduate education and a few select graduate programs. Teaching load should be 9-12 semester hours. They should only be allowed to run Ph.D. programs in select disciplines if those programs are viable and only if they are in collaboration with Research 1 or Research 2 universities. They should have larger class sizes and must accommodate as many students as possible. Masters Granting Institutions: All state universities should have as their primary mission the provision of quality undergraduate education. They should expand their capacities to accommodate more students. They should hire more instructors with masters' degrees to meet such responsibilities. These masters' degree holders should concentrate on teaching lower level undergraduate courses- the freshman and sophomore level courses. The more experienced Ph.D. holders in each department should teach junior and senior level classes. Less research should be expected from the professors at these colleges especially for the sake of compensation, tenure, and promotion. These colleges can run masters programs in select and limited disciplines provided undergraduate teaching is not neglected.

Four-Year Colleges: All Federal and State Colleges of Education should be converted to degree awarding four-year colleges. They should run honors degree programs in education as well as in the liberal arts, basic sciences, and social sciences.

The mission of these institutions should be teaching and service. The Polytechnics and Institutes of Technology: The Polytechnics and Institutes of Technology should run four-year degree programs. The ND (National Diploma) curriculum should be the same as that of the first two years of 4-year degree program. This will enable a ND holder to transfer to any university for the sake of completion of his or her degree program in two or three years.

Two-Year Colleges: Because of the great demand for higher education in Nigeria, states with high population of high school graduates should consider the establishment of two year colleges. The curriculum of these two-year colleges should be the same as the first two years of the curriculum of four-year colleges. They should be feeders for four-year colleges. These two-year colleges should also be the center for the training of middle skilled technical manpower.

5. CURRICULUM INNOVATIONS AT THE TERTIARY LEVEL

The present curriculum (in all subjects and disciplines) at the tertiary level does not prepare the student for the work place or advanced education outside Nigeria. Let us illustrate this statement with an example the subject of chemistry. In the US universities, students are able to perform experiments, generate and analyze data using computers. They are exposed to different types of sophisticated equipment some of which they will use in the workplace. In fact, part of the requirement for graduation of chemistry students is to acquire some practical training in chemical manufacturing companies. This enables them to acquire hand-on skills in their discipline. On the other hand, the Nigerian chemistry graduate at the present time has minimum knowledge in both skills and the core. Very little time is spent in the classroom and the laboratories as professors are on strike most of the time. This results in the production of ill-prepared and academically weak graduate. Most of the university graduates have found an inconvenient way to deal with skill problems. Some of them enroll in computer training schools and acquire basic skills in word and data processing. This enhances their chances of securing jobs outside their areas of discipline. Others resort to accepting low paying jobs with the hope to gain skills and apply for better paying jobs.

Graduate education in the United States, Canada, Europe, and South American countries gives strong support to higher-level manpower training, as well as to academic and non-academic research. On the other hand, the present graduate education is viewed in Nigeria as advancing knowledge only in the individual subject areas and discipline, and emphasis placed more on theory rather than applications. In order to catch up with the developed world in the twenty-first century, there must be an overhaul of both curriculum and pedagogy at tertiary institutions. The future demands greater need for interdisciplinary-learning. This can be enhanced with the availability of information technology. The National Science Foundation Report Review of Undergraduate Education puts it more clearly "Many curricular and pedagogical improvements are mutually reinforcing. Also, very important is the observation made by many, particularly employers, that a well-designed, active learning environment assists in the development of other skills and traits they seek in the employees: cognitive skills (problem-solving, decision-making, learning how to learn) social skills (communications and teamwork), and positive personal traits (adaptability and flexibility, openness to new ideas, empathy for ideas of others, innovative and entrepreneurial outlook, and a strong work ethic)".

For the past fifteen years, most universities in Nigeria have lost the capacity to do pure and applied research. The low number of research reports and publications of scholarly papers in national and international journals manifest this. This setback is even worse in the disciplines of medicine, engineering, agriculture, science, and technology. Presently, our medical schools are ill equipped and the teaching hospitals lack basic facilities for theoretical and practical instructions. Professors do not have the privilege to attend international conferences which (In the past) afforded them the opportunities to interact with their counterparts in developed countries. This without a doubt reduces their capabilities to be familiar with the state of the art equipment, techniques, and resources in their respective fields. This can virtually be said about all disciplines.

There is no doubt that the quality of doctoral programs run by even the best Nigerian universities is in doubt as these universities lack the minimum facility support to run such programs effectively. Most universities lack professors who should supervise such programs. This chapter will address the panacea to these problems in the sequel.

One essential curriculum issue which has neither been tackled nor even reviewed by the Federal Ministry of Education, the National Universities Commission, or the colleges and universities themselves is the non uniformity of the undergraduate curriculum. At the present time, it is difficult if not impossible for a Sociology undergraduate from the University of Ibadan to transfer to the University of Lagos in the same discipline. This is essentially because the undergraduate courses of study in Sociology at these two universities are different. Although the courses of study in Sociology in these two universities may have similar content, there is no uniform delineation of course sequencing, making it extremely difficult for faculty advisors to match course by course the course of study for Sociology. The lack of uniformity in the undergraduate curriculum makes it difficult for students to transfer from one university to another. A student, who for whatever reason, cannot continue his education at one university will either start from the beginning at another university or loose his chance for college education. Faculties also have the same problem of mobility. Unless a special arrangement is made within the department, a faculty member cannot secure a job at another college or university without losing his benefits at the previous university. Several Nigerian Colleges and Universities adopted the credit-course system, which are common in American Universities. What they have not implemented adequately is the flexibility that comes with such credit-course system. If the credit-course system is adopted and adequately implemented, then, the flexibility that comes with it will be beneficial to the Nigerian undergraduate in many and varied ways.

Since College and university curriculum has to respond to societal demand, the need to create new degree programs and discontinuation of low demand and redundant disciplines need not be overemphasized. For the past fifteen years, our country has witnessed an upsurge in criminal behavior and different forms of deviant behavior. There is a need therefore to establish degree programs in criminology. This way, these negative issues that confront our nation at this present time will be carefully researched. A department of criminology should not only train the civilian workers for the prison system, security agencies, and employees dealing with law enforcement, it should also partake in the professional training of our police force. Indeed, it is feasible to establish a strong link between the Police Colleges and

Criminology Departments of the universities. This will undoubtedly enhance the capacities of our policemen and other law enforcement officers.

Another discipline that needs to be established in Nigerian Universities is Special Education. As the nation continues to develop in the twenty-first century, there is a greater societal responsibility to Individuals with Disabilities and other special needs. The present practice whereby the caring of such individuals is left for the their families or religious organizations, is no longer desirable. Individuals with Mental Retardation have same rights as other individuals in the society and must be accorded the right to education.

In order to achieve this in the next century, special education programs should be established to train teachers who will teach these individuals at the Elementary School and High School levels. There is doubt that cases like the ones made above can be made for other emerging disciplines. Social life for university and college students should not only be tolerated but also supported by the university administrators to the extent that it does not constitute a hindrance to the goals and mission of the university. Moreover, as young adults, they have the right to social life. Unfortunately, while the majority of college students are law-abiding citizens, there is a small percentage of them who should not be found at the college campuses. Deviant and decadent behavior, intimidation, murders, and occultism has no place on campuses. In the last fifteen years, occultism has taken over the social life of college students. Murder has become rampant as a result of occultism and this is not well investigated or prosecuted by the courts. The majority of college students live in fear as a result of this. Occultism has no place in the university and college environment.

Streamlining: If the federal and state governments are to realize the optimum benefits of investment in higher education, streamlining college and university curriculum as well as degree offerings must be addressed. While the supporters of higher education decry the poor funding of higher education, the nation must face the real fact that in this period of meager resources, duplication of degree offerings and the running of parallel programs in neighboring universities do not help the case. It is important therefore that the following important questions must be addressed:

(a) Do Nigerian Universities need to produce one thousand graduates with degrees in philosophy? If Nigerian universities produce them, is there any job market for them?

(b) The University of Lagos has undergraduate and graduate programs in Urban and City Planning (in the Geography Department). Does Lagos State University, The Federal University of Agriculture Abeokuta need to run the same program? Is this not a waste of National resources?

(c) Where should a degree program in Material Science be best run- The University of Illorin (which is close to Ajeokuta Steel Complex) or University of Maiduguri or University of Sokoto?

(d) Is it feasible that the University of Calabar run an independent Ph.D. program in Mathematics while the University of Port Harcourt, The Federal University of Technology Owerri run similar programs? Is there anyway these universities can share resources?

(e) Should every university in Nigeria be in the business of running Ph.D. programs? What quality of Ph.D. are these?

(f) Are Nigerian Colleges and Universities adequately responding to societal demands and the job market need or are they there to produce "half-backed" graduates with little or no skills?

(g) Is the teaching load of professors adequate or are they under utilized?

Some of the answers to these questions are obvious. Let us address the issue of sharing resources with a concrete example. The City of Owerri, the capital of Imo State, has four-degree granting institutions.

At the present time, none of these Universities has minimum resource to support the academic programs being offered at these institutions. In fact, the classrooms are inadequate and sometimes too small to accommodate enough students. The libraries are substandard with few books and most of which are old. Is it feasible for the government to build a well equipped library at one of these institutions and students, faculty, and staff at these colleges can share such a library resource? A good library costs millions of Dollars to build and millions more to maintain. The University of Port Harcourt has a Ph.D. program in Mathematics. The Federal University of technology Owerri (FUTO) does the same thing. These universities are seventy miles apart. There is a World Renowned expert in Partial Differential Equations at FUTO and an expert in Fluid Mechanics at the University of Port Harcourt. Is it not feasible for graduate students from Port Harcourt to take 3 courses in Owerri one semester and the graduate students of FUTO to take course in Port Harcourt the next Semester, and vice versa? It is my view that the National Universities Commission should stop the new federal and state universities from running doctoral programs.

They do not have the resources to do so. These resources should better be directed towards the improvement of undergraduate programs.

Barriers to curriculum changes at the college level (in the United States) have well documented in Toombs W, and Tierney W (1991). According to these authors, in order to implement these changes the following must be taken into account:

Create a climate, even a demand for change.
Diminish the threat associated with innovations and avoid hard-line approaches.
Avoid being timid.
Appreciate timing.
Gear the innovation to the organization.
Disseminate and evaluate information.
Communicate effectively.
Get organizational leaders behind the innovation.
Build a base of active support.
Establish rewards.
Plan for the period after adoption.

It is therefore clear that in order to effect any worthwhile changes in the tertiary education curriculum, government leaders, university and college professors, and the university teachers' union (ASU) must be brought on board. By doing this, the threat to innovation will be greatly diminished and tangible and effective changes can be implemented.

6. FUNDING OF EDUCATION IN NIGERIA

Events in the last twenty years suggest that it is impossible for the federal and state governments to adequately fund all levels of education in Nigeria.

It is essential therefore that funding of education has to be reexamined. In this section, we shall advocate for different sources for funding education. This will create financial stability for the Nigerian educational system.

Federal and State Funding for Education: The Federal and State governments should continue to lead in the funding of education in Nigeria.

Land grant Designation: Nigeria is endowed with abundant natural resources. However, funding for education has not benefited from the country's wealth for the last fifteen years. If the Federal Government is serious about educating Nigerians, there must be a percentage of the Federal budget allocated to education every year. This percentage cannot continue to fluctuate. Machinery must be put in place in order to make sure such monies reach the levels of Education and for the purpose for which it is allocated. In other words, there must be an efficient mechanism to direct the monies to accomplish specific goals. Apart from direct funding through the Federal Ministry of Education, the Federal Government must mandate all ministries to support education with parts of their budgets. Such funding may be in the form of research grants to professors, consultation with professors and provision of work experience for undergraduate and graduate students. The ministries and other independent federal parastatals should be encouraged to rent and utilize university facilities for training and retraining of their workers.

Nigerian Science Foundation: The Federal Government should establish the Nigerian Science Foundation- a Foundation similar to the National Science Foundation (NSF) of the United States.

This foundation should have as its primary mission the promotion of science research, teaching, and learning at all levels.

Education and Luxury-Tax: All taxpayers and companies should pay some percentage of their yearly net income as education tax. Individuals who have benefited from the society and who buy expensive vehicles, live in expensive houses, have private planes, yachts, and vacation homes should be made to pay taxes on their luxurious life-style. Vehicle license tags should be renewed every year and taxes should be paid on them.

Private Foundations: Nigeria has very affluent people. The private foundations in the United State support not only education and educational institutions in the United States, but all over the world. Grants awarded by the Ford Foundation helped several Nigerians earn Ph.D. in the sixties and seventies. The Nigeria government should encourage private individuals, communities, and companies to establish charitable foundations not only to support education, but also to support community development. Government can enhance this by giving tax incentives to such individuals and companies, as well as awarding nation honors for such benevolence.

7. CONCLUSION

The path to greatness requires very careful and sometimes radical changes in the national polity. If Nigeria is to become the great Nation it aspires to be the Nigerian education system must undergo radical changes. Several changes in both administration and curriculum have been suggested in this chapter. However, these suggestions are not exhaustive. It is my view that the Nigerian leadership must confront these problems in our educational system at all levels.

In order to achieve meaningful changes at all levels, those changes must begin in our tertiary institutions. Change requires financial support. Nigeria as a nation has the financial resources to improve its education system. It also has the human resources to do so. Financial support for education is inevitable if Nigeria is to have a competitive workforce in the twenty-first century.

MANAGING NIGERIA'S ECONOMIC SYSTEM IN THE THIRD REPUBLIC[*]

Adepoju Adeleke

INTRODUCTION

The five basic functions of management are generally identified as planning, organizing, mobilizing resources, directing and controlling the activities of men and machines towards the attainment of some objectives. The formulation of objectives is in addition considered an essential function of management. The exercise of these functions puts the manager in a decision situation. One way or the other, management is involved in decision making, and decision making involves problem solving. Generally, a decision situation exists when: there is a desired objectives, alternative courses of actions are available, there is uncertainty as to which course is best, and external factors are present which are outside the control of the decision maker.

The choosing of any course of action involves management in problem solving. Problem solving therefore has traditionally been taken as an essential function of management.

In an economy/country, two principal actors are normally involved in the management and control of the economy. These are the government and individuals sometimes acting as cooperate bodies. The degree of management and control of each of the actors depend on the economic system adopted in such an economy/country. A country's economic system therefore, is the way the economic problems of planning, organizing, controlling, coordinating, and harnessing of the resources of the country are solved. Different economies/countries have adopted different economic systems in the management of their economic system. Whatever the system is adopted, a number of things are common to each of them. First, there are factors of production; the factors are owned, the factors are combined in certain ways, the output is distributed and consumed. In the process, some surplus is left unconsumed. This is invested to form the basis for future consumption.

---

[*] Excerpted from *Nigeria's Third Republic: The Problems and Prospects of Political Transition to Civil Rule,* Ojo, Bamidele A., © Nova Science Publishers, Inc. 1998.

Whatever economic system is operated in a country, answers to the following principal questions are necessary in the management of the economy:

- Who should own the factors of production?
- How should the production output be distributed?
- How should the surplus that results from output being greater than consumption distributed?

Quite a number of economic systems have been tried to solve the problem of managing the economic system at different times since the existence of man on earth. These systems include feudalism, mercantilism, colonialism, slavery, communism, socialism, etc. In the world today, the dominant systems are capitalism and socialism. There are varieties of each of these two economic systems. At one end is pure capitalism in which all the factors of production are owned by the capitalist, who makes all the investment decisions and receives all the profits of the investment. Under capitalism, the workers supply the labor and receive wages which would depend on their trade unions' ability to negotiate with the owners.

At the other extreme is communism in which all the factors of production are owned by the people (represented by a centralized government), and they make the investments and provide the labor. The profits from the investments theoretically accrue to the people, and are expected to be shared according to the needs of the people.

Pure capitalism and pure communism cannot, in reality, exist. Thus, we have varieties of mixed economic systems in which the government and the capitalist co-exist. What the capitalist control is called the private sector of the economy and what the government controls is called the public sector. Under socialism, the government owns a large proportion of the factors of production and employs the workers who are paid wages according to their contribution. The profits-surplus thus accrues to the government, who uses it on behalf of the people.

ECONOMIC SYSTEMS IN NIGERIA BEFORE 1972

Over the years, different economic systems have been practiced in Nigeria. In the olden days, before the advent of colonial era, the economic system adopted in Nigeria was a sort of communism. By this system, the factors of production were land and labor. The land was communally owned and was held in trust for the people by the head of the commune and was divided among the families in the village. The labor was owned and supplied by the family. The productive process pursued was agriculture and the output consumed was agricultural product. What was not consumed was saved and planted (invested) during the next season.

The output usually varied according to the size of the family. Consumption also depended on the size of the family. Whatever was left out of output which was not consumed became a surplus that accrued to the whole family. Where there was a head chief or head of family, part of the surplus was paid to him.

When the British rule started in Nigeria, another economic system emerged. The economy was mainly agrarian and the colonial government claimed ownership of some of the factors of production-mainly things below the surface of the ground.

To this end, part of the surplus accrued to the colonial government and this was transferred out of the country. This formed a leakage from the economy. The advent of the Europeans also brought foreign investors into the country. These investors established subsidiary companies in Nigeria with headquarters in the home countries overseas. These subsidiary companies (who were in fact multinationals) were involved in trading: bringing into the country such manufactured goods as drinks, clothing materials, gun powder, cigarette, building materials, and stationaries. They bought from Nigerians agricultural products such as palm kernels, cotton, cola nuts, hides and skin, groundnuts and some other products. They often repatriate the surpluses accruing from their businesses to the home countries.

To a large extent, the management of the private sector of the economy was dominated by these multinationals. This system was in operation some years after the country became independent in 1960.

THE INDIGENIZATION OF 1972 AND AFTER

Some years after political independence, it became clear to Nigerians that political independence, for it to be meaningful, should be founded on a bedrock of economic independence. It was in the realization of this fact that in March 1972, the Nigerian government promulgated the Indigenization Decree. The decree compels some foreign business organizations to share the ownership of some of their business interests with Nigerians. Since 1972, other similar decrees have been promulgated, the most important of them being the decree of January 12, 1977.

The decree classified all enterprises in Nigeria into three schedules:

- Schedule 1 consists of enterprises which should be 100 percent owned and managed exclusively by Nigerians;
- Schedule 2 are enterprises where Nigerians should acquire up to 60 percent equity participation; while,
- Schedule 3 consists of enterprises with 40 percent equity participation by Nigerians.

The decree then stipulated that appropriate equities of those enterprises were to be sold or transferred to Nigerians not later than December 31 1978 (or June 30 1977 for some classes of businesses).

The principal objective of the indigenization decree therefore is to transfer the management of the Nigerian economy from expatriate domination to indigenous Nigerians. Thus, the decrees of 1972 and 1977 whatever may be their shortcomings, effected not only a change of ownership but also that of management of the Nigerian economy.

SOME POLICY CONSIDERATIONS FOR THE EFFECTIVE MANAGEMENT OF THE NIGERIAN ECONOMIC SYSTEM IN THE THIRD REPUBLIC

According to the political program of the present military administration, the third republic for Nigeria will commence as from 1 October 1992, when hopefully the military government will hand over power to an elected civilian administration. The principal questions to ask are: who should do the management of the Nigerian economy and how should it be managed in the third republic?

The first question appears to have been answered by the Indigenization decrees. That is, Nigerians forming public or private liability companies, partnership or further still sole proprietorship should be, by and large involved in the management of the economy. Multinationals with appropriate equity participation of Nigerians should also be involved in the management of the economy. This suggestion tend to attribute a greater percentage of the management of the economy to the private sector. This seems to be the spirit of the indigenization policy.

This policy should be allowed to operate in the overall interest of the nation. It is a free enterprise (laissez faire) policy which means minimum intervention of government and greater participation of private individuals in business management.

The management of the economy involves decision making, and decision making for effective management involves skill, precision, dynamism, risk-taking, foresight and entrepreneurship; government red-tape administrative process, bureaucracy, and the maintenance of status quo characteristics of public administration would not augur well for the rapid transformation and the effective management of the economy.

There is no system that has no limitation, however, the living experiences of the development gap between countries that adopt a free enterprise system and those that operate a government centrally controlled and managed economy is a pointer that the later *does not allow* for effective development of the economy. It is observed for example, that most countries of Western Europe that adopt free enterprise system in the management of their economy are better able to develop economically than their Eastern Europe counterparts whose economic system are centrally controlled and managed by the government.

Under the free enterprise system, Nigerians acting as corporate bodies or single individuals make nearly all the investment decisions in the economy, and also receive all the profits which accrue from their investment decisions while paying taxes to government. Workers supply the labor and receive wages which would depend on their trade unions' ability to negotiate with the owners and management of the enterprises. Government involvement in the management of the economy should be reduced to a minimum level.

Under this situation, the economic model that emerge could be depicted as follows - see figure 1 (p. 94): In which a greater percentage of investment decisions are made by Nigerians operating as individuals or as cooperate bodies. In the figure 1, some percentages of the total economy is reserved for the control and management of foreigners acting as multinationals. This structure upholds the spirit of the indigenization decree. This is because there are some areas of businesses which involve heavy capital outlay or high level technology for which Nigerians have not acquired the necessary capabilities and know how. Such areas of businesses should be left for the multinationals to operate. They should however go into these areas with appropriate equity participation of Nigerians as stipulated in the policy of indigenization. This is necessary because no country can develop all alone. It is pertinent therefore, to allow for flow of information, capital, ideas and technological know how. The multinationals, with their wealth of business acumen and know how would bring in these essential factors of economic development. Upon all, it is suggested that foreign investors should be encouraged to participate in the sectors of the economy which have been allocated to them in the indigenization decree.

The second question is thus answered. The distribution of production output should be left to the free interplay of demand and supply characteristics of free market economy.

What role for government in the management of the economy in the third republic? It is observed that the functions of government in any economy are to:

1. make laws and regulations -- - legislative functions
2. interpret laws and regulations -- - judiciary functions
3. execute laws and regulations -- - executive functions.

We tend to suggest that the Nigerian third republic government should limit its role to these areas as far as possible for the reasons which have been advanced above. Under this situation governments either at state or federal level should sell off some of the shares which they have acquired in the profit making enterprises in Nigeria. These shares should be sold to indigenous Nigerians.

However, government should be involved in infrastructural developments which are indispensable for economic development. These include uninterrupted electric supply, efficient network of roads, effective health care delivery system, effective telecommunications systems, portable water for domestic and industrial uses, air and sea ports, and other social services. In other to meet these challenges, government should set up effective machinery for revenue collection from the private and corporate business enterprises.

The government should also be responsible for formulating and implementing educational policies. However, private bodies who want to participate in the implementation of the educational policies should be allowed to do so at the primary and secondary level of the educational system. This will reduce the burden on the government's shoulder in view of the demographic profile of the country which is characterized by young population. It will be necessary however for the government to set necessary standards for the educational system.

In the industrial relations sphere, the role of government should be that of an impartial judge between labor unions and the management of business enterprises. We have earlier suggested (see Adeleke 1984) that government should uphold the doctrine of laissez-faire in industrial relations matters in Nigeria. The laissez-faire principle gives an individual the opportunity to enter into a free contractual relationship with whoever decides to employ him. This principle is based on the "Benthamite Utilitarian" principle that an individual who knows best his interest should be left free to pursue and maximize those interests, the sum total of which for the society as a whole would be greater good of the greatest number.

Laissez-faire also means that the government should assist both employers and unions to treat themselves as they thought best with themselves. It has also been said that the most effective way to having and maintaining industrial peace and harmony is for both employees and employers or their representatives to freely enter into contractual relationships through collective bargaining without intervention, involvement nor interference of any third party.

According to the United Committee of Central Labor Organization (UCLO 1970), the best form of salary structure and salaries and wages revision would be that evolved by the two sides in industry: labor and management through collective bargaining.

It has however been recognized that for collective bargaining to be really free and effective, it is essential for the bargaining strength of both employees and employers to be as far as possible equally matched. Fawehinmi(1976) suggested that one of the ways for achieving this is for the government to strengthen the capabilities of weaker party (usually the labor unions) so that they can bargain on equal footing with the employers. The principle of having equal capability is based on the Asby's (1964) Law of Requisite Variety.

That "ONLY VARIETY ABSORBS VARIETY" i.e. 'iron sharpens iron'.... In figure 2 below, the role of government in the industrial relations system in the third republic is to amplify the capacity of the unions (employees) so that they can have equal bargaining power with that of the employers(management).See Figure 2: The Role of Government in The Nigeria's Industrial Relations System In The Third Republic (page 94 below). on the other hand, government should reduce the excesses of employers (management) so that they will be able and willing to negotiate with unions. The role of government as far as this suggestion is concerned is reduced to that of variety engineering, and maintaining the balance of power between the parties. In making this suggestion, government is being looked at as the supreme authority of the state and not that of government as the owner of investments and the overall employer of labor.

The most effective ways to maintain this balance of power is for government to enact laws which could make collective bargaining and joint consultation effective in work environment. Such laws would determine the scope, functions, structure and methods of operations of the agreements as may be appropriate to the conditions in the various undertakings. Having presented what should be the role of government in the management of the Nigerian economy in the third republic, we consider it necessary to discuss some basic principles towards the management of the economy.

SOME PRINCIPLES FOR THE MANAGEMENT OF THE NIGERIAN ECONOMY

Since the time of Taylor (1911), or rather before him, it has been recognized that there are approaches (principles) for the effective management of an Organization or an economy. It was in recognition of this truism that Taylor proposed his famous "Principles of Scientific Management". The author observed through a series of simple illustrations both at the national level and the private level where he was a foreman of a steel company that the whole country (U.S.A) was suffering from a great loss due to inefficiency in the production processes.

Taylor then proposed that the inefficiency can be reduced or eliminated through a scientific principles of management. The dominating interests of the author was how the Organization could be made more efficient. In arriving at proposing a "Scientific Principle of Management", Taylor conducted a time and motion studies to determine how tasks should be organized towards increased productivity. He observed that rests periods during the working day were necessary in order to recover from psychological fatigue. The author conceived man (employee) as an economic man that can only be motivated by wages and incentives pays.

Although, the scientific management approach dealt almost exclusively with the production structure of the Organization, and little to say about the institutional and managerial structures of an Organization, the approach seem to offer an insight into how tasks can be organized for productive efficiency. The Nigerian Managers have a lot to benefit from Taylor's proposition of a scientific approach to management of an Organization.

The industrial relations approach to management pioneered by Elton Mayo and his colleagues (1927-1933) at Hawthorne in USA ended up by emphasizing the importance of interpersonal and group relations as a factor of organizational efficiency. The approach sees people in Organization not merely as individuals responding to the formal requirements of their roles, but as group members developing their own norms and their own cohesion. They therefore work in Organization partly to satisfy their social needs and not mainly for economic gains.

As a result of the studies of Mayo and his colleagues, the industrial relations approach to management lay emphasis on people in Organization and their motivation as important factors of organizational effectiveness. It has been observed that one of the methods for managing business concerns or any Organization for that matter for effectiveness is also by "Management by Objectives". Drucker(1968), noted that Management by Objectives (MBO) is a principle of management that gives common direction of vision and effort, establish team work and harmonize the goals of the individual with the common goal. For Ejiofor(1981), Management by objectives is a method of management whereby the superior and subordinate managers of an Organization agree on its broad goals, translate these goals into a chain of specific short-term goals, define each individual's major areas of responsibility in terms of results expected, continually review the accomplishment of the subordinate, and use goals accomplishment as the sole basis of accessing and rewarding the subordinate.

From this conception, Management by Objectives has five key features:

1. organizational or departmental goals are jointly set by the manager and his superior,
2. Broad long-term goals are translated into a chain of specific interrelated short term goals,
3. Continual guidance of subordinate by superior,
4. Continual review of accomplishment by subordinate and superior,
5. Contribution towards goal achievement serves as sole basis of subordinate rewards.

The ultimate objective of MBO is to increase the effectiveness and efficiency of an organization through optimum performance of its members. This is realized by making all members of an organization committed to achieving the organizational objectives.

Another approach to management is the systems approach. This approach to management of an organization or an economy is an emerging paradigm for inquiring into the complexly of social, managerial, organizational and technological problems of a given situation. The approach starts with the definition of objectives, and ends with the implementation of the objectives. It gives a description or a design of an harmonious optimum ensemble of the required men and machines with such a corollary network of flow of information and materials needed to operate in order to achieve the given objectives.

The basic notion of a system is simply that it is a set of inter-related parts. Implicit in these concepts is a degree of wholeness which makes the whole something different from, and more than the individual units considered separately. The systems approach emphasizes looking at a problem in its entirety, taking into account all the interdependent parameters. It is a process for understanding how those parameters interact with one another and how they can be brought into proper relationships for attaining the given objectives.

It is noted that no system, existing either as an economy or an organization exists in an isolation. A system normally exist in an environment which in itself exist in a larger environment. An understanding of the strength and weakness of the larger environment is therefore imperative for effective management of the system.

To be effective, managers in the Nigerian economic system must understand organization-environment relationships. They must take cognizance of the ways organizations are tied to other structures - the political influences, technological developments, global world economies and markets, and societal values. An understanding of these phenomenon is likely to offer the managers a knowledge of the relationships which their organizations will require to assure their own survival in the complex environment in which they operate. The system approach provides an insight on how to manage complex organizations in an environment.

Which management principle is appropriate for Nigeria in the management of the economy in the third republic?

The Japanese have risen to become a world economic power of our time. One of the factors which have helped the Japanese is partly their approach to management of organizations. This approach is based solidly on the cultural values of the Japanese people - love of Japan, organizational and job commitment, trust, cooperation, collective decision - making, collective responsibility and rewards, implicit controls, holistic relationship, tolerance of ambiguity and emphasis on interdependency. The processes and issues which underline these are essential to cooperative and productive effort.

One of the distinctive features of Japanese management philosophy is not so much of basic skills transfer but of sharing of organizational philosophies, values and beliefs which of course are based on the society's values and aspirations.

As we move towards 1992, the era of the third republic, Nigerians have a lot to learn from the Japanese experience in the management of the economy for effectiveness.

First, a more concerted effort is needed to understand our culture from the perspective of how it enhances or hinders productive efforts. To do so will require an in depth study of our traditional social institutions and values. From the studies, we will be able to evolve a management philosophy appropriate to our environment and which enhances productive efforts and organizational effectiveness. In fact, Nigerians must be prepared to learn in the third republic.

CONCLUSION

The implications of this chapter for better management of the Nigeria's economic system can be summarized four sentences. First, to a large extent, the ownership, control and management of business organizations in Nigeria should be left in the hands of Nigerians operating either as an individual or corporate bodies. Second, the government should uphold the principles of laissez-faire in industries consisting of the total economy. Third, collective bargaining should be allowed to operate in industry. Fourth, Nigerians who are involved in the management of the economy must be prepared to learn in the third republic.

Over the years, the determinants of operational performance and effectiveness of an economy has been a subject of several studies. In this chapter we offer suggestions which might usher in a new era of self reliance and effective performance of the Nigerian economy. We observe that our suggestions are in line with the current global thinking on how an economic system can be managed in the overall interest of the society. It is hoped that the implementation of these suggestions would lead to an improved performance of the Nigerian's economic system in the third republic.

NOTES

Adeleke A (1984): "The Role of Government in the Nigerian Industrial Relations Systems: A Critical View" in Hashim I (ed): *Issues in Public Sector Management In Nigeria* (Zaria: Nigeria: Ahmadu Bello University Press Ltd.)

Ashby R (1964): *An Introduction to Cycbernetics* (London: Menthien and Co Ltd)

Drucker P.F *(1968): The Practice of Management* (London: Pan Books Ltd).

Ejiofor P (1981): *Management in Nigeria: Theories and Issues* (Onitsha, Nigeria:African Educational Publishers (Nig) Ltd.) Fawehinmi M.A.(1967): "Industrial Relations In Nigeria"

Paper presented at a *10-day National Seminar* on *Labor Management* organized by the Nigerian Workers Council, British Council, Ibadan: Nigeria

Mayo E *(1933): The Human Problems of an Industrial Civilization* (New York: Macmillan).

Taylor F.W (1923): *The Principles of Scientific Management* (New York: Harper and Row)

The Nigerian Enterprises Promotion Decree 1972, Decree No 4

The Nigerian Enterprises Promotion Decree 1977, Decree No 3

United Committee of Central Labor Organization (UCLO) 1970

"Equitable Demands for Economic Growth and National Prosperity" *Memorandum No 123* (Geneva)

NIGERIA: A COUNTRY STUDY[*]

Helen Chapin Metz (Editor)

COUNTRY PROFILE

Geography

Size: 923,768 square kilometers.

Boundaries: Southern limits set by Gulf of Guinea (bights of Benin and Biafra); inland frontiers shared with Cameroon (east), Chad (northeast), Niger (north), and Benin (west). No demarcation reached regarding Nigeria-Chad-Niger-Cameroon boundary in Lake Chad, leading to disputes.

Topography: Five major geographic divisions: low coastal zone along Gulf of Guinea; succeeded northward by hills and low plateaus; Niger-Benue river valley; broad stepped plateau stretching to northern border with highest elevations over 1,200 meters; mountainous zone along eastern border, which includes country's highest point (2,042 meters).

Climate: Tropical with variations governed by interaction of moist southwest monsoon and dry northeast winds. Mean maximum temperatures of 30-32°C (south), 33-35°C (north). High humidity in south February-November, June-September in north; low humidity during dry season. Annual rainfall decreases northward; about 2,000 millimeters in coastal zone (Niger Delta averages over 3,550 millimeters); 500 to 750 millimeters in north.

Society

Population: Population and growth estimates varied widely. World Bank estimated 1990 population at 119 million; however, 1991 preliminary census figures published in 1992 gave population total of 88.5 million. Growth rate in 1990 estimated about 3.3 percent; 28 percent of population urban in 1985.

---

[*] Excerpted from the Library of Congress Website.

Ethnic Groups: 250 to 400 or more recognized groups, many divided into subgroups of considerable social and political importance. Most important ethnolinguistic categories: Hausa and Fulani in north, Yoruba in southwest, and Igbo in southeast, all internally subdivided. Next major groups: Kanuri, Ibibio, Tiv, and Ijaw.

Languages: Number of languages estimated at 350 to 400, many with dialects. Most important: Hausa, Yoruba, and Igbo. Hausa major language in north. English official language used in government, large-scale business, mass media, and education beyond primary school. Several other languages also recognized for primary education. Classical Arabic of religious significance in north.

Religion: In last officially accepted census (1963), about 47 percent of population self-identified as Muslims (chiefly adherents of Sunni Islam), nearly 35 percent as Christians, and more than 18 percent as other (almost entirely adherents of indigenous religions). Majority of north Muslim; south mainly non-Muslim, primarily Christian; middle belt mixed faiths. Mission-related Christian churches (Anglican, Roman Catholic, Methodist, and others), African independent churches, and Aladura Church present.

Education: Universal primary education (six-year program) responsibility of state and local governments. Great increase in enrollments (about 12 million in government primary schools, additional millions in Muslim and Christian private schools in 1985). Responsibility for secondary education shared by federal and state governments; also some private schools; 3.7 million in government secondary schools in 1985. In 1990 between 150,000 and 200,000 in thirty-five colleges, universities, and higher technical schools.

Health: Major prevalent diseases included cerebrospinal meningitis, yellow fever, Lassa fever, acquired immune deficiency syndrome (AIDS), malaria, guinea worm, schistosomiasis, onchocerciasis, and malnutrition among young children. Medical establishments owned by federal, state, and local governments and private groups. Shortage of medical facilities and physicians in rural areas. Primary Health Care Plan launched in late 1980s, including expanded immunization campaign.

Economy

Gross National Product (GNP): US$30.0 billion, 1989; US$230 per capita, 1990.

Agriculture, Forestry, and Fishing: Agriculture represented 39.1 percent of gross domestic product (GDP) in 1988. In 1990, 34 million hectares, or 42 percent of arable land under cultivation; 18 million hectares of pastureland; 20 million hectares of forests. 1991 drought forced substantial increase in food imports. Cash crops: cocoa, palm oil, rubber, cotton, peanuts. Major food crops: cassava, yams, taro, sweet potatoes, sorghum, millet, corn, rice. Livestock: cattle, goats, sheep, horses, camels, pigs, poultry, representing 2.0 percent of GDP. Forests used extensively, and government engaged in afforestation projects. Fisheries catch did not meet domestic needs; modernization projects underway.

Industry: Constituted 10.0 percent of GDP in 1988. Primary processing industries: palm oil, peanuts, rubber, petroleum, wood, hides and skins. Manufacturing industries: food products, textiles, cement, building materials, footwear, chemical products, ceramics, small appliances.

Mining, Petroleum, and Energy: Main items mined: coal, tin, columbite for domestic use. Nigeria world's sixth largest oil exporter; domestic consumption 250,000 barrels per day; 11 percent of extracted oil refined domestically. Natural gas constituted more than 20 percent of commercial energy sources in 1990. Emphasis on expanding hydroelectric power (14 percent of energy consumed in 1980s) and oil- and gas-generated electricity.

Exports: Petroleum, cocoa.

Imports: Machinery, transportation equipment, chemicals, manufactured goods, food, live animals.

Major Trading Partners: United States, Britain, other European Economic Community countries, Japan, Canada. Nigeria had negative trade balance.

Currency: Naira (N); 1 naira = 100 kobo; average exchange rate in 1990: N8.04 per US$1.00.

Transportation and Communications

Roads: In 1990, 108,000 kilometers of roads, of which 30,000 kilometers paved, 25,000 kilometers gravel; rest unimproved earth. Most state capitals and large towns accessible by paved road.

Railroads: In 1990, 3,500 kilometers of narrow-gauge (1.067 meter) track. Nigerian Railway Corporation declared bankruptcy in 1988 and system in serious operational difficulties.

Civil Aviation: Three airports handled international flights: Murtala Muhammad International at Lagos, Aminu Kano International at Kano, and Port Harcourt. Twenty-nine other airports with paved runways. Nigeria Airways parastatal with domestic and international flights.

Ports: Three major complexes: Lagos (including Apapa and Tin Can Island), which handled majority of cargo, Delta (including Warri and Sapele on Niger River), and Rivers (including Port Harcourt); Calabar (on Cross River), major eastern port. Crude oil exported through Bonny, near Port Harcourt, and Burutu, near Warri.

Communications: Telecommunications being expanded in 1990; domestic satellite system linked all major urban areas; good international telecommunications system. Also 65 AM radio stations and various television stations.

Government and Politics

Government: Federal republic under strong presidential administration. Became parliamentary democracy at independence; under military rule 1966 to 1979, 1983- . Constitution of 1979 amended February 1984. New constitution promulgated 1989 and scheduled to take effect January 1993; provides for three independent branches of government: executive, legislative, judicial. National Assembly dissolved in 1983, had not been reinstated as of mid-1991. Transition to civilian rule scheduled to be completed January 1993.

Administrative Divisions: Thirty states divided into local councils; Federal Capital Territory of Abuja projected to become partially operational as national capital in 1991 as federal departments transfer from Lagos.

Judicial System: Legal system based on English common law modified by Nigerian rulings, constitution of 1979, legislative enactments, and decrees of military government in effect. Draft constitution of 1989 to take effect at start of Third Republic. Customary and Muslim sharia law recognized in personal status matters. Federal system included Supreme Court, federal courts of appeal, and federal high courts. Supreme Court had original jurisdiction in constitutional disputes.

Politics: In 1989 two political parties established by government: National Republican Convention, slightly right of center, and Social Democratic Party, slightly left of center. Presidential elections scheduled for December 1992.

Foreign Relations: Nonaligned; active member of United Nations, Organization of African Unity, Commonwealth of Nations, and Economic Community of West African States. Main principles of foreign policy: noninterference in internal affairs and inviolability of national borders in Africa.

National Security

Armed Forces: In 1990 armed forces totaled at least 94,500; components were army, 80,000; navy, 5,000; and air force, 9,500; no organized reserves; service entirely voluntary.

Major Tactical Units: Army had two mechanized infantry divisions, one armored division, and one airborne division; air force tactical command had three interceptor/strike squadrons, one maritime reconnaissance squadron, and five transport squadrons. Equipment inventory over 260 aircraft. Navy equipped with modern fleet of frigates, corvettes, transports, and patrol craft; defended territorial waters and was developing amphibious warfare capability.

Major Military Suppliers: Diversified military procurement sources included Italy, Germany, Britain, United States, and Eastern Europe. Small but important domestic defense industry.

Military Costs: Between 1977 and 1987, military spending decreased 80 percent to less than 1 percent of GNP; in 1990 defense budget N2.19 billion, or about US$277 million.

Security Forces: Size of national police (Nigeria Police Force) variously estimated at between 20,000 and 152,000, organized into seven area commands under Nigeria Police Council that included president, chief of staff, minister of internal affairs, and police inspector general. Also Port Security Police (total about 12,000) and Quick Intervention Force (number not known) in each state. Security services reorganized in 1986 into State Security Service for domestic intelligence, National Intelligence Agency for foreign intelligence and counterintelligence, and Defence Intelligence Agency for military intelligence.

INTRODUCTION

The most populous country in Africa and the largest in area of the West African states, Nigeria was an early twentieth century colony that became an independent nation in 1960. A country of great diversity because of the many ethnic, linguistic, and religious groups that live within its borders, Nigeria is also a country with a long past. The history of the peoples that constitute the present state dates back more than 2,000 years. The earliest archaeological finds were of the Nok, who inhabited the central Jos Plateau between the Niger and Benue rivers between 300 B.C. and 200 A.D. A number of states or kingdoms with which contemporary ethnic groups can be identified existed before 1500. Of these, the three dominant regional groups were the Hausa in the northern kingdoms of the savanna, the Yoruba in the west, and the Igbo in the south.

The European slave trade that occurred in Africa as early as the late fifteenth century and that crested between the 1650s and the 1850s had a significant impact on Nigeria. Britain declared the slave trade illegal in 1807 and sent its navy to West African waters to enforce the ban. Britain's action led ultimately to British intervention in Nigeria, which had become a major area for the slave trade. Meanwhile, whereas European missionaries were bringing Christianity to the peoples of southern Nigeria, Islam had been introduced along the caravan routes of northern Nigeria. The jihad, or holy war, waged within what became the Sokoto Caliphate between 1804 and 1808, was instrumental in spreading the Muslim faith not only in the north but also into adjacent regions, such as the area that came to be known as the middle belt, running from the Niger River valley in the west to the Cameroon Highlands in the east.

Initially, the slave trade had been the area's primary attraction for the European powers, but other products, including palm oil and cocoa, also played a role. To safeguard trade from the instability resulting from the ongoing Yoruba wars that began in the 1830s, Britain established a colony in Lagos as early as 1861. The Royal Niger Company was chartered for trading purposes in 1886, shortly after the Berlin Conference of 1885 had sought to resolve overlapping European colonial activities on the African continent. Until 1900 British control of the area was limited to the coastal region and Lokoja, at the confluence of the Niger and Benue rivers. In that year, Britain named Frederick Lugard high commissioner of the Protectorate of Northern Nigeria. His tenure, which lasted until 1918, stressed indirect British control using local rulers. When Northern Nigeria and Southern Nigeria were united in 1914, Lugard continued as Britain's chief representative. Hugh Clifford, who succeeded him as governor from 1919 to 1925, sought to bring Western economic development, to build on educational progress made in the south, and to introduce new governmental structures such as the 1922 constitution and the Legislative Council.

British rule and economic and educational development produced a rising nationalism that was reflected particularly in the organized labor movement and the creation of various political parties during World War II. Following the war, Nigeria developed under two colonial constitutions, those of 1946 and 1951. They expanded the Legislative Council and introduced the federal principle, combining regional autonomy with federal union and stipulating that civil service personnel and personnel in other public spheres should reflect the various parts of the country. In 1952-53 a census indicated that 54 percent of the population resided in the northern part of the country. Because population was the basis for allocating revenues as well as political representation, census findings always aroused considerable controversy as to their accuracy. The 1962 census was voided, and the 1963 census has become the accepted basis for planning purposes. The 1973 census, which claimed that 64 percent of the population lived in the north, was subsequently disallowed. (The November 1991 census was conducted by restricting movement of the population for two days in 250,000 enumeration areas, In mid-March 1992 the government announced that the overall population was only 88.5 million considerably less than anticipated.

Nigeria gained its independence on October 1, 1960, and the First Republic is generally held to have begun then, although the nation actually became a republic on October 1, 1963. The political scene, unfortunately, was clouded by the trial of two leading politicians, who were charged with conspiracy; and widespread political abuses and corruption caused the electorate to become disillusioned. The 1964-65 elections saw very low voter participation, followed by increasing violence that led to the death of as many as 2,000 persons. After an abortive coup attempt in January 1966, the army took over under Major General Johnson Aguiyi Ironsi, an Igbo, and a Federal Military Government was formed. Ironsi's tenure was short-lived because northern officers staged a countercoup in July, in which Ironsi was killed and Lieutenant Colonel Yakubu Gowon, a Christian from the middle belt area, took control. Tension increased between the infantry, who were mainly of northern origin, and the Igbo soldiers in the south. The conflict led to the bloody civil war of 1967-70 (also known as the Biafran War) that took the lives of about 2 million persons.

Gowon, who intended that his be an interim rule preparing for return to civilian government, concentrated on economic development. In the late 1960s, the discovery of petroleum in commercial quantities caused oil to replace cocoa, peanuts, and palm products as Nigeria's major foreign exchange earner; and in 1971 Nigeria became a member of the Organization of the Petroleum Exporting Countries (OPEC). The economy suffered, however, from the 1972-74 drought and rising unemployment as farm workers flocked into the cities.

Discontent increased, and in 1975 military forces deposed Gowon in a bloodless coup. They brought in Brigadier General Murtala Muhammad, who began demobilizing the military, cutting the civil service, and creating new states (the number of states eventually came to nineteen) in order to weaken regional ethnic ties. Dissatisfaction within the military over these measures led to Murtala Muhammad's assassination in 1976. He was succeeded by his next in command, Lieutenant General Olusegun Obasanjo, who concentrated on preparing the country for civilian rule in accordance with the draft of the constitution, which was promulgated in 1979, and the elections held under it.

The resulting Second Republic lasted from 1979 to 1983 under civilian president Shehu Shagari. The weak political coalition government, the end of the oil boom, the strain of recession, and fraud in the 1983 elections caused the army to step in again at the end of December 1983 January 1984 under Major General Muhammadu Buhari, who sought to end widespread corruption. The army removed Buhari in August 1985, substituting Major General Ibrahim Babangida and the calling the new governing military body Armed Forces Ruling Council. Babangida also attempted to prepare Nigeria for civilian government, initially through economic measures. He declared a National Economic Emergency in 1986 and undertook Nigeria's own version of a rigorous structural adjustment program (SAP), as a result of which it received aid from the World Bank (see Glossary).

Economic measures designed to raise the overall standard of living of Nigerians had to take into account the pluralistic nature of the society. The country contained between 250 and 400 ethnic groups (depending on the way they were defined), speaking about 400 languages.

Of these, the Hausa were the dominant group in the northern area, followed by the Kanuri; the Nupe and Tiv predominated in the middle belt; and the southern area was fragmented: the major groups being the Yoruba concentrated in the southwest and the Igbo in the southeast. Whereas 80 percent of Nigeria's population in 1990 lived in farming villages, the country experienced perhaps the fastest growing urbanization in the world in the 1970s and had the largest total urban population of any state in sub-Saharan Africa. The search for employment drew males to the cities, leaving most rural areas with a population composed largely of women, children, and the elderly.

Religion also has been pluralist. The far northern areas of Nigeria have commonly been considered Muslim, but the middle belt has a mixture of Muslim and Christian adherents. In the south, traditionally considered Christian and featuring Protestant and Africanized churches, such as the Aladura movement among the Yoruba and Roman Catholicism among the Igbo, there was also a sizeable Muslim population in 1990. In addition, traditional religion, characterized by worship of primordial spirits, dead ancestors, and spirits of places, is practiced, especially in rural areas.

Education, too, has followed a varied pattern. By 1992, Nigeria had a nationwide indigenous system in which English had come to be the language of instruction beyond primary school; traditional Quranic schools, both in the rural and urban areas of the north; and private and parochial schools in the cities, which provided a European-style education (such schools were taken over by the government in the mid-1970s but allowed to resume private operation in 1990).

Health facilities were uneven in quality as of 1990. Babangida launched a Primary Health Care plan in 1987 designed to expand immunization and improve inadequate rural health facilities and the geographic maldistribution of medical facilities. Significant health progress had been made nationally, however, since World War II. One of the most challenging health problems of the early 1990s was the prevalence of acquired and human services immune deficiency syndrome (AIDS). In the spring of 1992, the minister of health announced that about 400,000 Nigerians (nearly 0.5 percent of the population) were carriers of the virus that caused AIDS.

The relatively high percentage of secondary school and university graduates in Nigeria represented both an asset and a liability to the economy. Although an educated work force was useful in promoting technology and the professions, in the recession of the late 1980s, Nigeria had an unemployment rate for secondary school graduates of 35 to 40 percent, a potential source of unrest. Efforts to decrease unemployment were hampered by the dependence of the economy on petroleum. In 1988 oil produced 87 percent of the country's export income and 77 percent of total federal revenues. This situation made the economy very vulnerable to world oil price fluctuations. For example, the fall in oil prices and output in the latter 1980s caused a drastic decline in Nigeria's gross national product (GNP--see Glossary). GNP went from US$830 per capita in 1983 to US$250 per capita in 1989. As a result, in 1989, for the first time, Nigeria was listed by the World Bank as a low-income country. The fall in the price of oil caused Nigeria not only to incur a trade deficit but also to begin foreign borrowing, resulting in 1989 in the largest public debt of any sub-Saharan state.

In addition to petroleum, Nigeria's major exports in the early 1990s continued to be primary products such as cocoa and, to a lesser degree, peanuts, cotton, and palm oil products. (In 1990 a law was passed banning the export of cocoa beans as of January 1991 in order to promote domestic processing. This law caused concern because despite various projects for establishing processing plants, Nigeria was unable to process all the cocoa beans produced.) The United States replaced Britain in the later 1980s as Nigeria's best customer, but Britain remained Nigeria's largest single source of imports.

Babangida's introduction of the SAP in 1986 represented an effort to increase domestic production and to institute financial and import restrictions that would strengthen the economy. Measures taken under the SAP entailed control of the value of the naira (see Glossary) by creating the second-tier foreign exchange market, strict control of the money supply and credits, a budget deficit limited to 4 percent of gross domestic product (GDP--see Glossary), privatization of major state-owned companies together with a new industrial policy, easing of trade restrictions, and debt rescheduling. The SAP was still in place in early 1992; the floating of the naira against international currencies in March 1992 was a bold step but was expected to result in further inflation.

Babangida's SAP was not Nigeria's first attempt at economic planning. Early government planning efforts, beginning in the late 1940s, had limited results; therefore, in 1990 Nigeria adopted a three-year rolling plan system that could readily be modified when changed circumstances required. The major goals were to reduce inflation, which had averaged 20 percent or more annually between 1973 and 1984; to maintain the infrastructure-- Nigeria had one of the best-developed transportation systems in Africa but maintenance had been poor; to achieve agricultural self-sufficiency, and to reduce the SAP burden. As with most other developing countries, the share that agriculture contributed to GDP declined. It went from 65.7 percent in fiscal year (see Glossary) 1959 to 39.2 percent in 1988. Moreover, Nigerian's hope of achieving food self-sufficiency was at least temporarily dashed when in early 1991 drought forced Nigeria to increase substantially its food imports. Manufacturing's share in GDP gradually rose from 4.4 percent in fiscal year 1959 to 10.0 percent in 1988. The growth in manufacturing resulted in part from the Nigerian Enterprises Promotion decrees of 1972, 1977, and 1981 that facilitated indigenous majority ownership. These decrees were relaxed in 1985, however, to encourage foreign investment and thus stimulate the economy.

The major goals of economic development were integrating agriculture and industry more closely, including privatization or commercialization of a number of parastatals and government-owned enterprises; improving the infrastructure with particular reference to increasing electric power generation, enlarging and modernizing communications systems, and performing needed maintenance on existing transportation systems; reducing dependence on oil; and creating an effective national planning body. By the end of 1991, privatization measures had taken effect in such areas as agriculture, banking, railroads, and telecommunications. Nigeria, however, for the most part lacked the capital necessary for large-scale development and depended upon foreign loans to implement its programs. For example, it received a 1990 European Economic Community grant for rural development and telecommunications of 3.54 billion naira (for value of the naira--see Glossary) under the (Fourth) Lomé Convention (see Glossary) and a 1991 British loan of £23.3 million to expand the electric power system. As a result of such borrowing, at the end of 1991 Nigeria owed an estimated US$34 billion in external debt, 44 percent was owed to members of the Paris Club (see Glossary) and 20 percent to foreign commercial banks. Throughout 1990 and 1991, Nigeria engaged in extensive debt rescheduling with Paris Club countries such as Britain, Italy, Japan, and Sweden.

Among other major development projects that Nigeria was pursuing was the large Ajaokuta steelworks, begun with Soviet funding and subsequently funded by the World Bank, due for completion at the end of 1992. On a smaller scale was a European currency unit (ECU) 48 million loan from the European Investment Bank under the Third Lomé Convention for the development of palm oil refining facilities. In addition, despite its efforts to diversify its economy, Nigeria was expanding its oil production. The expansion came, most notably, through the discovery of an offshore field near Akwa Ibom, which was scheduled to increase oil production by one-third by 1994. Expansion also resulted from the renovation of oil refineries at Warri and Kaduna; the development of petrochemical plants; an oil condensate project at Oso on the Niger Delta coast; and the planned construction, beginning in 1992, of facilities to enable the export of liquefied natural gas from Bonny.

Despite this economic progress, the implementation of the SAP led to decreased spending on social programs in the late 1980s. The decrease caused some domestic dissatisfaction, which was reflected in strikes and student demonstrations. Since achieving independence in 1960, Nigeria has faced a number of incidents reflecting domestic discontent; in many instances the incidents were initiated by the army or its leaders. Such dissension, of which the most serious outbreak was the Biafran civil war, has led to twenty-two years of military rule; democratic government under the First Republic and the Second Republic was limited to ten years. Sources of military dissatisfaction have arisen not only from the personal ambitions of various military leaders but also from general dismay at the corruption, bribery, favoritism, and inefficiency prevalent in the government. Many Nigerians initially saw the army as the most effective body to control the country, but with the understanding that military rule was an interim measure and that plans must go forward for the transition to democratic government. In support of this view, a number of organized interest groups, such as professional associations, trade unions, student associations, women's organizations, and the media have exerted pressures in favor of democratic processes.

The 1989 constitution that Nigeria adopted as the basis for its transition to democratic government was modeled on the United States federal system. It provided for a president; two legislative houses, one based on population and the other on states; and an independent judiciary. A timetable was established for a series of elections at the local government area, state, and national levels. At first, officeholders in any previous government were barred from holding office in an attempt to eliminate corruption and undue political influence; in mid-December 1991 the ban was lifted, making only Babangida ineligible.

In 1989 Babangida also rejected the applications of all political entities to be recognized as political parties and instead in October 1989 created two parties: the Republican National Convention, "a little to the right of center," and the Social Democratic Party, "a little to the left of center." This action, which generated considerable controversy, was designed to create parties that would cross ethnic, religious, regional, and socioeconomic lines. Results of the various elections held in 1991 appeared to indicate that previously cohesive blocs were indeed being eroded. On August 27, 1991, the number of states was increased from twenty-one to thirty (see fig. 1). Irregularities in the gubernatorial primaries in October 1991 in nine states caused the election results to be canceled in November and new elections to be rescheduled for early December, with the final state gubernatorial and state assembly elections occurring in mid-December. Although by Nigerian standards the elections went relatively smoothly, there was some criticism of the system of open balloting by which voters stood behind a photograph of their chosen candidate and were counted.

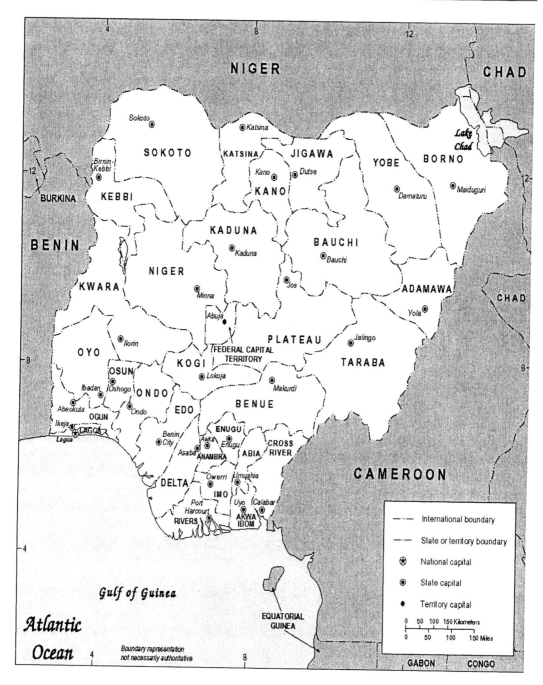

Figure 1. Administrative Divisions of Nigeria as of August 1991

Among the difficulties involved in encouraging the democratic process have been ethnic and religious tensions arising among the multitudinous groups in the country. Outbreaks of violence caused by religious tensions resulting in losses of life have occurred in the past and recurred in the 1980s and 1990s. Most recently, in 1991 and 1992 they took place in Bauchi, Benue, Kaduna, Kano, Taraba, and other states. Desire for ethnic self-assertion and for the power and financial wherewithal resulting from statehood have largely constituted the basis for the creation of new states. Nigeria has moved from three regions at independence to four regions in 1963, twelve states in 1967, nineteen states in 1976, twenty-one states in 1987, and thirty states in August 1991. Government leaders including Babangida have endeavored, however, to diversify ethnic representation in a state so as to prevent the dominance of a single group. The move of the federal capital from Lagos to Abuja in December 1991 resulted not only from the tremendous overcrowding and pressure on transportation and other infrastructure facilities in Lagos but also from the desire to locate the capital in a central area that lacked association with a particular ethnic group. Some issues continued to be controversial, such as the impact the move to Abuja would have on Lagos. Moreover, the relationship of states to the federal government, with particular reference to the division of revenues among them, had as of early 1992 not been resolved to general satisfaction, nor had the highly controversial matter of the establishment of Muslim sharia courts of appeal in southern states.

Despite these domestic difficulties, Nigeria has continued to play a prominent role not only in West Africa but also in the world community. Nigeria was a prime organizer of the Economic Community of West African States (ECOWAS) and of the ECOWAS Cease-fire Monitoring Group (ECOMOG) that stemmed from it. ECOMOG provided a peacekeeping force for Liberia to which Nigeria contributed 900 personnel in August 1990 as well as leadership. To reduce the financial burden on Nigeria of participation in African peacekeeping forces, Babangida, at the 27th annual meeting of the Organization of African Unity (OAU), held in Abuja in June 1991, again raised the matter of a volunteer pan-African defense force, suggesting that such a force be organized on a regional basis.

In 1991-92 Babangida served as president of the OAU, thereby enhancing his mediator role. During this period, he met with the prime ministers of Chad and Niger and the president of Cameroon concerning border problems between Nigeria and these countries. A meeting of the four states in July 1990 had failed to resolve the Lake Chad boundary question, and in the summer of 1991 Cameroon had occupied nine Nigerian border villages or islands. Because it had a higher standard of living than its neighbors, Nigeria was also facing an influx of workers from surrounding countries. In November 1991, in an attempt to deal with the problem, Nigeria announced that it planned to create a frontier force to control illegal immigration. Nigeria's major role in the African continent was particularly highlighted by the visit of South African president Frederick W. de Klerk to Nigeria in early April 1992. The visit laid a foundation for possible future recognition of a transitional South African government by the OAU and other African states.

Nigeria has sought to play a responsible role in OPEC as well as in various United Nations bodies. Nigeria's position toward the Arabs-Israeli dispute has been influenced by its domestic religious divisions. Babangida reinstated Nigeria's diplomatic relations with Israel in August 1991, and shortly thereafter invited Palestine Liberation Organization head Yasser Arafat to visit, greeting him with a twenty-one-gun salute reserved for heads of state. The same month Babangida suspended Nigeria's membership in the Organization of the Islamic Conference. He had initiated membership in 1986 without any prior consultation, that a move had created a furore among Nigerian Christians. Because of its position as a former British colony, its membership in the British Commonwealth of Nations, and its position as a world oil producer, Nigeria's national interests have led it to align itself primarily with the West, including the European Economic Community.

Nigeria's role as an African regional leader, peacekeeper, and mediator has emerged at the same time that the country's army was being drastically reduced from approximately 250,000 personnel during the civil war to about 80,000 in 1991. Additional cuts were projected in order to bring the forces to approximately 60,000. This process, together with a large-scale restructuring of the armed forces beginning in 1990 and still underway in early 1992, occurred in preparation for civilian government under the transition to the Third Republic.

The size of the armed forces reflected not only Nigeria's expanse but also the domestic instability the country had experienced since achieving independence in 1960. In the period between 1966 and 1985, Nigeria underwent no less than six coups d'état, in addition to several attempted coups. (A serious recent failed coup was that led by Major Gideon Ockar, a middle belt Christian, in April 1991. He advocated the "excising" from Nigeria of the five northern Muslim states--the coup attempt occurred prior to the creation of Nigeria's nine additional states--on the grounds that the true Nigeria was the Christian southern part of the country.)

Economic and social conditions worsened in the 1980s, increasing the discontent resulting from ethnic, sectional, and religious cleavages. To these forces for instability were added such factors as the potential for foreign subversion, caused in part by the large number of illegal workers from other African states; the fluctuation of oil prices and particularly the impact of decreasing oil income on the economy; the pressures of the rising foreign debt; and the growing Islamism, or Islamic, activism (sometimes seen as fundamentalism), as well as increasing Christian fundamentalism.

Public disenchantment with the military in the 1980s and 1990s caused increasing demands for democracy, the elimination of military tribunals, and an end to Decree Number 2, passed during the Buhari regime. In 1992 this decree still permitted the jailing of individuals for up to six weeks without charge and set limits on freedom of speech and the press. Pressure groups, such as labor unions, academic, and student groups, and especially the media, agitated for reforms and a greater role in government decision making, particularly in the economic field. Such activity led the government to jail various individuals on a number of occasions. Another public concern was the rising crime rate, especially in urban areas, and the marked increase in drug- related crime and international narcotics trafficking. Numerous jail sentences resulted, leading to overcrowding and causing periodic amnesties to empty penal facilities.

Despite Nigeria's recent history of military domination of politics, in April 1992 Babangida appeared committed to turning over power to a new civilian government in January 1993. Part of Babangida's transition process entailed the demilitarization of the government. Demilitarization was accomplished in part in September 1990 by retiring from military service all cabinet ministers except for Babangida and the minister of defense. The officers continued to serve in a civilian capacity. The post of chief of the General Staff was likewise eliminated; the incumbent, Vice Admiral Augustus Aikhomu, who had also been retired from the military, was named vice president. In addition, numerous state military governors were retired and replaced by lower-ranking officers; in each state, a civilian deputy governor served under the military governor in order to become familiar with the duties entailed. In December 1991, the newly elected civilian governors took office.

Serious questions remained, however, as to whether or not Babangida's goals for the professionalization of the armed forces and the reeducation of the military concerning their subordinate role in a forthcoming civilian government were attainable. Concurrently, Babangida stressed educating the citizenry about their responsibilities for active, knowledgeable participation in government. The question was also raised as to whether or not democracy could be achieved by a military government that established rules for the transition but that simultaneously imposed strict limits on the democratic process and sought to silence critics both of the domestic political scene and of the government's economic policies, particularly the SAP. The House of Representatives elections and the Senate elections (which will return senators from each state and one from Abuja to the newly structured 61-member Senate) scheduled for November 1992 and the presidential elections scheduled for December 1992 would be the final test in the transition to the Third Republic slated to occur in January 1993.

HISTORICAL SETTING

Like so many other modern African states, Nigeria is the creation of European imperialism. Its very name--after the great Niger River, the country's dominating physical feature--was suggested in the 1890s by British journalist Flora Shaw, who later became the wife of colonial governor Frederick Lugard. The modern history of Nigeria--as a political state encompassing 250 to 400 ethnic groups of widely varied cultures and modes of political organization--dates from the completion of the British conquest in 1903 and the amalgamation of northern and southern Nigeria into the Colony and Protectorate of Nigeria in 1914. The history of the Nigerian people extends backward in time for some three millennia. Archaeological evidence, oral traditions, and written documentation establish the existence of dynamic societies and well-developed political systems whose history had an important influence on colonial rule and has continued to shape independent Nigeria. Nigerian history is fragmented in the sense that it evolved from a variety of traditions, but many of the most outstanding features of modern society reflect the strong influence of the three regionally dominant ethnic groups--the Hausa in the north, the Yoruba in the west, and the Igbo in the east.

There are several dominant themes in Nigerian history that are essential in understanding contemporary Nigerian politics and society. First, the spread of Islam, predominantly in the north but later in southwestern Nigeria as well, began a millennium ago. The creation of the Sokoto Caliphate in the jihad (holy war) of 1804-8 brought most of the northern region and adjacent parts of Niger and Cameroon under a single Islamic government. The great extension of Islam within the area of present-day Nigeria dates from the nineteenth century and the consolidation of the caliphate. This history helps account for the dichotomy between north and south and for the divisions within the north that have been so strong during the colonial and postcolonial eras.

Second, the slave trade, both across the Sahara Desert and the Atlantic Ocean, had a profound influence on virtually all parts of Nigeria. The transatlantic trade in particular accounted for the forced migration of perhaps 3.5 million people between the 1650s and the 1860s, while a steady stream of slaves flowed north across the Sahara for a millennium, ending at the beginning of the twentieth century. Within Nigeria, slavery was widespread, with social implications that are still evident today. The Sokoto Caliphate, for example, had more slaves than any other modern country, except the United States in 1860. Slaves were also numerous among the Igbo, the Yoruba, and many other ethnic groups. Indeed, many ethnic distinctions, especially in the middle belt--the area between the north and south--were reinforced because of slave raiding and defensive measures that were adopted for protection against enslavement. Conversion to Islam and the spread of Christianity were intricately associated with issues relating to slavery and with efforts to promote political and cultural autonomy.

Third, the colonial era was relatively brief, lasting only six decades or so, depending upon the part of Nigeria, but it unleashed such rapid change that the full impact was still felt in the contemporary period. On the one hand, the expansion of agricultural products as the principal export earner and the corresponding development of infrastructure resulted in severely distorted economic growth that has subsequently collapsed. On the other hand, social dislocation associated with the decline of slavery and the internal movement of population between regions and to the cities necessitated the reassessment of ethnic loyalties, which in turn have been reflected in politics and religion.

In the three decades since the independence of Nigeria in 1960, a period half as long as the colonial era, Nigeria has experienced a number of successful and attempted military coups d'état and a brutal civil war, let corrupt civilian governments siphon off the profits from the oil boom of the 1970s, and faced economic collapse in the 1980s. As the most populous country in Africa, and one of the ten most populous countries in the world, Nigeria has a history that is important in its own right but that also bears scrutiny if for no other reason than to understand how and why this nation became as it is today.

EARLY HISTORY

All evidence suggests the early settlement of Nigeria millennia before the spread of agriculture 3,000 years ago, and one day it probably will be possible to reconstruct the high points of this early history. Although archaeological research has made great strides in identifying some major developments, comparatively little archaeological work has been undertaken. Consequently, it is possible only to outline some of the early history of Nigeria.

The earliest known example of a fossil skeleton with negroid features, perhaps 10,000 years old, was found at Iii Ileru in western Nigeria and attests to the antiquity of habitation in the region. Stone tools, indicating human settlement, date back another 2,000 years. Microlithic and ceramic industries were developed by pastoralists in the savanna from at least the fourth millennium B.C. and were continued by grain farmers in the stable agricultural communities that subsequently evolved there. To the south, hunting and gathering gradually gave way to subsistence farming on the fringe of the forest in the first millennium B.C. The cultivation of staple foods, such as yams, later was introduced into forest clearings. The stone ax heads, imported in great quantities from the north and used in opening the forest for agricultural development, were venerated by the Yoruba descendants of neolithic pioneers as "thunderbolts" hurled to earth by the gods.

The primitive iron-smelting furnaces at Taruga dating from the fourth century B.C. provide the oldest evidence of metalworking in West Africa, while excavations for the Kainji Dam revealed the presence of ironworking there by the second century B.C. The transition from Neolithic times to the Iron Age apparently was achieved without intermediate bronze production. Some scholars speculate that knowledge of the smelting process may have been transmitted from the Mediterranean by Berbers who ventured south. Others suggest that the technology moved westward across the Sudan (see Glossary) from the Nile Valley, although the arrival of the Iron Age in the Niger River valley and the forest region appears to have predated the introduction of metallurgy in the upper savanna by more than 800 years. The usefulness of iron tools was demonstrated in the south for bush cutting and in the north for well digging and the construction of irrigation works, contributing in both regions to the expansion of agriculture.

The earliest culture in Nigeria to be identified by its distinctive artifacts is that of the Nok people. These skilled artisans and ironworkers were associated with Taruga and flourished between the fourth century B.C. and the second century A.D. in a large area above the confluence of the Niger and Benue rivers on the Jos Plateau. The Nok achieved a level of material development not repeated in the region for nearly 1,000 years. Their terra-cotta sculpture, abstractly stylized and geometric in conception, is admired both for its artistic expression and for the high technical standards of its production.

Information is lacking from the "silent millennium" (first millennium A.D.) that followed the Nok ascendancy, apart from evidence of iron smelting on Dala Hill in Kano from about 600 to 700 A.D. It is assumed, however, that trade linking the Niger region with North Africa played a key role in the continuing development of the area. Certainly by the beginning of the second millennium A.D., there was an active trade along a north-south axis from North Africa through the Sahara to the forest, with the savanna people acting as intermediaries in exchanges that involved slaves, ivory, salt, glass beads, coral, cloth, weapons, brass rods, and other goods.

EUROPEAN SLAVE TRADE IN WEST AFRICA

A desire for glory and profit from trade, missionary zeal, and considerations of global strategy brought Portuguese navigators to the West African coast in the late fifteenth century. Locked in a seemingly interminable crusading war with Muslim Morocco, the Portuguese conceived of a plan whereby maritime expansion might bypass the Islamic world and open new markets that would result in commercial gain. They hoped to tap the fabled Saharan gold trade, establish a sea route around Africa to India, and link up with the mysterious Christian kingdom of Prester John. The Portuguese achieved all these goals. They obtained access to the gold trade by trading along the Gulf of Guinea, establishing a base at Elmina ("the mine") on the Gold Coast (Ghana), and they made their way into the Indian Ocean, militarily securing a monopoly of the spice trade. Even the Christian kingdom turned out to be real; it was Ethiopia, although Portuguese adventures there turned sour very quickly. Portugal's lasting legacy for Nigeria, however, was its initiation of the transatlantic slave trade.

By 1471 Portuguese ships had reconnoitered the West African coast south as far as the Niger Delta, although they did not know that it was the delta, and in 1481 emissaries from the king of Portugal visited the court of the *oba* of Benin. For a time, Portugal and Benin maintained close relations. Portuguese soldiers aided Benin in its wars; Portuguese even came to be spoken at the *oba*'s court. Gwatto, the port of Benin, became the depot to handle the peppers, ivory, and increasing numbers of slaves offered by the *oba* in exchange for coral beads; textile imports from India; European-manufactured articles, including tools and weapons; and *manillas* (brass and bronze bracelets that were used as currency and also were melted down for objets d'art). Portugal also may have been the first European power to import cowrie shells, which were the currency of the far interior.

Benin profited from its close ties with the Portuguese and exploited the firearms bought from them to tighten its hold on the lower Niger area. Two factors checked the spread of Portuguese influence and the continued expansion of Benin, however. First, Portugal stopped buying pepper because of the availability of other spices in the Indian Ocean region. Second, Benin placed an embargo on the export of slaves, thereby isolating itself from the growth of what was to become the major export from the Nigerian coast for 300 years. Benin continued to capture slaves and to employ them in its domestic economy, but the Edo state remained unique among Nigerian polities in refusing to participate in the transatlantic trade. In the long run, Benin remained relatively isolated from the major changes along the Nigerian coast.

The Portuguese initially bought slaves for resale on the Gold Coast, where slaves were traded for gold. For this reason, the southwestern coast of Nigeria and neighboring parts of the present-day Republic of Benin (not to be confused with the kingdom of Benin) became known as the "slave coast." When the African coast began to supply slaves to the Americas in the last third of the sixteenth century, the Portuguese continued to look to the Bight of Benin as one of its sources of supply. By then they were concentrating activities on the Angolan coast, which supplied roughly 40 percent of all slaves shipped to the Americas throughout the duration of the transatlantic trade, but they always maintained a presence on the Nigerian coast.

The Portuguese monopoly on West African trade was broken at the end of the sixteenth century, when Portugal's influence was challenged by the rising naval power of the Netherlands. The Dutch took over Portuguese trading stations on the coast that were the source of slaves for the Americas. French and English competition later undermined the Dutch position. Although slave ports from Lagos to Calabar would see the flags of many other European maritime countries (including Denmark, Sweden, and Brandenburg) and the North American colonies, Britain became the dominant slaving power in the eighteenth century. Its ships handled two-fifths of the transatlantic traffic during the century. The Portuguese and French were responsible for another two-fifths.

Nigeria kept its important position in the slave trade throughout the great expansion of the transatlantic trade after the middle of the seventeenth century. Slightly more slaves came from the Nigerian coast than from Angola in the eighteenth century, while in the nineteenth century perhaps 30 percent of all slaves sent across the Atlantic came from Nigeria. Over the period of the whole trade, more than 3.5 million slaves were shipped from Nigeria to the Americas. Most of these slaves were Igbo and Yoruba, with significant concentrations of Hausa, Ibibio, and other ethnic groups. In the eighteenth century, two polities--Oyo and the Aro confederacy--were responsible for most of the slaves exported from Nigeria. The Aro confederacy continued to export slaves through the 1830s, but most slaves in the nineteenth century were a product of the Yoruba civil wars that followed the collapse of Oyo in the 1820s.

The expansion of Oyo after the middle of the sixteenth century was closely associated with the growth of slave exports across the Atlantic. Oyo's cavalry pushed southward along a natural break in the forests (known as the Benin Gap, i.e., the opening in the forest where the savanna stretched to the Bight of Benin), and thereby gained access to the coastal ports.

Oyo experienced a series of power struggles and constitutional crises in the eighteenth century that directly related to its success as a major slave exporter. The powerful Oyo Mesi, the council of warlords that checked the king, forced a number of kings to commit suicide. In 1754 the head of the Oyo Mesi, *basorun* Gaha, seized power, retaining a series of kings as puppets. The rule of this military oligarchy was overcome in 1789, when King Abiodun successfully staged a countercoup and forced the suicide of Gaha. Abiodun and his successors maintained the supremacy of the monarchy until the second decade of the nineteenth century, primarily because of the reliance of the king on a cavalry force that was independent of the Oyo Mesi. This force was recruited largely from Muslim slaves, especially Hausa, from farther north.

The other major slave-exporting state was a loose confederation under the leadership of the Aro, an Igbo clan of mixed Igbo and Ibibio origins, whose home was on the escarpment between the central Igbo districts and the Cross River. Beginning in the late seventeenth century, the Aro built a complex network of alliances and treaties with many of the Igbo clans. They served as arbiters in villages throughout Igboland, and their famous oracle at Arochukwu, located in a thickly wooded gorge, was widely regarded as a court of appeal for many kinds of disputes. By custom the Aro were sacrosanct, allowing them to travel anywhere with their goods without fear of attack. Alliances with certain Igbo clans who acted as mercenaries for the Aro guaranteed their safety. As oracle priests, they also received slaves in payment of fines or dedicated to the gods by their masters as scapegoats for their own transgressions. These slaves thereby became the property of the Aro priests, who were at liberty to sell them.

Besides their religious influence, the Aro established their ascendancy through a combination of commercial acumen and diplomatic skill. Their commercial empire was based on a set of twenty-four-day fairs and periodic markets that dotted the interior. Resident Aro dominated these markets and collected slaves for export. They had a virtual monopoly of the slave trade after the collapse of Oyo in the 1820s. Villages suspected of violating treaties with the Aro were subject to devastating raids that not only produced slaves for export but also maintained Aro influence. The Aro had treaties with the coastal ports from which slaves were exported, especially Calabar, Bonny, and Elem Kalabari. The people of Calabar were Efik, a subsection of Ibibio, while Bonny and Elem Kalabari were Ijaw towns.

The Ijaw, who occupied the tidal area in proximity to the Igbo, had wrested a frugal living from the sale of dried fish and sea salt to the inland communities for centuries before the rise of the slave trade. Traditionally, they had lived in federated groups of villages with the head of the ranking village presiding over general assemblies attended by all the males. During the heyday of the slave trade in the eighteenth century, the major Ijaw villages grew into cities of 5,000 to 10,000 inhabitants ruled by local strongmen allied with the Aro. Their economies were based on the facilities they offered to slave traders. They were entrepreneurial communities, receiving slaves from the Aro for resale to European agents. Personal wealth rather than status within a lineage group was the basis for political power and social status. Government typically was conducted by councils composed of leading merchants and headed by an *amanyanabo* (chief executive), an office that in time became hereditary.

By the end of the eighteenth century, the area that was to become Nigeria was far from a unified country. Furthermore, the orientation of the north and the south was entirely different. The savanna states of Hausaland and Borno had experienced a difficult century of political insecurity and ecological disaster but otherwise continued in a centuries-long tradition of slow political and economic change that was similar to other parts of the savanna. The southern areas near the coast, by contrast, had been swept up in the transatlantic slave trade. Political and economic change had been rapid and dramatic. By 1800 Oyo governed much of southwestern Nigeria and neighboring parts of the modern Republic of Benin, while the Aro had consolidated southeastern Nigeria into a confederation that dominated that region. The Oyo and the Aro confederations were major trading partners of the slave traders from Europe and North America.

THE NINETEENTH CENTURY: REVOLUTION AND RADICAL ADJUSTMENT

In the first decade of the nineteenth century, two unrelated developments that were to have a major influence on virtually all of the area that is now Nigeria ushered in a period of radical change. First, between 1804 and 1808, the Islamic holy war of Usman dan Fodio established the Sokoto Caliphate, which not only expanded to become the largest empire in Africa since the fall of Songhai but also had a profound influence on much of Muslim Africa to the west and to the east (see fig. 2). Second, in 1807 Britain declared the transatlantic slave trade to be illegal, an action that occurred at a time when Britain was responsible for shipping more slaves to the Americas than any other country. Although the transatlantic slave trade did not end until the 1860s, it was gradually replaced by other commodities, especially palm oil; the shift in trade had serious economic and political consequences in the interior, which led to increasing British intervention in the affairs of Yorubaland and the Niger Delta. The rise of the Sokoto Caliphate and the economic and political adjustment in the south strongly shaped the course of the colonial conquest at the end of the nineteenth century.

COLONIAL NIGERIA

Prodded by the instability created by the Yoruba wars and by the activities of other European powers, Britain moved cautiously but inexorably toward colonial domination of the lower Niger Basin. In the decades that followed its abolition of the slave trade, British diplomacy wove a fabric of treaties with kings and chieftains whose cooperation was sought in suppressing the traffic. British interests also dictated occasional armed intervention by the Royal Navy and by the Royal Niger Company Constabulary to staunch the flow of slaves to the coast, to protect legitimate commerce, and to maintain peace. Moreover, the missionaries cried out for protection and assistance in stamping out slavery and other "barbarous practices" associated with indigenous religions. Finally, the posting of consular officials by the Foreign Office to service the increasing amount of trade in the ports of the bights of Benin and Biafra helped project British influence inland.

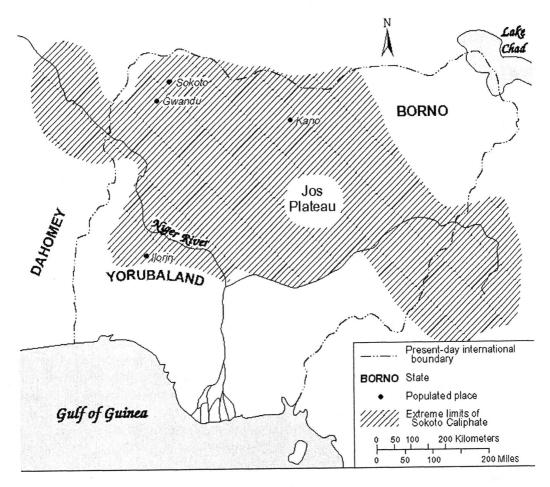

Figure 2. The Sokoto Caliphate, Mid-Nineteenth Century

For many years, official hesitation about adding tropical dependencies to the British Empire outweighed these factors. The prevailing sentiment, even after Lagos became a colony in 1861, was expressed in a parliamentary report in 1865 urging withdrawal from West Africa. Colonies were regarded as expensive liabilities, especially where trading concessions could be exercised without resorting to annexation. Attitudes changed, however, as rival European powers, especially France and Germany, scurried to develop overseas markets and annexed territory (see fig. 3).

Inevitably, imperial ambitions clashed when the intentions of the various European countries became obvious. In 1885 at the Berlin Conference, the European powers attempted to resolve their conflicts of interest by allotting areas of exploitation. The conferees also enunciated the principle, known as the dual mandate, that the best interests of Europe and Africa would be served by maintaining free access to the continent for trade and by providing Africa with the benefits of Europe's civilizing mission. Britain's claims to a sphere of influence in the Niger Basin were acknowledged formally, but it was stipulated here as elsewhere that only effective occupation would secure full international recognition. In the end, pressure in the region from France and Germany hastened the establishment of effective British occupation.

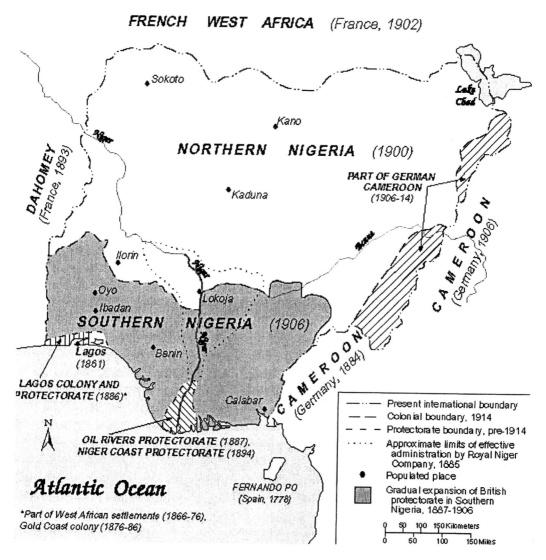

Figure 3. British Presence in the Niger Region, 1861-1914

EMERGENCE OF NIGERIAN NATIONALISM

British colonialism created Nigeria, joining diverse peoples and regions in an artificial political entity. It was not unusual that the nationalism that became a political factor in Nigeria during the interwar period derived both from an older political particularism and broad pan-Africanism rather than from any sense of a common Nigerian nationality. Its goal initially was not self-determination, but rather increased participation in the governmental process on a regional level. Inconsistencies in British policy reinforced cleavages based on regional animosities by attempting simultaneously to preserve the indigenous cultures of each area and to introduce modern technology and Western political and social concepts. In the north, appeals to Islamic legitimacy upheld the rule of the emirs, so that nationalist sentiments there were decidedly anti-Western. Modern nationalists in the south, whose thinking was shaped by European ideas, opposed indirect rule, which had entrenched what was considered to be an anachronistic ruling class in power and shut out the Westernized elite.

The ideological inspiration for southern nationalists came from a variety of sources, including prominent American-based activists such as Marcus Garvey and W.E.B. Du Bois. Nigerian students abroad joined those from other colonies in pan-African groups, such as the West African Students Union, founded in London in 1925. Early nationalists tended to ignore Nigeria as the focus of patriotism; rather, the common denominator was based on a newly assertive ethnic consciousness, particularly Yoruba and Igbo. Despite their acceptance of European and North American influences, the nationalists were critical of colonialism for its failure to appreciate the antiquity of indigenous cultures. They wanted self-government, charging that only colonial rule prevented the unshackling of progressive forces in Africa.

Political opposition to colonial rule often assumed religious dimensions. Independent Christian churches had emerged at the end of the nineteenth century because many European missionaries were racist and blocked the advancement of a Nigerian clergy. European interpretations of Christian orthodoxy also refused to allow the incorporation of local customs and practices, even though the various mission denominations themselves interpreted Christianity very differently. It was acceptable for the established missions to differ, but most Europeans were surprised and shocked that Nigerians would develop new denominations independent of European control. Christianity long had experienced "protestant" schisms; the emergence of independent Christian churches in Nigeria was another phase of this history. The pulpits of the independent congregations provided one of the few available avenues for the free expression of attitudes critical of colonial rule.

In the 1920s, there were several types of associations that were ostensibly nonpolitical. One group consisted of professional and business associations, such as the Nigerian Union of Teachers, which provided trained leadership for political groups; the Nigerian Law Association, which brought together lawyers, many of whom had been educated in Britain; and the Nigerian Produce Traders' Association, led by Obafemi Awolowo.

Ethnic and kinship organizations that often took the form of a tribal union also emerged in the 1920s. These organizations were primarily urban phenomena that arose after large numbers of rural migrants moved to the cities. Alienated by the anonymity of the urban environment and drawn together by ties to their ethnic homelands--as well as by the need for mutual aid--the new city dwellers formed local clubs that later expanded into federations covering whole regions. By the mid-1940s, the major ethnic groups had formed such associations as the Igbo Federal Union and the Egbe Omo Oduduwa (Society of the Descendants of Oduduwa), a Yoruba cultural movement, in which Awolowo played a leading role.

A third type of organization that was more pointedly political was the youth or student group, which became the vehicle of intellectuals and professionals. They were the most politically conscious segment of the population and stood in the vanguard of the nationalist movement. Newspapers, some of which were published before World War I, provided coverage of nationalist views.

The opportunity afforded by the 1922 constitution to elect a handful of representatives to the Legislative Council gave politically conscious Nigerians something concrete to work on. The principal figure in the political activity that ensued was Herbert Macauley, often referred to as the father of Nigerian nationalism. He aroused political awareness through his newspaper, the Lagos *Daily News*, while leading the Nigerian National Democratic Party (NNDP), which dominated elections in Lagos from its founding in 1922 until the ascendancy of the National Youth Movement (NYM) in 1938. His political platform called for economic and educational development, Africanization of the civil service, and self-government for Lagos. Significantly, however, Macauley's NNDP remained almost entirely a Lagos party, popular only in the area with experience in elective politics.

The NYM first used nationalist rhetoric to agitate for improvements in education. The movement brought to public notice a long list of future leaders, including H.O. Davies and Nnamdi Azikiwe. Although Azikiwe later came to be recognized as the leading spokesman for national unity, his orientation on return from university training in the United States was pan-African rather than nationalist, emphasizing the common African struggle against European colonialism. He betrayed much less consciousness of purely Nigerian goals than Davies, a student of Harold Laski at the London School of Economics, whose political orientation was considered left-wing.

By 1938 the NYM was agitating for dominion status within the British Commonwealth of Nations, so that Nigeria would have the same status as Canada and Australia. In elections that year, the NYM ended the domination of the NNDP in the Legislative Council and moved to establish a genuinely national network of affiliates. This promising start was stopped short three years later by internal divisions in which ethnic loyalties emerged triumphant. The departure of Azikiwe and other Igbo members of the NYM left the organization in Yoruba hands; during World War II, it was reorganized into a predominantly Yoruba political party, the Action Group, by Awolowo. Yoruba-Igbo rivalry had become a major factor in Nigerian politics (see Ethnic Relations).

During World War II, three battalions of the Nigeria Regiment fought in the Ethiopian campaign. Nigerian units also contributed to two divisions serving with British forces in Palestine, Morocco, Sicily, and Burma, where they won many honors. Wartime experiences provided a new frame of reference for many soldiers, who interacted across ethnic boundaries in ways that were unusual in Nigeria. The war also made the British reappraise Nigeria's political future. The war years, moreover, witnessed a polarization between the older, more parochial leaders inclined toward gradualism and the younger intellectuals, who thought in more immediate terms.

The rapid growth of organized labor in the 1940s also brought new political forces into play. During the war, union membership increased sixfold to 30,000. The proliferation of labor organizations, however, fragmented the movement, and potential leaders lacked the experience and skill to draw workers together.

In the postwar period, party lines were sharply drawn on the basis of ethnicity and regionalism. After the demise of the NYM, the nationalist movement splintered into the Hausa- and Fulani- backed Northern People's Congress (NPC), the Yoruba-supported Action Group, and the Igbo-dominated National Council of Nigeria and the Cameroons (NCNC, later the National Council of Nigerian Citizens). These parties negotiated with the British government over constitutional changes, but cooperation among them was the result of expediency rather than an emerging sense of national identity. Because of the essentially regional political alignments of the parties, the British government decided to impose a political solution for Nigeria based on a federally structured constitution.

Nigeria's first political party to have nationwide appeal was the NCNC, founded in 1944 when Azikiwe encouraged activists in the National Youth Movement to call a conference in Lagos of all major Nigerian organizations to "weld the heterogeneous masses of Nigeria into one solid bloc." The aged Macauley was elected president of the new group, and Azikiwe became its secretary general. The party platform renewed the National Youth Movement's appeal for Nigerian self-government within the Commonwealth under a democratic constitution.

At its inception, party membership was based on affiliated organizations that included labor unions, social groups, political clubs, professional associations, and more than 100 ethnic organizations. These bodies afforded unusual opportunities for political education in existing constituencies, but the NYM, which was fading out, was absent from the list of NCNC affiliates. Leadership of the NCNC rested firmly with Azikiwe, in large part because of his commanding personality but also because of the string of newspapers he operated and through which he argued the nationalist cause. In the late 1940s, the NCNC captured a majority of the votes in the predominantly Yoruba Western Region, but increasingly it came to rely on Igbo support, supplemented by alliances with minority parties in the Northern Region. The NCNC backed the creation of new regions, where minorities would be ensured a larger voice, as a step toward the formation of a strong unitary national government.

The Action Group arose in 1951 as a response to Igbo control of the NCNC and as a vehicle for Yoruba regionalism that resisted the concept of unitary government. The party was structured democratically and benefited from political spadework done by the NCNC in the Western Region in the late 1940s. As a movement designed essentially to exploit the federal arrangement to attain regional power, however, the Action Group became the NCNC's competitor for votes in the south at the national level and at the local level in the Western Region.

The Action Group was largely the creation of Awolowo, general secretary of Egbe Omo Oduduwa and leader of the Nigerian Produce Traders' Association. The Action Group was thus the heir of a generation of flourishing cultural consciousness among the Yoruba and also had valuable connections with commercial interests that were representative of the comparative economic advancement of the Western Region. Awolowo had little difficulty in appealing to broad segments of the Yoruba population, but he strove to prevent the Action Group from being stigmatized as a "tribal" group. Despite his somewhat successful efforts to enlist non-Yoruba support, the regionalist sentiment that had stimulated the party initially could hardly be concealed.

Another obstacle to the development of the Action Group was the animosity between segments of the Yoruba community--for example, many people in Ibadan opposed Awolowo on personal grounds because of his identification with the Ijebu Yoruba. Despite these difficulties, the Action Group rapidly built an effective organization. Its program reflected greater planning and was more ideologically oriented than that of the NCNC. Although he did not have Azikiwe's compelling personality, Awolowo was a formidable debater as well as a vigorous and tenacious political campaigner. He used for the first time in Nigeria modern, sometimes flamboyant, electioneering techniques. Among his leading lieutenants were Samuel Akintola of Ibadan and the *oni* of Ife.

The Action Group was a consistent supporter of minority-group demands for autonomous states within a federal structure, and it even supported the severance of a midwest state from the Western Region. This move assumed that comparable alterations would be made elsewhere, an attitude that won the party minority voting support in the other regions. It also backed Yoruba irredentism in the Fulani-ruled emirate of Ilorin in the Northern Region and separatist movements among non-Igbo in the Eastern Region.

The Northern People's Congress (NPC) was organized in the late 1940s by a small group of Western-educated northern Muslims who obtained the assent of the emirs to form a political party capable of counterbalancing the activities of the southern-based parties. It represented a substantial element of reformism in the Muslim north. The most powerful figure in the party was Ahmadu Bello, the *sardauna* (war leader) of Sokoto, a controversial figure who aspired to become the sultan of Sokoto, still the most important political and religious position in the north. Often described by opponents as a "feudal" conservative, Bello had a consuming interest in the protection of northern social and political institutions from southern influence. He also insisted on maintaining the territorial integrity of the Northern Region, including those areas with non-Muslim populations. He was prepared to introduce educational and economic changes to strengthen the north. Although his own ambitions were limited to the Northern Region, Bello backed the NPC's successful efforts to mobilize the north's large voting strength so as to win control of the national government.

The NPC platform emphasized the integrity of the north, its traditions, religion, and social order. Support for broad Nigerian concerns occupied a clear second place. A lack of interest in extending the NPC beyond the Northern Region corresponded to this strictly regional orientation. Its activist membership was drawn from local government and emirate officials who had access to means of communication and to repressive traditional authority that could keep the opposition in line.

The small contingent of northerners who had been educated abroad--a group that included Abubakar Tafawa Balewa and Aminu Kano--was allied with British-backed efforts to introduce gradual change to the emirates. The support given by the emirs to limited modernization was motivated largely by fear of the unsettling presence of southerners in the north and by the equally unsettling example of improving conditions in the south. Those northern leaders who were committed to modernization were firmly connected to the traditional power structure. Most internal problems within the north--peasant disaffection or rivalry among Muslim factions--were concealed, and open opposition to the domination of the Muslim aristocracy was not tolerated. Critics, including representatives of the middle belt who plainly resented Muslim domination, were relegated to small, peripheral parties or to inconsequential separatist movements.

In 1950 Aminu Kano, who had been instrumental in founding the NPC, broke away to form one such party, the Northern Elements Progressive Union (NEPU), in protest against the NPC's limited objectives and what he regarded as a vain hope that traditional rulers would accept modernization. NEPU formed a parliamentary alliance with the NCNC.

The NPC continued to represent the interests of the traditional order in the preindependence deliberations. After the defection of Kano, the only significant disagreement within the NPC related to the awareness of moderates, such as Balewa, that only by overcoming political and economic backwardness could the NPC protect the foundations of traditional northern authority against the influence of the more advanced south.

In all three regions, minority parties represented the special interests of ethnic groups, especially as they were affected by the majority. The size of their legislative delegations, when successful in electing anyone to the regional assemblies, was never large enough to be effective, but they served as a means of public expression for minority concerns. They received attention from major parties before elections, at which time either a dominant party from another region or the opposition party in their region sought their alliance.

The political parties jockeyed for positions of power in anticipation of the independence of Nigeria. Three constitutions were enacted from 1946 to 1954 that were subjects of considerable political controversy in themselves but inevitably moved the country toward greater internal autonomy, with an increasing role for the political parties. The trend was toward the establishment of a parliamentary system of government, with regional assemblies and a federal House of Representatives.

In 1946 a new constitution was approved by the British Parliament and promulgated in Nigeria. Although it reserved effective power in the hands of the governor and his appointed executive council, the so-called Richards Constitution (after Governor Arthur Richards, who was responsible for its formulation) provided for an expanded Legislative Council empowered to deliberate on matters affecting the whole country. Separate legislative bodies, the houses of assembly, were established in each of the three regions to consider local questions and to advise the lieutenant governors. The introduction of the federal principle, with deliberative authority devolved on the regions, signaled recognition of the country's diversity. Although realistic in its assessment of the situation in Nigeria, the Richards Constitution undoubtedly intensified regionalism as an alternative to political unification.

The pace of constitutional change accelerated after the promulgation of the Richards Constitution, which was suspended in 1950. The call for greater autonomy resulted in an interparliamentary conference at Ibadan in 1950, when the terms of a new constitution were drafted. The so-called Macpherson Constitution, after the incumbent governor, went into effect the following year.

The most important innovations in the new charter reinforced the dual course of constitutional evolution, allowing for both regional autonomy and federal union. By extending the elective principle and by providing for a central government with a Council of Ministers, the Macpherson Constitution gave renewed impetus to party activity and to political participation at the national level. But by providing for comparable regional governments exercising broad legislative powers, which could not be overridden by the newly established 185-seat federal House of Representatives, the Macpherson Constitution also gave a significant boost to regionalism. Subsequent revisions contained in a new constitution the Lyttleton Constitution, enacted in 1954, firmly established the federal principle and paved the way for independence.

In 1957 the Western and the Eastern regions became formally self-governing under the parliamentary system. Similar status was acquired by the Northern Region two years later. There were numerous differences of detail among the regional systems, but all adhered to parliamentary forms and were equally autonomous in relation to the federal government at Lagos. The federal government retained specified powers, including responsibility for banking, currency, external affairs, defense, shipping and navigation, and communications, but real political power was centered in the regions. Significantly, the regional governments controlled public expenditures derived from revenues raised within each region.

Ethnic cleavages intensified in the 1950s. Political activists in the southern areas spoke of self-government in terms of educational opportunities and economic development. Because of the spread of mission schools and wealth derived from export crops, the southern parties were committed to policies that would benefit the south of the country. In the north, the emirs intended to maintain firm control on economic and political change. Any activity in the north that might include participation by the federal government (and consequently by southern civil servants) was regarded as a challenge to the primacy of the emirates. Broadening political participation and expanding educational opportunities and other social services also were viewed as threats to the status quo. Already there was an extensive immigrant population of southerners, especially Igbo, in the north; they dominated clerical positions and were active in many trades.

The cleavage between the Yoruba and the Igbo was accentuated by their competition for control of the political machinery. The receding British presence enabled, local officials and politicians to gain access to patronage over government jobs, funds for local development, market permits, trade licenses, government contracts, and even scholarships for higher education. In an economy with many qualified applicants for every post, great resentment was generated by any favoritism authorities showed to members of their own ethnic group.

In the immediate post-World War II period, Nigeria benefited from a favorable trade balance. The principal exports were agricultural commodities--peanuts and cotton from the Northern Region, palm products from the Eastern Region, and cocoa from the Western Region. Marketing boards, again regionally based, were established to handle these exports and to react to price fluctuations on the world market. During the 1950s, the marketing boards accumulated considerable surpluses. Initially, imports lagged behind exports, although by the mid-1950s imports began to catch up with exports, and the surpluses decreased. Expansion in the nonagricultural sectors required large imports of machinery, transport equipment and, eventually, intermediate materials for industry. In time there also were increased administrative costs to be met. Although per capita income in the country as a whole remained low by international standards, rising incomes among salaried personnel and burgeoning urbanization expanded consumer demand for imported goods.

In the meantime, public sector spending increased even more dramatically than export earnings. It was supported not only by the income from huge agricultural surpluses but also by a new range of direct and indirect taxes imposed during the 1950s. The transfer of responsibility for budgetary management from the central to the regional governments in 1954 accelerated the pace of public spending on services and on development projects. Total revenues of central and regional governments nearly doubled in relation to the gross domestic product (GDP--see Glossary) during the decade.

The most dramatic event, having a long-term effect on Nigeria's economic development, was the discovery and exploitation of petroleum deposits. The search for oil, begun in 1908 and abandoned a few years later, was revived in 1937 by Shell and British Petroleum. Exploration was intensified in 1946, but the first commercial discovery did not occur until 1956, at Olobiri in the Niger Delta. In 1958 exportation of Nigerian oil was initiated at facilities constructed at Port Harcourt. Oil income was still marginal, but the prospects for continued economic expansion appeared bright and further accentuated political rivalries on the eve of independence.

The election of the House of Representatives after the adoption of the 1954 constitution gave the NPC a total of seventy-nine seats, all from the Northern Region. Among the other major parties, the NCNC took fifty-six seats, winning a majority in both the Eastern and the Western regions, while the Action Group captured only twenty-seven seats. The NPC was called on to form a government, but the NCNC received six of the ten ministerial posts. Three of these posts were assigned to representatives from each region, and one was reserved for a delegate from the Northern Cameroons.

As a further step toward independence, the governor's Executive Council was merged with the Council of Ministers in 1957 to form the all-Nigerian Federal Executive Council. NPC federal parliamentary leader Balewa was appointed prime minister. Balewa formed a coalition government that included the Action Group as well as the NCNC to prepare the country for the final British withdrawal. His government guided the country for the next three years, operating with almost complete autonomy in internal affairs.

The preparation of a new federal constitution for an independent Nigeria was carried out at conferences held at Lancaster House in London in 1957 and 1958 and presided over by the British colonial secretary. Nigerian delegates were selected to represent each region and to reflect various shades of opinion. The delegation was led by Balewa of the NPC and included party leaders Awolowo of the Action Group, Azikiwe of the NCNC, and Bello of the NPC; they were also the premiers of the Western, Eastern, and Northern regions, respectively. Independence was achieved on October 1, 1960.

Elections were held for a new and greatly enlarged House of Representatives in December 1959; 174 of the 312 seats were allocated to the Northern Region on the basis of its larger population. The NPC, entering candidates only in the Northern Region, confined campaigning largely to local issues but opposed the addition of new regimes. The NCNC backed creation of a midwest state and proposed federal control of education and health services. The Action Group, which staged a lively campaign, favored stronger government and the establishment of three new states, while advocating creation of a West Africa Federation that would unite Nigeria with Ghana and Sierra Leone. The NPC captured 142 seats in the new legislature. Balewa was called on to head a NPC-NCNC coalition government, and Awolowo became official leader of the opposition.

INDEPENDENT NIGERIA

By an act of the British Parliament, Nigeria became an independent country within the Commonwealth on October 1, 1960. Azikiwe was installed as governor general of the federation and Balewa continued to serve as head of a democratically elected parliamentary, but now completely sovereign, government. The governor general represented the British monarch as head of state and was appointed by the crown on the advice of the Nigerian prime minister in consultation with the regional premiers. The governor general, in turn, was responsible for appointing the prime minister and for choosing a candidate from among contending leaders when there was no parliamentary majority. Otherwise, the governor general's office was essentially ceremonial.

The government was responsible to a parliament composed of the popularly elected 312-member House of Representatives and the 44-member Senate, chosen by the regional legislatures.

In general, the regional constitutions followed the federal model, both structurally and functionally. The most striking departure was in the Northern Region, where special provisions brought the regional constitution into consonance with Islamic law and custom. The similarity between the federal and regional constitutions was deceptive, however, and the conduct of public affairs reflected wide differences among the regions.

Abubakar Tafawa Balewa, first prime minister (1960-66), speaking at Organization of African Unity meeting in Addis Ababa -- Courtesy Embassy of Nigeria, Washington

In February 1961, a plebiscite was conducted to determine the disposition of the Southern Cameroons and Northern Cameroons, which were administered by Britain as United Nations Trust Territories. By an overwhelming majority, voters in the Southern Cameroons opted to join formerly French-administered Cameroon over integration with Nigeria as a separate federated region. In the Northern Cameroons, however, the largely Muslim electorate chose to merge with Nigeria's Northern Region.

Third session of the Enugu Provincial Assembly in the early 1960s
Courtesy Embassy of Nigeria, Washington

Politics in the Crisis Years

During the first three years after independence, the federal government was an NPC-NCNC coalition, despite the conflicting natures of the two partners. The former was regionalist, Muslim, and aristocratic; the latter was nationalist, Christian, and populist. Moreover, the NCNC supported opponents of the NPC in regional elections in the Northern Region. Although a more natural ideological alignment of the Action Group and the NCNC was called for by some Action Group leaders, it held no attraction for the NCNC as long as the NPC was assured of a parliamentary majority.

Domination of the Northern Region by the NPC and NCNC control of the Eastern Region were assured. Action Group control of the Western Region, however, was weakened and then collapsed because of divisions within the party that reflected cleavages within Yoruba society. This loss of stability in one region gradually undermined the political structure of the whole country.

The leadership of the Action Group, which formed the official opposition in the federal parliament, split in 1962 as a result of a rift between Awolowo and Akintola, prime minister of the Western Region. Awolowo favored the adoption of democratic socialism as party policy, following the lead of Kwame Nkrumah's regime in Ghana. The radical ideology that Awolowo expressed was at variance with his earlier positions, however, and was seen as a bid to make the Action Group an interregional party that drew support across the country from educated younger voters, whose expectations were frustrated by unemployment and the rising cost of living. Akintola, in reaction, attempted to retain the support of conservative party elements who were disturbed by Awolowo's rhetoric. He called for better relations with the NPC and an allparty federal coalition that would remove the Action Group from opposition and give its leaders greater access to power.

Awolowo's radical majority staged the expulsion of Akintola from the party. The governor of the Western Region demanded Akintola's resignation as prime minister (although he had not lost a vote of confidence in the regional legislature) and named a successor recommended by the Action Group to head the government. Akintola immediately organized a new party, the United People's Party, which pursued a policy of collaboration with the NPC-NCNC government in the federal parliament.

Akintola's resignation in May 1962 sparked bloody rioting in the Western Region and brought effective government to an end as rival legislators, following the example in the streets, introduced violence to the floor of the regional legislature. The federal government declared a state of emergency, dissolved the legislature, and named a federal administrator for the Western Region. One of his first acts was to place many Action Group leaders under house arrest.

Investigations by the federal administrator led to accusations of criminal misuse of public funds against Awolowo and other Action Group leaders. A special commission found that Awolowo had funneled several million pounds from public development corporations to the Action Group through a private investment corporation when he was prime minister of the Western Region in the 1950s. The regional government seized the corporation's assets and pressed legal claims against the Action Group.

In the course of the financial investigation, police uncovered evidence linking Awolowo with a conspiracy to overthrow the government. With a number of other Action Group leaders, he was arrested and put on trial for treason. Authorities charged that 200 activists had received military training in Ghana and had smuggled arms into Nigeria in preparation for a coup d'état. Awolowo was found guilty, along with seventeen others, and was sentenced to ten years in prison. Anthony Enahoro, Awolowo's chief lieutenant who had been abroad at the time of the coup, was extradited from Britain and also was convicted of treason and imprisoned.

In the meantime, the state of emergency was lifted and Balewa, determining that Akintola had been improperly dismissed, obtained his reinstatement as prime minister of the Western Region at the head of a coalition between the NCNC and the United People's Party. The Action Group successfully contested the legality of this action in the courts, but a retroactive amendment to the Western Region's constitution that validated Akintola's reappointment was quickly enacted. As Balewa told parliament, the legalities of the case "had been overtaken by events."

Later in 1963, Nigeria became a republic within the Commonwealth. The change in status called for no practical alteration of the constitutional system. The president, elected to a five-year term by a joint session of the parliament, replaced the crown as the symbol of national sovereignty and the British monarchy as head of state. Azikiwe, who had been governor general, became the republic's first president.

Popular Disillusionment and Political Realignment

The conspiracy trials that led to the conviction of two of the country's most dynamic politicians, Awolowo and Enahoro, severely weakened public confidence in the political and judicial systems. Abuses were widespread, including intimidation of opponents by threats of criminal investigation, manipulation of the constitution and the courts, diversion of public funds to party and private use, rigging of elections, and corruption of public officials whose political patrons expected them to put party interests ahead of their legal responsibilities. Popular disillusion also intensified because politicians failed to produce benefits commensurate with constituents' expectations.

The volatile political scene leading up to elections in 1964 was ominous. The Action Group virtually disappeared from the federal parliament as a result of the Awolowo affair, thereby fundamentally altering political alignments at the national level. By early 1964, therefore, the federal parliament no longer had a recognized opposition. Akintola's party, which was renamed the Nigerian National Democratic Party in an effort to attract more support, now dominated the Western Region. The federal government nominally consisted of a consensus of the ruling parties of all four regions, but it was a fragile alliance at best and had emerged as a result of heavy-handed tactics. The NCNC had strengthened its position by gaining firm control of the Midwestern Region, so that it dominated two of the four regions. Akintola managed to undermine the NCNC in the Western Region, even though nationally he was pledged to an alliance with the NCNC. For its part, the NCNC denounced Akintola's party as a "tool of the NPC" and allied itself with remnants of the Action Group.

Political realignment was deceptive, however, because the basic divisions within the country remained unaltered. The NPC was reasonably secure in the Northern Region, despite the presence of minor parties, but it could not govern Nigeria alone, and alliances with any of the southern parties were ideologically incompatible and very tenuous. The NPC continued its dominance because of the inability of the other parties to find common ground among themselves and with northern progressives. Awolowo's pointed remarks in 1963 that democracy could be secured only if the Action Group and the NCNC could reach an accommodation that would remove the deadweight of the NPC from power fueled NPC concerns. The detention of Awolowo prevented that alliance from maturing, but it did not result in greater political stability. Indeed the alliance between the NPC and NCNC, which had dominated federal politics and destroyed the Action Group, now fell apart.

Civil War

Throughout the remainder of 1966 and into 1967, the FMG sought to convene a constituent assembly for revision of the constitution that might enable an early return to civilian rule. Nonetheless, the tempo of violence increased. In September attacks on Igbo in the north were renewed with unprecedented ferocity, stirred up by Muslim traditionalists with the connivance, Eastern Region leaders believed, of northern political leaders. The army was sharply divided along regional lines. Reports circulated that troops from the Northern Region had participated in the mayhem. The estimated number of deaths ranged as high as 30,000, although the figure was probably closer to 8,000 to 10,000. More than 1 million Igbo returned to the Eastern Region. In retaliation, some northerners were massacred in Port Harcourt and other eastern cities, and a counterexodus of non-Igbo was under way.

The Eastern Region's military governor, Lieutenant Colonel Chukwuemeka Odumegwu Ojukwu, was under pressure from Igbo officers to assert greater independence from the FMG. Indeed, the eastern military government refused to recognize Gowon's legitimacy on the ground that he was not the most senior officer in the chain of command. Some of Ojukwu's colleagues questioned whether the country could be reunited amicably after the outrages committed against the Igbo in the Northern Region. Ironically, many responsible easterners who had advocated a unitary state now called for looser ties with the other regions.

The military commanders and governors, including Ojukwu, met in Lagos to consider solutions to the regional strife. But they failed to reach a settlement, despite concessions offered by the northerners, because it proved impossible to guarantee the security of Igbo outside the Eastern Region. The military conferees reached a consensus only in the contempt they expressed for civilian politicians. Fearing for his safety, Ojukwu refused invitations to attend subsequent meetings in Lagos.

In January 1967, the military leaders and senior police officials met at Aburi, Ghana, at the invitation of the Ghanaian military government. By now the Eastern Region was threatening secession. In a last-minute effort to hold Nigeria together, the military reached an accord that provided for a loose confederation of regions. The federal civil service vigorously opposed the Aburi Agreement, however. Awolowo, regrouping his supporters, demanded the removal of all northern troops garrisoned in the Western Region and warned that if the Eastern Region left the federation, the Western Region would follow. The FMG agreed to the troop withdrawal.

In May Gowon issued a decree implementing the Aburi Agreement. Even the Northern Region leaders, who had been the first to threaten secession, now favored the formation of a multistate federation. Meanwhile, the military governor of the Midwestern Region announced that his region must be considered neutral in the event of civil war.

The Ojukwu government rejected the plan for reconciliation and made known its intention to retain all revenues collected in the Eastern Region in reparation for the cost of resettling Igbo refugees. The eastern leaders had reached the point of ruptive in their relations with Lagos and the rest of Nigeria. Despite offers made by the FMG that met many of Ojukwu's demands, the Eastern Region Consultative Assembly voted May 26 to secede from Nigeria. In Lagos Gowon proclaimed a state of emergency and unveiled plans for abolition of the regions and for redivision of the country into twelve states. This provision broke up the Northern Region, undermining the possibility of continued northern domination and offering a major concession to the Eastern Region. It was also a strategic move, which won over eastern minorities and deprived the rebellious Igbo heartland of its control over the oil fields and access to the sea. Gowon also appointed prominent civilians, including Awolowo, as commissioners in the federal and new state governments, thus broadening his political support.

On May 30, Ojukwu answered the federal decree with the proclamation of the independent Republic of Biafra, named after the Bight of Biafra. He cited as the principal cause for this action the Nigerian government's inability to protect the lives of easterners and suggested its culpability in genocide, depicting secession as a measure taken reluctantly after all efforts to safeguard the Igbo people in other regions had failed.

Initially the FMG launched "police measures" to restore the authority of Lagos in the Eastern Region. Army units attempted to advance into secessionist territory in July, but rebel troops easily stopped them. The Biafrans retaliated with a surprise thrust into the Midwestern Region, where they seized strategic points. However, effective control of the delta region remained under federal control despite several rebel attempts to take the non-Igbo area. The federal government began to mobilize large numbers of recruits to supplement its 10,000-member army.

By the end of 1967, federal forces had regained the Midwestern Region and secured the delta region, which was reorganized as the Rivers State and Southeastern State, cutting off Biafra from direct access to the sea. But a proposed invasion of the rebel-held territory, now confined to the Igbo heartland, stalled along the stiffened Biafran defense perimeter.

A stalemate developed as federal attacks on key towns broke down in the face of stubborn Biafran resistance. Ill-armed and trained under fire, rebel troops nonetheless had the benefit of superior leadership and superb morale. Although vastly outnumbered and outgunned, the Biafrans probed weak points in the federal lines, making lightning tactical gains, cutting off and encircling advancing columns, and launching commando raids behind federal lines. Biafran strikes across the Niger managed to pin down large concentrations of federal troops on the west bank.

In September 1968, Owerri was captured by federal troops advancing from the south, and early in 1969 the federal army, expanded to nearly 250,000 men, opened three fronts in what Gowon touted as the "final offensive." Although federal forces flanked the rebels by crossing the Niger at Onitsha, they failed to break through. The Biafrans subsequently retook Owerri in fierce fighting and threatened to push on to Port Harcourt until thwarted by a renewed federal offensive in the south. That offensive tightened the noose around the rebel enclave without choking it into submission.

Biafran propaganda, which stressed the threat of genocide to the Igbo people, was extremely effective abroad in winning sympathy for the secessionist movement. Food and medical supplies were scarce in Biafra. Humanitarian aid, as well as arms and munitions, reached the embattled region from international relief organizations and from private and religious groups in the United States and Western Europe by way of nighttime airlifts over the war zone. The bulk of Biafra's military supplies was purchased on the international arms market with unofficial assistance provided by France through former West African colonies. In one of the most dramatic episodes of the civil war, Carl Gustav von Rosen, a Swedish count who at one time commanded the Ethiopian air force, and several other Swedish pilots flew five jet trainers modified for combat in successful strikes against Nigerian military installations.

Biafra's independence was recognized by Tanzania, Zambia, Gabon, and the Ivory Coast, but it was compromised in the eyes of most African states by the approval of South Africa, Southern Rhodesia, and Portugal. Britain extended diplomatic support and limited military assistance to the federal government. The Soviet Union became an important source of military equipment for Nigeria. Modern Soviet-built warplanes, flown by Egyptian and British pilots, interdicted supply flights and inflicted heavy casualties during raids on Biafran urban centers. In line with its policy of noninvolvement, the United States prohibited the sale of military goods to either side while continuing to recognize the FMG.

In October 1969, Ojukwu appealed for United Nations (UN) mediation for a cease-fire as a prelude to peace negotiations. But the federal government insisted on Biafra's surrender, and

Gowon observed that "rebel leaders had made it clear that this is a fight to the finish and that no concession will ever satisfy them." In December federal forces opened a four-pronged offensive, involving 120,000 troops, that sliced Biafra in half. When Owerri fell on January 6, 1970, Biafran resistance collapsed. Ojukwu fled to the Ivory Coast, leaving his chief of staff, Philip Effiong, behind as "officer administering the government." Effiong called for an immediate, unconditional cease-fire January 12 and submitted to the authority of the federal government at ceremonies in Lagos.

Estimates in the former Eastern Region of the number of dead from hostilities, disease, and starvation during the thirty-month civil war are estimated at between 1 million and 3 million. The end of the fighting found more than 3 million Igbo refugees crowded into a 2,500-square-kilometer enclave. Prospects for the survival of many of them and for the future of the region were dim. There were severe shortages of food, medicine, clothing, and housing. The economy of the region was shattered. Cities were in ruins; schools, hospitals, utilities, and transportation facilities were destroyed or inoperative. Overseas groups instituted a major relief effort, but the FMG insisted on directing all assistance and recovery operations and barred some agencies that had supplied aid to Biafra.

Because charges of genocide had fueled international sympathy for Biafra, the FMG allowed a team of international experts to observe the surrender and to look for evidence. Subsequently, the observers testified that they found no evidence of genocide or systematic destruction of property, although there was considerable evidence of famine and death as a result of the war. Furthermore, under Gowon's close supervision, the federal government ensured that Igbo civilians would not be treated as defeated enemies. A program was launched to reintegrate the Biafran rebels into a unified Nigeria. A number of public officials who had "actively counselled, aided, or abetted" secession were dismissed, but a clear distinction was made between them and those who had simply carried out their duties. Igbo personnel soon were being reenlisted in the federal armed forces. There were no trials and few people were imprisoned. Ojukwu, in exile, was made the scapegoat, but efforts to have him extradited failed.

An Igbo official, Ukapi "Tony" Asika, was named administrator of the new East Central State, comprising the Igbo heartland. Asika had remained loyal to the federal government during the civil war, but as a further act of conciliation, his all-Igbo cabinet included members who had served under the secessionist regime. Asika was unpopular with many Igbo, who considered him a traitor, and his administration was characterized as inept and corrupt. In three years under his direction, however, the state government achieved the rehabilitation of 70 percent of the industry incapacitated during the war. The federal government granted funds to cover the state's operating expenses for an interim period, and much of the war damage was repaired. Social services and public utilities slowly were reinstituted, although not to the prewar levels.

THE FEDERAL MILITARY GOVERNMENT IN THE POSTWAR ERA

In the postwar period, all significant political power remained concentrated in the FMG. None of the three major ethnic groups had a powerful voice in its executive element, which was disproportionately composed of representatives of middle belt minorities and to a lesser extent of Muslim Yoruba and of Ijaw and Ibibio from the Eastern Region. The Northern Region had been divided into six states in 1967, which left the area without its former power base in the federation. The decision was accepted by northerners in part because of the military government's relative strength in comparison with earlier civilian governments. Acceptance also was motivated by the fact that northerners were less fearful of the Igbo or a southern coalition. Only the Yoruba power base in the west retained its prewar characteristics. The 1967 administrative structure also made national unity attractive to the westerners because, with the creation of a Yoruba state (Kwara) in the north, their position seemed stronger relative to the northerners. Remaining points of conflict included the number of civil service posts to be allotted to each ethnic group and the assignment of civil servants from former regional services to states other than their own.

Railroad construction project in 1963 to open market for a
gricultural produce in northeastern Nigeria -- Courtesy World Bank

Economic Development

After the civil war, the FMG moved to resurrect the six-year development plan inaugurated in 1962. The First National Development Plan charted Nigeria's transition from an essentially agricultural economy to a mixed economy based on agricultural expansion and limited industrial growth. Government was heavily involved in the economy because locally generated private investment was unable to generate sufficient capital for development. New development plans were instituted in 1970 and 1975, but the goals set in all three plans proved unrealistic.

By the late 1960s, oil had replaced cocoa, peanuts, and palm products as the country's biggest foreign exchange earner. In 1971 Nigeria--by then the world's seventh-largest petroleum producer--became a member of the Organization of the Petroleum Exporting Countries (OPEC). The dramatic rise in world oil prices in 1974 caused a sudden flood of wealth that can be described as "dynamic chaos." Much of the revenue was intended for investment to diversify the economy, but it also spurred inflation and, coming in the midst of widespread unemployment, underscored inequities in distribution. In 1975 production fell sharply as a result of the sudden decrease in world demand, and prices moved downward until late in the year when OPEC intervened to raise prices. Nigeria fully supported OPEC policies.

In 1972 the government issued an indigenization decree, the first of a number of Nigerian Enterprises Promotion decrees, that barred aliens from investing in specified enterprises and reserved participation in certain trades to Nigerians. At the time, about 70 percent of commercial firms operating in Nigeria were foreign-owned. In 1975 the federal government bought 60 percent of the equity in the marketing operations of the major oil companies in Nigeria, but full nationalization was rejected as a means of furthering its program of indigenization.

Unemployment constituted an increasingly serious problem. Large numbers of farm workers, who had gone to urban areas in search of higher wages, remained in the cities even if they failed to find jobs, while school graduates and dropouts flooded the labor market at a rate of 600,000 a year in the mid-1970s. Unemployment reached its highest levels in the crowded Igbo areas in the east, where the economy still was recovering from the effects of the war. Skilled workers were reluctant to leave the east in search of work, although eventually the shortage of skilled workers in other parts of the country began to have its effect in overcoming Igbo fears. The dangers involved in discharging large numbers of soldiers who had no job prospects made demobilization of the costly military establishment undesirable. Substantial increases in public-sector employment promised to absorb some of the soldiers, but they lacked training. These economic problems assumed an imposing political dimension. To some extent, they reflected a pattern in the world economic situation, but the popular imagination blamed corruption and mismanagement and held the Gowon regime responsible.

The regime also had to deal with a severe drought that struck the northern states between 1972 and 1974. The drought was the most serious since that of 1913-14. The drought and resulting famine affected the Sahel countries to the west, north, and east far more than Nigeria, but considerable numbers of refugees poured into Nigeria from Niger. Famine conditions also prevailed in some parts of the north of Nigeria. In the long run, however, Nigerian agriculture benefited from the rise in prices that resulted from crop failures in other parts of the Sahel. In the short run, the drought influenced policy decisions about the necessity of promoting irrigation schemes and reforestation.

Crime, Corruption, and Political Turbulence

In 1972 Gowon partially lifted the ban on political activity that had been in force since 1966 in order to permit a discussion of a new constitution that would prepare the way for civilian rule. The debate that followed was ideologically charged. Awolowo's call for a transition to "democratic socialism" made the military particularly nervous. The press, trade unions, and universities demanded a quick return to the democratic process. The call for new states was loud, but there was no agreement over how many there should be. Gowon abruptly ended public discussion, explaining that "peace is more important than politics."

The decennial census was scheduled for 1973. Under the banner "Prepare to be Counted," the military government conducted a public campaign that emphasized the technical rather than political dimensions of the exercise. The procedure was to be supervised by a committee whose members were selected carefully for geographical and ethnic balance, and computers were to be used for processing the returns. Despite measures taken to ensure a more accurate count than had been possible before, the results once again confounded demographers: the census found that Nigeria's population had increased by nearly 44 percent in 10 years, a rate of growth unprecedented in any developing country. According to the returns submitted, the north contained 64 percent of the total population, compared with 53.7 percent in 1963, a figure even then believed to be exaggerated. The 1973 census, on which representation in a new, elected parliament would be based, revived fears that one ethnic group would permanently dominate the others. It also meant that a considerable share of oil revenues would flow to the northern states under the existing system of allocation. The government failed in its efforts to sell the census as a technical exercise because the political implications were widely understood and hotly debated, despite the ban on political discussion.

The Gowon regime came under fire because of widespread and obvious corruption at every level of national life. Graft, bribery, and nepotism were an integral part of a complex system of patronage and "gift" giving through which influence and authority were asserted. Although the military had pledged to rid the government of corruption, the public became increasingly aware of abuses, primarily because of daily exposés in the press. In 1973 the federal government established a special anticorruption police force--the "X-Squad"--whose subsequent investigations revealed ingenious forms of extortion and fraud-- not only in government and public corporations but in private business and in the professions as well.

A major scandal that had international implications and reached the highest levels of government and the business community took place in the mid-1970s; it involved the purchase abroad of construction materials by state agents at prices well above market values. Rake-offs were pocketed by public officials and private contractors. Other scandals in hospitals and orphanages shocked the populace, while corruption in importing medical drugs whose effective dates long since had expired revealed that even the health of Nigerians was at risk.

Inefficiencies compounded the impact of corruption. In mid1975 , 400 cargo ships--250 of them carrying 1.5 million tons of cement--clogged the harbor of Lagos, which had been paralyzed for fifteen months with vessels waiting to be unloaded. To compound the error, spoiled and inferior-grade cement was concealed by mixing it with acceptable material for use in public building projects. Later, buildings collapsed or had to be dismantled because of the inferior product. New roads washed away because of bad construction and inadequate controls. In these scandals, as in others, the culprits were a combination of Nigerian businessmen, government officials, and foreign companies. Few people and few projects seemed exempt from the scourge.

Crime posed a threat to internal security and had a seriously negative impact on efforts to bring about economic development. Armed gangs, often composed of former soldiers, roamed the countryside engaging in robbery, extortion, and kidnapping. The gangs sometimes operated with the connivance of the police or included moonlighting soldiers. Pirates raided cargo ships awaiting entry to ports or unloaded them at the piers ahead of the stevedores. Drug trafficking and smuggling were prevalent. Punishment was meted out to large batches of convicted and suspected criminals, who were dispatched by firing squads in public executions meant to impress spectators with the seriousness of the offenses and with the government's concern to curb crime. These measures had no noticeable effect on the crime rate, however, but seemed rather to provoke a callous public attitude toward violence.

In January 1975, Gowon revamped the membership of the Federal Executive Council, increasing the number of military ministers. He depended more and more on a small group of advisers and became increasingly inaccessible to his military colleagues. Without broad consultation, he backed off from the 1976 date set for a return to civilian rule, explaining that to adhere rigidly to it would "amount to a betrayal of a trust" and "certainly throw the nation back into confusion." Public employees staged protest strikes in May and June that brought essential services to a standstill. The government responded by granting retroactive wage increases that averaged 30 percent, which fed inflation and led to industrial strikes as union members demanded parallel raises.

The political atmosphere deteriorated to the point that Gowon was deposed in a bloodless coup d'état July 29, 1975--the ninth anniversary of the revolt that had brought him to power. At the time, Gowon was at an OAU summit meeting in Kampala, Uganda. The perpetrators of the coup included many of the officers who had participated in the July 1966 coup. Even the officers responsible for Gowon's security were involved. Gowon pledged his full loyalty to the new regime and left for exile in Britain, where he received a pension from the Nigerian government.

THE SECOND REPUBLIC, 1979-83

The first elections under the 1979 constitution were held on schedule in July and August 1979, and the FMG handed over power to a new civilian government under President Shehu Shagari on October 1, 1979. Nigeria's Second Republic was born amid great expectations. Oil prices were high and revenues were on the increase. It appeared that unlimited development was possible. Unfortunately, the euphoria was short-lived, and the Second Republic did not survive its infancy.

Five major parties competed for power in the first elections in 1979. As might be expected, there was some continuity between the old parties of the First Republic and the new parties of the Second Republic. The National Party of Nigeria (NPN), for example, inherited the mantle of the Northern People's Congress, although the NPN differed from the NPC in that it obtained significant support in the non-Igbo states of southeastern Nigeria. The United Party of Nigeria (UPN) was the successor to the Action Group, with Awolowo as its head. Its support was almost entirely in the Yoruba states. The Nigerian People's Party (NPP), the successor to the NCNC, was predominantly Igbo and had Azikiwe as its leader. An attempt to forge an alliance with nonHausa -Fulani northern elements collapsed in the end, and a breakaway party with strong support in parts of the north emerged from the failed alliance. This northern party was known as the Great Nigerian People's Party under the leadership of Waziri Ibrahim of Borno. Finally, the People's Redemption Party was the successor to the Northern Elements Progressive Union and had Aminu Kano as its head.

Just as the NPC dominated the First Republic, its successor, the NPN, dominated the Second Republic. Shagari won the presidency, defeating Azikiwe in a close and controversial vote. The NPN also took 36 of 95 Senate seats, 165 of 443 House of Representatives seats and won control of seven states (Sokoto, Niger, Bauchi, Benue, Cross River, Kwara, and Rivers). The NPN lost the governorship of Kaduna State but secured control of the Kaduna legislature. The NPN failed to take Kano and lacked a majority in either the Senate or House of Representatives. It was forced to form a shaky coalition with the NPP, the successor of the NCNC, the old coalition partner of the NPC. The NPP took three states (Anambra, Imo, and Plateau), sixteen Senate seats and seventy-eight House of Representatives seats, so that in combination with the NPN the coalition had a majority in both the House of Representatives and the Senate. Nonetheless, the interests of the two parties were often in conflict, which forced the NPN to operate alone in most situations. Even though the presidential form of constitution was intended to create a stronger central government, the weakness of the coalition undermined effective central authority.

The UPN came in with the second largest number of seats and effectively formed the official opposition, just as the Action Group had done in the First Republic. The UPN took five states (Lagos, Oyo, Ogun, Ondo, and Bendel), 28 Senate seats, and 111 House seats. Awolowo continued as spokesman for the left of center. The Great Nigerian People's Party managed to win two states (Borno and Gongola), eight Senate seats, and forty-three House of Representatives seats. The People's Redemption Party, which was the most radical of the parties, won Kano and the governorship of Kaduna, seven Senate seats, and forty-nine House of Representatives seats.

A number of weaknesses beset the Second Republic. First, the coalition that dominated federal politics was not strong, and in effect the NPN governed as a minority because no coalition formed to challenge its supremacy. Second, there was lack of cooperation between the NPN-dominated federal government and the twelve states controlled by opposition parties. Third, and perhaps most important, the oil boom ended in mid-1981, precisely when expectations of continuous growth and prosperity were at a height.

There were many signs of tension in the country. The Bakalori Project, an irrigation scheme in Sokoto, for example, became the focus of serious unrest in the late 1970s when thousands of farmers protested the loss of their land, and police retaliated by burning villages and killing or wounding hundreds of people. Widespread dissatisfaction became apparent with the Maitatsine, or Yan Tatsine (followers of the Maitatsine), a quasi-Muslim fringe group that who sparked religious riots in Kano in 1980, and Kaduna, and Maiduguri in 1982 after police tried to control this activities (see Islam). The disturbance in Kano alone resulted in the deaths of 4,177 people between December 18 and 29, 1980. In 1981 teachers staged a strike because they had not been paid. As the political situation deteriorated, the federal government looked for scapegoats and found them in the large number of foreign workers who had come to Nigeria in response to the jobs created by the oil boom. In the crackdown on illegal immigration, an estimated 2 million foreigners were expelled in January and February 1983, of whom 1 million were from Ghana and 150,000 to 200,000 from Niger.

The recession that set in with the fall in oil prices after the middle of 1981 put severe strains on the Second Republic. For political reasons, government spending continued to accelerate, and the frictions among the political parties and between the federal government and the states only reinforced financial irresponsibility. Nigeria's foreign debt increased from N3.3 billion (for value of the naira--see Glossary) in 1978 to N14.7 billion in 1982. By 1983 the nineteen state governments had run up a combined debt of N13.3 billion. Heavy investment in economic development continued unabated. In addition to finishing a steel mill at Ajaokuta in Kwara State, for example, a second plant opened at Aladje, near Warri, in 1982. Steel-rolling mills also were built at Jos, Oshogbo, and Katsina--sites chosen for political reasons. By 1987 N5 billion had been spent on the steel industry alone, most of this committed under the Second Republic, even although the economics of steel development were questionable.

Corruption once again was rampant under the Second Republic. It had been a serious problem since the civil war, when wartime contracts often were awarded under dubious circumstances. Corruption became more serious after the war, most notably in connection with the cement scandal of the early 1970s, the Festival of African Culture (FESTAC) in Lagos, and the development of Abuja as the new federal capital. Corruption under the Second Republic was even greater. Major scandals involved the Federal Housing Scheme, the National Youth Service Corps, the Nigerian External Telecommunications, the Federal Mortgage Bank, the Federal Capital Territory Administration, the Central Bank of Nigeria, and the Nigerian National Supply Company. In addition, the halfhearted attempts to license imports and to control inflation encouraged smuggling, which became a major crime that went virtually unchecked. Umaru Dikko came to the attention of the international community because of an abortive plot to kidnap him in London and return him to Nigeria to stand trial for corruption. British authorities found him in a shipping crate on a runway moments before he was to be sent to Nigeria. Dikko was involved in many scandals, including the issuance of licenses to import rice--rice imports had risen from 50,000 tons in 1976 to 651,000 tons in 1982.

As elections approached in August 1983, economic decline that reflected low oil prices, widespread corruption, and continued government spending at record levels was proof to many that the Second Republic was in sad shape. The lack of confidence was evident in the massive flight of capital--estimated at US$14 billion between 1979 and 1983. The second elections under the Second Republic were to be its last. When the results were tallied in 1983, it was clear that there had been fraud (see The Second Republic). The NPN increased its control of states from seven to twelve, including Kano and Kaduna. Shagari was reelected president, and the NPN gained 61 of 95 Senate seats and 307 of 450 House of Representatives seats. Not even the supporters of the NPN expected such results. Considering the state of the economy and the public outcry over the rigged election, the Shagari government stayed in power for a surgprisingly long time.

RETURN TO MILITARY RULE

On December 31, 1983, the military seized power once again, primarily because there was virtually no confidence in the civilian regime. The fraudulent election was used as an excuse for the takeover, although the military was in fact closely associated with the ousted government. More serious still, the economy was in chaos. The true cost of the failure to use earlier revenues and foreign reserves to good effect now became apparent.

The leader of the coup d'état was Major General Muhammadu Buhari of Katsina, whose background and political loyalties tied him closely to the Muslim north and the deposed government. Buhari had been director of supply and services in the early 1970s, military governor of Northeast State at the time it was divided into three states, and federal commissioner for petroleum and mines (1976-78) during the height of the oil boom. At the time of the coup, he was commander of the Third Armored Division in Jos.

Buhari tried to restore public accountability and to reestablish a dynamic economy without altering the basic power structure of the country. The military had become impatient with the civilian government. Corruption in particular was out of control, and the fraudulent election had been too obvious. Because the civilians in the NPN could not control the situation, the military would try its hand. Nonetheless, Buhari's political and economic aims were almost identical to those of the NPN.

The military regime conducted tribunals to curb corruption, and many scandals were revealed. Once again the civil service was cleansed, although on a smaller scale than the purge of 1975. This time, however, the military tried to achieve two aims. First, it attempted to secure public support by reducing the level of corruption; second, it demonstrated its commitment to austerity by trimming the federal budget. As a further attempt to mobilize the country, Buhari launched a War Against Indiscipline in spring 1984. This national campaign, which lasted fifteen months, preached the work ethic, emphasized patriotism, decried corruption, and promoted environmental sanitation.

The campaign was a military program for reform and mobilization that achieved few of its aims. In practice, unemployment was on the rise as the recession worsened, so that speeches about working hard seemed out of place. The appeal to Nigerian nationalism had the negative effect of restricting the flexibility of the government in international negotiations over the debt. The campaign was enforced haphazardly; some people were executed or given long jail terms while others were allowed off if they were well-connected. Environmental sanitation meant that the state capitals had to be cleaned up, and the principal target was the petty bourgeoisie that eked a living out of selling services or retailing commodities on a small scale. Their "illegal structures"--market stalls and workshops along the streets--were destroyed, and widespread resentment resulted among the small traders, repairmen, and others in the self-employed service sector.

The regime attempted to stifle criticism. Journalists were harassed, and many critics were arrested. Symbolically, the arrest of the popular musician, Fela Ransome-Kuti, personified the crackdown. Ransome-Kuti's lyrics sharply mocked the government's inability to deal with national problems. The National Security Organisation (NSO) became the principal instrument of repression. The NSO, created in 1976, had played only a marginal role in Nigerian politics until the Buhari regime. Buhari appointed Rafindadi, a civilian, as head of the NSO, and under Rafindadi, Nigeria experienced the harassment and insecurity of a secret police force for the first time. Fortunately, the NSO proved to be inefficient, and subsequent reaction to its operations led to its reorganization.

Buhari's biggest problem was Nigeria's foreign debt. Negotiations with the International Monetary Fund (IMF--see Glossary) dragged on, and in the end efforts to reschedule the debt failed. Although Buhari was committed to austerity, the IMF insisted on even more drastic measures to cut spending, devalue the currency, and otherwise restructure the economy than most Nigerians were willing to accept. Buhari had to accede to the strong and vocal opposition to the IMF terms. Nigerian nationalism won out over economic necessity, at least in the short run. Furthermore, by the end of 1985 there was considerable frustration within the army. The army had been reduced in size steadily since the end of the civil war, from a total of about 275,000 in 1969 to about 80,000 by the end of the 1980s. The economic crisis, the campaign against corruption, and civilian criticism of the military undermined Buhari's position, and in August 1985 a group of officers under Major General Ibrahim Babangida removed Buhari from power.

The officers who staged the coup were mostly from the north, but unlike Buhari (of Hausa origin), they were mostly from minority ethnic groups. Babangida, for example, was of Gwari origin from Niger state. He was a member of the Supreme Military Council under the Murtala Muhammad, Obasanjo, and Buhari regimes and had been involved in the 1975 and 1984 coups. Lieutenant General Domkat Bali became chairman of the Joint Chiefs of Staff. The Armed Forces Ruling Council (which succeeded the Supreme Military Council) was dominated by minority groups from the north. Some radicals and technocrats were appointed to ministerial positions.

The new regime was committed to a return to civilian rule and supported the 1979 constitution. Babangida assumed the title of president, which he justified in terms of the Constitution. Furthermore, he tried to assuage the unrest in the country by correcting the excesses of the Buhari regime. The NSO was abolished in 1986, and its duties were reassigned to less threatening bodies. The freewheeling press was allowed fuller rein again, although there was still occasional harassment. Trials of former politicians were ended, and many former officials who had been convicted were released from jail. In 1987 the regime decreed that all politicians who had held office since 1960 and who had been convicted of criminal offenses were banned from politics.

The Babangida regime had a rocky start. A countercoup in December 1985 failed but made it clear that not everyone in the military sided with the Armed Forces Ruling Council. The most serious opposition centered in the labor movement and on the university campuses. In May 1986, students at Ahmadu Bello University and Kaduna Polytechnic staged demonstrations that led to military occupation of those campuses and to the deaths of a number of students. The student movement had considerable support at other universities. On June 4, 1986, the Nigerian Labour Congress in alliance with students and university teachers organized a national day of sympathy, which led to the arrest of many union leaders. There was also considerable controversy over Nigeria's entry into the Organization of the Islamic Conference, an international body of Muslim states, in 1986. Buhari's regime had made the application, which Babangida allowed to stand. The strong reaction among many Christians, led by the Christian Association of Nigeria (formed in 1976), proved to be an embarrassment to the regime.

Babangida addressed the worsening recession through the structural adjustment program of 1986. By 1986, 44 percent of export earnings was being used to service the foreign debt.

Austerity was not enough; rescheduling the foreign debt was essential, but public opinion was against an IMF loan. The government already was committed to many of the conditions for the IMF loan, including even more austere measures. However, it resisted pressures to reduce the petroleum subsidy, to allow trade liberalization, and to devalue the naira. Although negotiations with the IMF were suspended, the federal budget of 1986 still imposed many of the IMF conditions. On October 1, 1986, the government declared a National Economic Emergency, which lasted for fifteen months. Under the emergency, the government de-emphasized large-scale agricultural projects and introduced salary and wage reductions for armed forces and for public- and private-sector employees. Import restrictions were intensified, including a 30-percent surcharge on imports. Officially, the government now encouraged foreign investment and promoted privatization. Finally, the petroleum subsidy was cut back. Despite these drastic moves, efforts to reschedule the foreign debt without an IMF loan failed, and a drop in world oil prices further compounded Nigeria's situation.

Eventually the World Bank stepped into the breach and provided US$4.2 billion over three years to support the structural adjustment program. The eligible debt finally was rescheduled in early 1988. There was heavy devaluation of the naira in 1986, followed by even more drastic reductions in 1989 and early 1990. As a result of the recession, there was a drop in real income, especially for urban dwellers, while unemployment rose steadily from a low in 1980 to almost 12 percent in 1986. The situation in the second half of the 1980s was even worse, with per capita income falling below US$300 in 1988.

The Babangida regime appointed a new body, the Political Bureau, in January 1986 to make recommendations on the return to civilian rule. Its report, submitted in March 1987, was decidedly at odds with the government's structural adjustment program. The Political Bureau, composed of academics and civil servants, wanted to maintain a strong state presence in the economy, while the military regime was steadily moving away from that position. The bureau also favored creation of a two-party political system that would be broadly social democratic in ideology, as a means of escaping from the ethnic-based political parties of the past. The Political Bureau also recommended creation of at least two new states, Katsina and Akwa Ibom, this was accomplished in 1987 (see fig. 4). Although the Babangida regime did not like many of the Political Bureau's recommendations, a Constitution Review Committee was formed in September 1987.

This process of review and discussion convinced the military regime that the transition to civilian rule should be gradual. The perceived mistakes of 1979 and the creation of the Second Republic would not be repeated, it was hoped. The military would stay in power through 1989 to oversee the transition. The first stage was local elections, held in December 1987. No political parties were allowed, and in many districts, especially in Lagos, the results were overturned and new elections held. In 1990 the military continued in power but still promised a return to civilian rule.

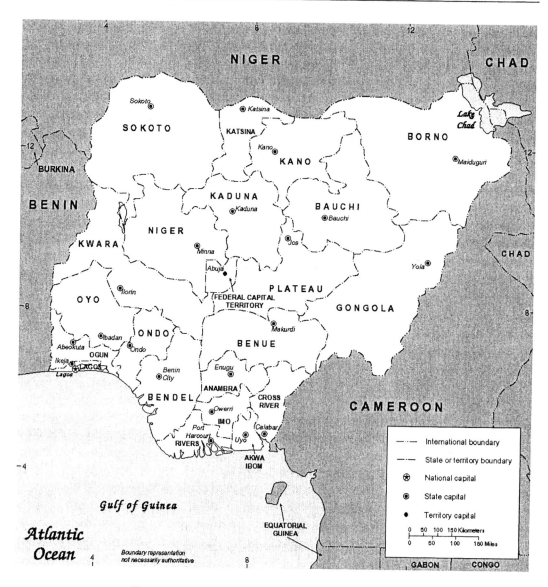

Figure 4. Administrative Division, 1987-August 1991

THE SOCIETY AND ITS ENVIRONMENT

Nigeria, the most populous country in Africa and the tenth largest country by population in the world, is located at the eastern terminus of the bulge of West Africa. As with many of the other nations of Africa, Nigeria's national boundaries result from its colonial history and cut across a number of cultural and physical boundaries. Nigeria has a total area of 923,768 square kilometers, about 60 percent the size of the state of Alaska, and the greatest area of the nations along the coast of West Africa (although in Africa as a whole, it is only the fourteenth largest country by area). The maximum north-south distance within the country is about 1,040 kilometers, while the maximum east-west distance is about 1,120 kilometers. Although it represents only about 3 percent of the surface area of Africa, Nigeria contains about 20 percent of total African population. In this and other respects, it is arguably the single most important country on the continent.

PHYSICAL SETTING

Relief and Main Physical Features

Much of Nigeria's surface consists of ancient crystalline rocks of the African Shield. Having been subject to weathering and erosion for long periods, the characteristic landscape of this area is extensive level plains interrupted by occasional granite mountains. These features form a major landscape type of Nigeria and of West Africa as a whole. There are also smaller areas of younger granites found, for example, on the Jos Plateau.

Sedimentary strata dating from various periods overlay the older rocks in many areas. The sedimentary areas typically consist of flat-topped ridges and dissected plateaus and a characteristic landscape of extensive plains and no major rocky outcrops. This landscape is generally true of the basins of the Niger and Benue rivers as well as the depressions of the Chad and Sokoto basins in the far northeast and northwest of the country, respectively. The most dramatic of the sedimentary landscapes are in southeastern Nigeria, where thick sedimentary beds from the Abakaliki Uplift to the Anambra Basin have been tilted and eroded. This process has resulted in a rugged scarp land topography with east-facing cliffs at in the Udi Hills, north of Enugu, and in the area around Nanka and Agulu.

Although relatively little of the Nigerian landscape has been shaped by volcanic episodes, there are two main areas of volcanic rock. They are found on the Biu Plateau in the northeast, extending into some localized volcanic areas along the eastern border with Cameroon, and on the Jos Plateau in the northern center of the country.

The elevational pattern of most of Nigeria consists of a gradual rise from the coastal plains to the northern savanna regions, generally reaching an elevation of 600 to 700 meters. Higher altitudes, reaching more than 1,200 meters in elevation, are found only in isolated areas of the Jos Plateau and in parts of the eastern highlands along the Cameroon border. The coastal plain extends inland for about ten kilometers and rises to an elevation of forty to fifty meters above sea level at its northern boundary. The eastern and western sections of the coastal plain are separated by the Niger Delta, which extends over an area of about 10,000 square kilometers. Much of this is swampland, separated by numerous islands. The coastal plain region penetrates inland about seventy-five kilometers in the west but extends farther in the east. This region is gently undulating with elevation increasing northward and a mean elevation of about 150 meters above sea level. Much of the population of southern Nigeria is located in these eastern and western coastal plains and in some of the contiguous areas of the coast and the lower Niger Basin.

Separating the two segments of the coastal plain and extending to the northeast and northwest are the broad river basins of the Niger and Benue rivers. The upper reaches of these rivers form narrow valleys and contain falls and rapids. Most of the lower portions, however, are free from rapids and have extensive floodplains and braided stream channels. To the north of the Niger and Benue basins are the broad, stepped plateau and granite mountains that characterize much of northern Nigeria. Such mountains are also found in the southwest, in the region between the western coastal plains and the upper Niger Basin. The western wedge between Abeokuta and Ibadan and the Niger Basin reaches elevations of 600 meters or more, while the extensive northern savanna region, stretching from Kontagora to Gombe and east to the border, includes extensive areas with elevations of more than 1,200 meters or more at its center. The mountainous zone along the middle part of the eastern border, the Cameroon Highlands, includes the country's highest point (2,042 meters). In the far northeast and northwest, elevation falls again to below 300 meters in the Chad Basin in the far northeast and the Sokoto Basin in the northwest.

Climate

As in most of West Africa, Nigeria's climate is characterized by strong latitudinal zones, becoming progressively drier as one moves north from the coast. Rainfall is the key climatic variable, and there is a marked alternation of wet and dry seasons in most areas. Two air masses control rainfall--moist northward-moving maritime air coming from the Atlantic Ocean and dry continental air coming south from the African landmass. Topographic relief plays a significant role in local climate only around the Jos Plateau and along the eastern border highlands.

In the coastal and southeastern portions of Nigeria, the rainy season usually begins in February or March as moist Atlantic air, known as the southwest monsoon, invades the country. The beginning of the rains is usually marked by the incidence of high winds and heavy but scattered squalls. The scattered quality of this storm rainfall is especially noticeable in the north in dry years, when rain may be abundant in some small areas while other contiguous places are completely dry. By April or early May in most years, the rainy season is under way throughout most of the area south of the Niger and Benue river valleys. Farther north, it is usually June or July before the rains really commence. The peak of the rainy season occurs through most of northern Nigeria in August, when air from the Atlantic covers the entire country. In southern regions, this period marks the August dip in precipitation. Although rarely completely dry, this dip in rainfall, which is especially marked in the southwest, can be useful agriculturally, because it allows a brief dry period for grain harvesting.

From September through November, the northeast trade winds generally bring a season of clear skies, moderate temperatures, and lower humidity for most of the country. From December through February, however, the northeast trade winds blow strongly and often bring with them a load of fine dust from the Sahara. These dust-laden winds, known locally as the harmattan, often appear as a dense fog and cover everything with a layer of fine particles. The harmattan is more common in the north but affects the entire country except for a narrow strip along the southwest coast. An occasional strong harmattan, however, can sweep as far south as Lagos, providing relief from high humidities in the capital and pushing clouds of dust out to sea.

Given this climatological cycle and the size of the country, there is a considerable range in total annual rainfall across Nigeria, both from south to north and, in some regions, from east to west. The greatest total precipitation is generally in the southeast, along the coast around Bonny (south of Port Harcourt) and east of Calabar, where mean annual rainfall is more than 4,000 millimeters. Most of the rest of the southeast receives between 2,000 and 3,000 millimeters of rain per year, and the southwest (lying farther north) receives lower total rainfall, generally between 1,250 and 2,500 millimeters per year. Mean annual precipitation at Lagos is about 1,900 millimeters; at Ibadan, only about 140 kilometers north of Lagos, mean annual rainfall drops to around 1,250 millimeters. Moving north from Ibadan, mean annual rainfall in the west is in the range of 1,200 to 1,300 millimeters.

North of Kaduna, through the northern Guinea savanna and then the Sudan (see Glossary) savanna zones, the total rainfall and the length of the rainy season decline steadily. The Guinea savanna starts in the middle belt, or southern part of northern Nigeria. It is distinguished from the Sudan savanna because it has more trees whereas the Sudan few trees. Rainy seasons decline correspondingly in length as one moves north, with Kano having an average rainy period of 120 to 130 days, and Katsina and Sokoto having rainy seasons 10 to 20 days shorter. Average annual rainfall in the north is in the range of 500 to 750 millimeters.

The regularity of drought periods has been among the most notable aspects of Nigerian climate in recent years, particularly in the drier regions in the north. Experts regard the twentieth century as having been among the driest periods of the last several centuries; the well publicized droughts of the 1970s and 1980s were only the latest of several significant such episodes to affect West Africa in this century. At least two of these droughts have severely affected large areas of northern Nigeria and the Sahel region farther north. These drought periods are indications of the great variability of climate across tropical Africa, the most serious effects of which are usually felt at the drier margins of agricultural zones or in the regions occupied primarily by pastoral groups.

Temperatures throughout Nigeria are generally high; diurnal variations are more pronounced than seasonal ones. Highest temperatures occur during the dry season; rains moderate afternoon highs during the wet season. Average highs and lows for Lagos are 31° C and 23° C in January and 28° C and 23° C in June. Although average temperatures vary little from coastal to inland areas, inland areas, especially in the northeast, have greater extremes. There, temperatures reach as high as 44° C before the onset of the rains or drop as low as 6° C during an intrusion of cool air from the north from December to February.

POPULATION

The size of its population is one of Nigeria's most significant and distinctive features. With probably more than 100 million people in 1990--the precise figure is uncertain because there has been no accepted census since 1963, although a census was scheduled for the fall of 1991--Nigeria's population is about twice the size of that of the next largest country in Africa, Egypt, which had an estimated mid-1989 population of 52 million. Nigeria represents about 20 percent of the total population of sub-Saharan Africa. The population is unevenly distributed, however; a large percentage of the total number live within several hundred kilometers of the coast but population is also dense along the northern river basin areas such as Kano and Sokoto. Population densities, especially in the southwest near Lagos and the rich agricultural regions around Enugu and Owerri, exceed 400 inhabitants per kilometer (see table 1). None of the neighboring states of West or Central Africa approaches the total level of Nigerian population or the densities found in the areas of greatest concentration in Nigeria. Several of Nigeria's twenty-one states have more people than a number of other countries in West Africa, and some of the Igbo areas of the southeast have the highest rural densities in sub-Saharan Africa. In contrast, other areas of Nigeria are sparsely populated and have apparently remained so for a considerable time. This pattern of population distribution has major implications for the country's development and has had great impact on the nation's postindependence history.

Migration from rural to urban areas has accelerated in recent decades. Estimates of urban dwellers reveal this shift--in 1952, 11 percent of the total population was classified as urban; in 1985, 28 percent. One-sixth of the urban population, or approximately 6 million people, lived in Lagos, and in 1985 eight other cities had populations of more than 500,000.

Table 1. Population Estimates by State, 1987

State	Population	State	Population
Akwa Ibom	5,100,000	Kwara	3,400,000
Anambra	7,200,000	Lagos	4,100,000
Bauchi	4,800,000	Niger	2,200,000
Bendel	4,900,000	Ogun	3,100,000
Benue	4,800,000	Ondo	5,500,000
Borno	6,000,000	Oyo	10,400,000
Cross River	1,900,000	Plateau	4,000,000
Gongola	5,200,000	Rivers	3,400,000
Imo	7,300,000	Sokoto	9,000,000
Kaduna	3,300,000	Federal Capital Territory (Abuja)	300,000
Kano	11,500,000	TOTAL	112,300,000
Katsina	4,900,000		

Source: Based on information from Economist Intelligence Unit, *Country Report: Nigeria* [London], No. 1, 1990, 10.

ETHNICITY

Ethnicity is one of the keys to understanding Nigeria's pluralistic society. It distinguishes groupings of peoples who for historical reasons have come to be seen as distinctive--by themselves and others--on the basis of locational origins and a series of other cultural markers. Experience in the postindependence period fostered a widespread belief that modern ethnicity affects members' life chances. In Nigerian colloquial usage, these collectivities were commonly called "tribes." In the emergent Nigerian national culture, this topic was discussed widely as "tribalism," a morally reprehensible term whose connotations were similar to American terms, such as "discrimination," "racism," or "prejudice." Nigerian national policies have usually fostered tolerance and appreciation for cultural differences, while trying at the same time to suppress unfair treatment based on ethnic prejudice. This long-term campaign involved widespread support in educated circles to replace the term "tribe" or "tribal" with the more universally applicable concept of ethnicity. Nevertheless, older beliefs died slowly, and ethnic identities were still a vital part of national life in 1990.

The ethnic variety was dazzling and confusing. Estimates of the number of distinct ethnic groupings varied from 250 to as many as 400. The most widely used marker was that of language. In most cases, people who spoke a distinct language having a separate term for the language and/or its speakers saw themselves, or were viewed by others, as ethnically different. Language groupings were numbered in the 1970s at nearly 400, depending upon disagreements over whether or not closely related languages were mutually intelligible. Language groupings sometimes shifted their distinctiveness rather than displaying clear boundaries. Manga and Kanuri speakers in northeastern Nigeria spoke easily to one another. But in the major Kanuri city of Maiduguri, 160 kilometers south of Manga-speaking areas, Manga was considered a separate language. Kanuri and Manga who lived near each other saw themselves as members of the same ethnic group; others farther away did not.

Markers other than language were also used to define ethnicity. Speakers of Bura (a Chadic language closely related to Marghi) saw themselves traditionally as two ethnic groups, Bura and Pabir, a view not necessarily shared by others. Bura mostly adhered to Christianity or to a local indigenous religion, and a few were Muslims. They lived originally in small, autonomous villages of 100 to 500 persons that and expanded split as the population grew. The Pabir had the same local economy as the Bura, but they were Muslim, they lived in larger (originally walled) villages of 400 to 3,000 with more northerly architectural styles, they resisted splitting up into subgroups, and they recognized a central ruler (emir) in a capital town (Biu). There was a strong movement in the 1980s among many Bura speakers to unite the two groups based on their common language, location, and interests in the wider society. Given long-standing conflicts that separated them as late as 1990, however, their common ethnicity was open to question.

The official language of the country is English, which is taught in primary schools and used for instruction in secondary schools and universities. All officials with education to secondary school level or beyond spoke English and used it across language barriers formed by Nigeria's ethnic diversity. Many in the university-trained elite used English as one of the languages in their homes and/or sent their children to preschools that provided a head start in English-language instruction. In addition to English, pidgin has been used as a lingua franca in the south (and in adjoining Cameroon) for more than a century among the nonschool population. In 1990 it was used in popular songs, radio and television dramas, novels, and even newspaper cartoons. In the north, southerners spoke pidgin to one another, but Hausa was the lingua franca of the region and was spreading rapidly as communications and travel provided a need for increased intelligibility. Counting English, the use of which was expanding as rapidly as Hausa, many Nigerians were at least trilingual. This language facility usually included a local vernacular, a wider African lingua franca, and English. Given the long history of trade and markets that stimulated contacts across local ethnic units, multilingualism was a very old and established adaptation. Such multilingualism enabled communication among different ethnic groups in the century.

Ethnic Relations

Relations between ethnic groups remained a major problem for such a large and pluralistic society in 1990. In precolonial times, interethnic relations were often mistrustful, or discriminatory, and sometimes violent. At the same time, there were relationships, such as trade, that required peaceful communications. The most widespread communication was in the north between pastoral and agricultural peoples who traded cattle for farm products, and pasturage rights for manuring. Farmers might also buy a few cattle and have them cared for by pastoralists. Emirate rulers who normally raided and pillaged among non-Muslim village groups often established peaceful "trust" relations with residents of one or two villages; those residents then acted as hosts and guides for the raiders, in exchange for immunity for themselves. More subtle and peaceful exchanges involved smaller ethnic groups in the middle belt, each of which specialized in one or more commodities. In towns and along trade routes, occupations such as smithing, producing cotton, selling cattle, weaving, house building, and beer making were often confined to, or correlated with, ethnically defined units. Thus, ecological and economic specializations promoted peaceful interethnic relations. Conversely, promulgating conflict, mistrust, and stereotypes in ethnic relations were droughts; competition for control over trade routes or allies; resistance to, or the creation and maintenance of, exploitative relations; and other factors.

The civil war taught Nigerians that ethnic conflicts were among the most destructive forces in the life of the nation. By 1990 ethnic conflict was suppressed and carefully controlled so that any outbreak or seriously publicized discrimination on ethnic grounds was considered a matter of national security. In the few outbreaks that occurred since the war, the federal government acted swiftly to gain control and stop the conflict. Nevertheless, the way in which ethnic relations might threaten the security of individuals and groups was among the most serious issues in national life, especially for the millions of Nigerians who had to live and work in interethnic contexts.

Even in the more cosmopolitan cities, more than 90 percent of marriages were within rather than between ethnic units, or at least within identical regions and language groups. Marriages between subgroups of Igbo, Yoruba, Hausa, Fulani, or Kanuri occurred without stigma and had done so for many decades. But in the south, Yoruba-Igbo unions were uncommon, and north-south marriages were even rarer, especially between Hausa-Fulani or Kanuri and any person from southern Nigeria. Northern Muslim intermarriage was not uncommon, nor was intermarriage among peoples of the middle belt. But unions between middle belters and Muslims from emirates farther north remained rare. Migrants who could not find a spouse from their own ethnic group within the local enclave obtained a mate from the home community. Social pressure for ethnic endogamy was intense and persisted even among elites in business, universities, the military, religion, and politics. In the late 1980s and early 1990s, however, it appeared that marriages within the Christian and Muslim communities were increasingly transethnic.

The conjunction of location, language, religion, and common and differentiating customs created a strong sense of shared fate among coethnics and formed a constant basis for organizing ethnically related groupings into political constituencies. Thus, when political parties emerged, they represented the northern Muslim peoples, the Yoruba, and the Igbo; middle belters and others in between were courted from several directions (see The Second

Republic). Given the shortage of government jobs and the expanding numbers of qualified applicants coming out of the education system, ethnic rivalry for government posts exacerbated ethnic competition. It was also a driving force in the establishment of more states, with more state capitals and more locally controlled jobs. Such jobs were likely to be less competitive ethnically because the boundaries of local governments tended to correlate with ethnic units. Under such conditions, would-be leaders stimulated the fears of their ethnic constituents. Ethnic organizations and university students wrote letters to newspapers pressuring for greater representation, more development resources, and separate states or districts for their particular group. Countering this practice, after the civil war the new constitution of 1979 provided that no political party could be legalized unless it obtained support in all parts of the country. This attempt to crosscut ethnicity with rules of political party competition has gone far toward alleviating the problem.

People first looked for relatives when migrating into one of the country's many large cities, as an increasing number of Nigerians were doing. If they found none, they looked for coethnics from their own rural area who shared a network of friends, neighbors, and relations. They spoke the same language, went to the same church or mosque and helped one another to find a job and housing and to join ethnic associations. In the textile mills of Kaduna in the north, studies of "class formation" among workers indicated that ethnic groupings were far stronger and used more frequently by workers than were trade unions, unless working conditions became extremely bad. It was only then that union membership, interaction, strength, and unity rose. Otherwise, ethnicity was the primary dimension for worker relations and mutual aid. Studies elsewhere in the country produced similar results. The trade union movement in Nigeria was well established and strong, especially at times of severe economic downturn, such as the late 1980s and early 1990s, when the structural adjustment program (SAP) severely decreased real wages. Rivalry within unions, however, and worker associations for mutual aid, as well as normal social life at work and afterward, were strongly influenced by formal and informal ethnic affiliations.

Ethnic stereotypes remained strong. Each of the main groups had disparaging stories and sayings about the others that were discussed openly when a foreigner was alone with members of a single ethnic group. Such prejudices died slowly, especially when ethnic groups lived in enclaves, knew little of each other's customs, and often attended different schools. It was official policy, however, to protect the rights of minorities, and in several instances the will to do so was ably demonstrated. Thus, Igbo property abandoned in the north at the time of the civil war was maintained by local governments and later returned. Although there were problems, this property restitution, the attempt to ensure that Igbo were accepted at all major universities, and the placement of Igbo in civil service posts helped create a sense of nationhood and trust in the rule of law and in the good intentions of the federal government.

Contemporary Society

Nigerian history has provided an extraordinary set of pressures and events as a context for modern nation building. Under such circumstances--the imposition of colonial rule, independence, interethnic and interregional competition or even violence, military coups, a civil war, an oil boom that had government and individuals spending recklessly and often with corrupt intentions, droughts, and a debt crisis that led to a drastic recession and lowered standards of living--people tended to cleave to what they knew. That is to say, they adhered to regional loyalties, ethnicity, kin, and to patron-client relations that protected them in an unstable and insecure environment. Meanwhile, other factors and processes stimulated by education, jobs, politics, and urban and industrial development created crosscutting ties that linked people in new, more broadly national ways.

By 1990 both sets of distinctions operated at once and gave no sign of weakening. For example, from time to time labor unions were able to call widespread, even general, strikes. At other times, unorganized workers or farmers rioted over long-held or sudden grievances. Nevertheless, attempts to create national movements or political parties out of such momentary flare-ups failed. Instead, once the outburst was over, older linkages reasserted themselves. In effect, the structure of society in 1990 was the result of these two processes-- historical, locational, and ethnic on the one hand and socioeconomic on the other. In Nigeria the latter contact referred primarily to occupation, rural-urban residence, and formal education. Together these factors accounted for similarities and differences that were common across ethnic and regional groupings.

RELIGION

Several religions coexisted in Nigeria, helping to accentuate regional and ethnic distinctions. All religions represented in Nigeria were practiced in every major city in 1990. But Islam dominated in the north, Protestantism and local syncretic Christianity were most in evidence in Yoruba areas, and Catholicism predominated in the Igbo and closely related areas. The 1963 census indicated that 47 percent of Nigerians were Muslim, 35 percent Christian, and 18 percent members of local indigenous congregations. If accurate, this indicated a sharp increase in the number of Christians (up 13 percent); a slight decline among those professing indigenous beliefs, compared with 20 percent in 1953; and only a modest (4 percent) rise of Muslims. This surge was partly a result of the recognized value of education provided by the missions, especially in the previously non-Christian middle belt. It also resulted from 1963 census irregularities that artificially increased the proportion of southern Christians to northern Muslims. Since then two more forces have been operating. There has been the growth of the Aladura Church, an Africanized Christian sect that was especially strong in the Yoruba areas, and of evangelical churches in general, spilling over into adjacent and southern areas of the middle belt. At the same time, Islam was spreading southward into the northern reaches of the middle belt, especially among the upwardly mobile, who saw it as a necessary attribute for full acceptance in northern business and political circles. In general, however, the country should be seen as having a predominantly Muslim north and a non-Muslim, primarily Christian south, with each as a minority faith in the other's region; the middle belt was more heterogeneous.

Islam

Islam is a traditional religion in West Africa. It came to northern Nigeria as early as the eleventh century and was well established in the state capitals of the region by the sixteenth century, spreading into the countryside and toward the middle belt uplands. There, Islam's advance was stopped by the resistance of local peoples to incorporation into the emirate states. The Fulani-led jihad in the nineteenth century pushed Islam into Nupe and across the Niger River into northern Yoruba- speaking areas. The colonial conquest established a rule that active Christian proselytizing could not occur in the northern Muslim region, although in 1990 the two religions continued to compete for converts in the middle belt, where ethnic groups and even families had adherents of each persuasion.

The origins of Islam date to Muhammad (the Prophet), a prosperous merchant of the town of Mecca in Arabia. He began in A.D. 610 to preach the first of a series of revelations granted him by God (Allah) through the agency of the archangel Gabriel. The divine messages, received during solitary visits into the desert, continued during the remainder of his life.

Muhammad denounced the polytheistic paganism of his fellow Meccans; his vigorous and continuing censure ultimately earned him their bitter enmity. In 622 he and a group of followers accepted an invitation to settle in Yathrib, which became known as Medina (the city) through its association with him. The hijra, (known in the West as the hegira), or journey to Medina, marked the beginning of the Islamic calendar in the year 622. In Medina Muhammad continued his preaching, ultimately defeated his detractors in battle, and had consolidated the temporal as well as spiritual leadership of most Arabs before his death in 632.

After Muhammad's death, his followers compiled his words that were regarded as coming directly from God in a document known as the Quran, the holy scripture of Islam. Other sayings and teachings of the Prophet, as well as the precedents of his personal behavior as recalled by those who had known him, became the hadith ("sayings"). From these sources, the faithful have constructed the Prophet's customary practice, or sunna, which they endeavor to emulate. Together, these documents form a comprehensive guide to the spiritual, ethical, and social life of the faithful in most Muslim countries.

The *shahada* (profession of faith, or testimony) states succinctly the central belief, "There is no God but Allah, and Muhammad is his Prophet." The faithful repeat this simple profession on ritual occasions, and its recital designates the speaker as a Muslim. The term *Islam* means submission to God, and the one who submits is a Muslim.

The God preached by Muhammad was previously known to his countrymen, for *Allah* is the general Arabic term for the supreme being rather than the name of a particular deity. Rather than introducing a new deity, Muhammad denied the existence of the pantheon of gods and spirits worshipped before his prophethood and declared the omnipotence of God, the unique creator. Muhammad is the "Seal of the Prophets," the last of the prophetic line. His revelations are said to complete for all time the series of revelations that had been given earlier to Jews and Christians. God is believed to have remained one and the same throughout time, but humans are seen as having misunderstood or strayed from God's true teachings until set aright by Muhammad. Prophets and sages of the biblical tradition, such as Abraham, Moses, and Jesus, are recognized as inspired vehicles of God's will. Islam, however, reveres as sacred only the message. It accepts the concepts of guardian angels, the Day of Judgment, resurrection, and the eternal life of the soul.

The duties of the Muslim form the "five pillars" of the faith. These are *shahada, salat* (daily prayer), *zakat* (almsgiving), *sawm* (fasting), and hajj (pilgrimage). The believer prays facing Mecca at five specified times during the day. Whenever possible, men observe their prayers in congregation at a mosque under direction of an imam, or prayer leader, and on Fridays are obliged to do so. Women are permitted to attend public worship at the mosque, where they are segregated from men, but their attendance tends to be discouraged, and more frequently they pray in the seclusion of their homes.

In the early days of Islam, a tax for charitable purposes was imposed on personal property in proportion to the owner's wealth. The collection of this tax and its distribution to the needy were originally functions of the state. But with the breakdown of Muslim religiopolitical authority, alms became an individual responsibility.

The ninth month of the Muslim calendar is Ramadan, a period of obligatory fasting in commemoration of Muhammad's receipt of God's revelation. Throughout the month, all but the sick and the weak, pregnant or lactating women, soldiers on duty, travelers on necessary journeys, and young children are enjoined from eating, drinking, smoking, or sexual intercourse during daylight hours. Those adults excused are obliged to endure an equivalent fast at their earliest opportunity. A festive meal breaks the daily fast and inaugurates a night of feasting and celebration. Well-to-do believers usually do little or no work during this period, and some businesses close for all or part of the day. Because the months of the lunar year revolve through the solar year, Ramadan falls at various seasons in different years. A considerable test of discipline at any time of the year, a fast that falls in summertime imposes severe hardship on those who must do physical work.

Finally, at least once during their lifetime all Muslims should make the hajj, or pilgrimage, to the holy city of Mecca to participate in the special rites that occur during the twelfth month of the lunar calendar. For most well-to-do Nigerian traders and business people, the trip was so common that the honorific "hajji" (fem., *hajjia*), signifying a pilgrim, was routinely used to refer to successful traders.

Two features of Islam are essential to understanding its place in Nigerian society. They are the degree to which Islam permeates other institutions in the society, and its contribution to Nigerian pluralism. As an institution in emirate society, Islam includes daily and annual ritual obligations; the pilgrimage to Mecca; sharia, or religious law; and an establishment view of politics, family life, communal order, and appropriate modes of personal conduct in most situations. Thus, even in 1990, Islam pervaded daily life. Public meetings began and ended with Muslim prayer, and everyone knew at least the minimum Arabic prayers and the five pillars of the religion required for full participation. Public adjudication (by local leaders with the help of religious experts, or Alkali courts) provided widespread knowledge of the basic tenets of sharia law-- the Sunni school of law according to Malik ibn Anas, the jurist from Medina, was that primarily followed. Sunni (from sunna), or orthodox Islam, is the dominant sect in Nigeria and most of the Muslim world. The other sect is Shia Islam, which holds that the caliphs or successors to the Prophet should have been his relatives rather than elected individuals.

Every settlement had at least one place set aside for communal prayers. In the larger settlements, mosques were well attended, especially on Fridays when the local administrative and chiefly elites led the way, and the populace prayed with its leaders in a demonstration of communal and religious solidarity. Gaining increased knowledge of the religion, one or more pilgrimages to Mecca for oneself or one's wife, and a reputation as a devout and honorable Muslim all provided prestige. Those able to suffuse their everyday lives with the beliefs and practices of Islam were deeply respected.

Air transport had made the hajj more widely available, and the red cap wound with a white cloth, signifying its wearer's pilgrimage, was much more common in 1990 than twenty years previously. Upper-income groups went several times and sent or took their wives as well. The ancient custom of spending years walking across Africa to reach Mecca was still practiced, however, and groups of such pilgrims could be seen receiving charity at Friday prayers outside major mosques in the north.

Nigerian Islam was not highly organized. Reflecting the aristocratic nature of the traditional ruling groups, there were families of clerics whose male heirs trained locally and abroad in theology and jurisprudence and filled major positions in the mosques and the judiciary. These ulama, or learned scholars, had for centuries been the religious and legal advisers of emirs, the titled nobility, and the wealthy trading families in the major cities. Ordinary people could consult the myriads of would-be and practicing clerics in various stages of training, who studied with local experts, functioned at rites of passage, or simply used their religious education to gain increased "blessedness" for their efforts. Sufi brotherhoods, (from suf, or wool; the wearing of a woolen robe indicated devotion to a mystic life), a form of religious order based on more personal or mystical relations to the supernatural, were widespread, especially in the major cities. There the two predominant ones, Qadiriyah and Tijaniyah, had separate mosques and, in a number of instances, a parochial school system receiving grants from the state. The brotherhoods played a major role in the spread of Islam in the northern area and the middle belt.

Islam both united and divided. It provided a rallying force in the north and into the middle belt, where it was spreading. The wide scope of Islamic beliefs and practices created a leveling force that caused Muslims in the north to feel that they were part of a common set of cultural traditions affecting family life, dress, food, manners, and personal qualities linking them to one another and a wider Islamic world. At the constitutional conference of 1978, Muslim delegates walked out as a unit over the issue of a separate Islamic supreme court, a demand they lost but which in 1990 remained a Muslim goal. To adapt fully to northern life, non-Muslims had to remain in an enclave, living quasi-segregated lives in their churches, their social clubs, and even their work. In contrast, becoming a convert to Islam was the doorway to full participation in the society. Middle belt people, especially those with ambitions in politics and business, generally adopted Islam. The main exception to this rule was Plateau State, where the capital, Jos, was as much a Christian as a Muslim community, and a greater accommodation between the two sets of beliefs and their adherents had occurred.

Divisions within the Muslim community existed, however. The nineteenth-century jihad that founded the Sokoto Caliphate was a regenerative and proselytizing movement within the community of the faithful. In major centers in 1990, the Sufi brotherhoods supported their own candidates for both religious and traditional emirate offices. These differences were generally not disruptive. Islamic activist preachers and student leaders who spread ideas about a return to extreme orthodoxy also existed. In addition, a fringe Islamic cult, known as the Maitatsine, started in the late 1970s and operated throughout the 1980s, springing up in Kano around a mystical leader (since deceased) from Cameroon who claimed to have had divine revelations superseding those of the Prophet. The cult had its own mosques and preached a doctrine antagonistic to established Islamic and societal leadership. Its main appeal was to marginal and poverty-stricken urban in-migrants, whose rejection by the more established urban groups fostered this religious opposition. These disaffected adherents ultimately lashed out at the more traditional mosques and congregations, resulting in violent outbreaks in several cities of the north (see Domestic Security).

Christianity

The majority of Christians were found in the south. A few isolated mission stations and mission bookstores, along with churches serving southern enclaves in the northern cities and larger towns, dotted the Muslim north. The Yoruba area traditionally has been Protestant and Anglican, whereas Igboland has always been the area of greatest activity by the Roman Catholic Church. Other denominations abounded as well. Presbyterians arrived in the early twentieth century in the Ibibio Niger Delta area and had missions in the middle belt as well. This latter area was an open one. Small missionary movements were allowed to start up, generally in the 1920s, after the middle belt was considered pacified. Each denomination set up rural networks by providing schooling and health facilities. Most such facilities remained in 1990, although in many cases schools had been taken over by the local state government in order to standardize curricula and indigenize the teaching staff. Pentecostals arrived mostly as indigenous workers in the postindependence period and in 1990 Perte costalism was spreading rapidly throughout the middle belt, having some success in Roman Catholic and Protestant towns of the south as well. There were also breakaway, or Africanized churches that blended traditional Christian symbols with indigenous symbols. Among these was the Aladura movement that was spreading rapidly throughout Yorubaland and into the non-Muslim middle belt areas.

Apart from Benin and Warri, which had come in contact with Christianity through the Portuguese as early as the fifteenth century, most missionaries arrived by sea in the nineteenth century. As with other areas in Africa, Roman Catholics and Anglicans each tended to establish areas of hegemony in southern Nigeria. After World War I, smaller sects such as the Brethren, Seventh Day Adventists, Jehovah's Witnesses, and others worked in interstitial areas, trying not to compete. Although less well-known, African-American churches entered the missionary field in the nineteenth century and created contacts with Nigeria that lasted well into the colonial period.

African churches were founded by small groups breaking off from the European denominations, especially in Yorubaland, where such independence movements started as early as the late nineteenth century. They were for the most part ritually and doctrinally identical to the pavent church, although more African music, and later dance, entered and mixed with the imported church services. A number also used biblical references to support polygyny. With political independence came African priests in both Roman Catholic and Protestant denominations, although ritual and forms of worship were strictly those of the home country of the original missionaries. By the 1980s, however, African music and even dancing were being introduced quietly into church services, albeit altered to fit into rituals of European origin. Southern Christians living in the north, especially in larger cities, had congregations and churches founded as early as the 1920s. Even medium-sized towns (20,000 persons or more) with an established southern enclave had local churches, especially in the middle belt, where both major religions had a strong foothold. The exodus of Igbo from the north in the late 1960s left Roman Catholic churches poorly attended, but by the 1980s adherents were back in even greater numbers, and a number of new churches had been built.

The Aladura, like several other breakaway churches, stress healing and fulfillment of life goals for oneself and one's family. African beliefs that sorcery and witchcraft are malevolent forces against which protection is required are accepted; rituals are warm and emotional, stressing personal involvement and acceptance of spirit possession. Theology is biblical, but some sects add costumed processions and some accept polygyny.

Major congregations of the larger Anglican and Roman Catholic missions represented elite families of their respective areas, although each of these churches had members from all levels and many quite humble church buildings. Nevertheless, a wedding in the Anglican cathedral in Lagos was usually a gathering of the elite of the entire country, and of Lagos and Yorubaland in particular. Such families had connections to their churches going back to the nineteenth century and were generally not attracted to the breakaway churches. All major urban centers, all universities, and the new capital of Abuja had areas set aside for the major religions to build mosques and churches and for burial grounds.

Interethnic conflict generally has had a religious element. Riots against Igbo in 1953 and in the 1960s in the north were said to be fired by religious conflict. The riots against Igbo in the north in 1966 were said to have been inspired by radio reports of mistreatment of Muslims in the south. In the 1980s, serious outbreaks between Christians and Muslims occurred in Kafanchan in southern Kaduna State in a border area between the two religions.

URBANIZATION

Throughout Africa societies that had been predominantly rural for most of their history were experiencing a rapid and profound reorientation of their social and economic lives toward cities and urbanism. As ever greater numbers of people moved to a small number of rapidly expanding cities (or, as was often the case, a single main city), the fabric of life in both urban and rural areas changed in massive, often unforeseen ways. With the largest and one of the most rapidly growing cities in sub-Saharan Africa, Nigeria has experienced the phenomenon of urbanization as thoroughly as any African nation, but its experience has also been unique--in scale, in pervasiveness, and in historical antecedents.

Modern urbanization in most African countries has been dominated by the growth of a single primate city, the political and commercial center of the nation; its emergence was, more often than not, linked to the shaping of the country during the colonial era. In countries with a coastline, this was often a coastal port, and in Nigeria, Lagos fitted well into this pattern. Unlike most other nations, however, Nigeria had not just one or two but several other cities of major size and importance, a number of which were larger than most other national capitals in Africa. In two areas, the Yoruba region in the southwest and the Hausa-Fulani and Kanuri areas of the north, there were numbers of cities with historical roots stretching back considerably before the advent of British colonizers, giving them distinctive physical and cultural identities. Moreover, in areas such as the Igbo region in the southeast, which had few urban centers before the colonial period and was not highly urbanized even at independence, there has been a massive growth of newer cities since the 1970s, so that these areas in 1990 were also highly urban.

Cities are not only independent centers of concentrated human population and activity; they also exert a potent influence on the rural landscape. What is distinctive about the growth of cities in Nigeria is the length of its historical extension and the geographic pervasiveness of its coverage.

Students at recess in a Lagos primary school
Courtesy Embassy of Nigeria, Washington

EDUCATION

There were three fundamentally distinct education systems in Nigeria in 1990: the indigenous system, Quranic schools, and formal European-style education institutions. In the rural areas where the majority lived, children learned the skills of farming and other work, as well as the duties of adulthood, from participation in the community. This process was often supplemented by age-based schools in which groups of young boys were instructed in community responsibilities by mature men. Apprentice systems were widespread throughout all occupations; the trainee provided service to the teacher over a period of years and eventually struck out on his own. Truck driving, building trades, and all indigenous crafts and services from leather work to medicine were passed down in families and acquired through apprenticeship training as well. In 1990 this indigenous system included more than 50 percent of the school-age population and operated almost entirely in the private sector; there was virtually no regulation by the government unless training included the need for a license. By the 1970s, education experts were asking how the system could be integrated into the more formal schooling of the young, but the question remained unresolved by 1990.

Outdoor class at a Quran school in Lagos in the early 1960s
Courtesy Embassy of Nigeria, Washington

Islamic education was part of religious duty. Children learned up to one or two chapters of the Quran by rote from a local *mallam*, or religious teacher, before they were five or six years old. Religious learning included the Arabic alphabet and the ability to read and copy texts in the language, along with those texts required for daily prayers. Any Islamic community provided such instruction in a *mallam*'s house, under a tree on a thoroughfare, or in a local mosque. This primary level was the most widespread. A smaller number of those young Muslims who wished, or who came from wealthier or more educated homes, went on to examine the meanings of the Arabic texts. Later, grammar, syntax, arithmetic, algebra, logic, rhetoric, jurisprudence, and theology were added; these subjects required specialist teachers at the advanced level. After this level, students traditionally went on to one of the famous Islamic centers of learning.

For the vast majority, Muslim education was delivered informally under the tutelage of *mallams* or ulama, scholars who specialized in religious learning and teaching. Throughout the colonial period, a series of formal Muslim schools were set up and run on European lines. These schools were established in almost all major Nigerian cities but were notable in Kano, where Islamic brotherhoods developed an impressive number of schools. They catered to the children of the devout and the well-to-do who wished to have their children educated in the new and necessary European learning, but within a firmly religious context. Such schools were influential as a form of local private school that retained the predominance of religious values within a modernized school system. Because the government took over all private and parochial schools in the mid-1970s and only allowed such schools to exist again independently in 1990, data are lacking concerning numbers of students enrolled.

Western-style education came to Nigeria with the missionaries in the mid-nineteenth century. Although the first mission school was founded in 1843 by Methodists, it was the Anglican Church Missionary Society that pushed forward in the early 1850s to found a chain of missions and schools, followed quickly in the late 1850s by the Roman Catholics. In 1887 in what is now southern Nigeria, an education department was founded that began setting curricula requirements and administered grants to the mission societies. By 1914, when north and south were united into one colony, there were fifty-nine government and ninety-one mission primary schools in the south; all eleven secondary schools, except for King's College in Lagos, were run by the missions. The missions got a foothold in the middle belt; a mission school for the sons of chiefs was opened in Zaria in 1907 but lasted only two years. In 1909 Hans Vischer, an ex-Anglican missionary, was asked to organize the education system of the Protectorate Northern Nigeria. Schools were set up and grants given to missions in the middle belt. In 1914 there were 1,100 primary school pupils in the north, compared with 35,700 in the south; the north had no secondary schools, compared with eleven in the south. By the 1920s, the pressure for school places in the south led to increased numbers of independent schools financed by local efforts and to the sending of favorite sons overseas for more advanced training.

The education system focused strongly on examinations. In 1916 Frederick Lugard, first governor of the unified colony, set up a school inspectorate. Discipline, buildings, and adequacy of teaching staff were to be inspected, but the most points given to a school's performance went to the numbers and rankings of its examination results. This stress on examinations was still used in 1990 to judge educational results and to obtain qualifications for jobs in government and the private sector.

Progress in education was slow but steady throughout the colonial era until the end of World War II. By 1950 the country had developed a three-tiered system of primary, secondary, and higher education based on the British model of wide participation at the bottom, sorting into academic and vocational training at the secondary level, and higher education for a small elite destined for leadership. On the eve of independence in the late 1950s, Nigeria had gone through a decade of exceptional educational growth leading to a movement for universal primary education in the Western Region. In the north, primary school enrollments went from 66,000 in 1947 to 206,000 in 1957, in the west (mostly Yoruba areas) from 240,000 to 983,000 in the same period, and in the east from 320,000 to 1,209,000.

Secondary level enrollments went from 10,000 for the country as a whole in 1947 to 36,000 in 1957; 90 percent of these, however, were in the south.

Given the central importance of formal education, it soon became "the largest social programme of all governments of the federation," absorbing as much as 40 percent of the budgets of some state governments. Thus, by 1984-85 more than 13 million pupils attended almost 35,000 public primary schools. At the secondary level, approximately 3.7 million students were attending 6,500 schools (these numbers probably included enrollment in private schools), and about 125,000 postsecondary level students were attending 35 colleges and universities. The pressure on the system remained intense in 1990, so much so that one education researcher predicted 800,000 higher level students by the end of the 1990s, with a correlated growth in numbers and size of all education institutions to match this estimate.

Universal primary education became official policy for the federation in the 1970s. The goal has not been reached despite pressure throughout the 1980s to do so. In percentage terms, accomplishments have been impressive. Given an approximate population of 49.3 million in 1957 with 23 percent in the primary school age-group (ages five to fourteen), the country had 21 percent of its school-age population attending in the period just prior to independence, after what was probably a tripling of the age-group in the preceding decade. By 1985 with an estimated population of 23 million between ages five and fourteen, approximately 47 percent of the age-group attended school (see table 2). Although growth slowed and actually decreased in some rural areas in the late 1980s, it was projected that by the early part of the next century universal primary education would be achieved.

University education has a high priority. Main library, University of Lagos
Courtesy Orlando E. Pacheco

Secondary and postsecondary level growth was much more dramatic. The secondary level age-group (ages fifteen to twenty- four) represented approximately 16 percent of the entire population in 1985. Secondary level education was available for approximately 0.5

percent of the age-group in 1957, and for 22 percent of the age-group in 1985 (see table 3). In the early 1960s, there were approximately 4,000 students at six institutions (Ibadan, Ife, Lagos, Ahmadu Bello University, the University of Nigeria at Nsukka, and the Institute of Technology at Benin), rising to 19,000 by 1971 and to 30,000 by 1975 (see table 4). In 1990 there were thirty-five polytechnic institutes, military colleges, and state and federal universities, plus colleges of education and of agriculture; they had an estimated enrollment of 150,000 to 200,000, representing less than 1 percent of the twenty-one to twenty-nine-year-old age-group.

Table 2. Enrollment, Number of Schools, and Number of Teachers in Public Primary Schools by State, 1983-84 to 1985-86

State[1]	1983-84 Total Enroll-ment	Number of Schools	Number of Teachers	1984-85 Total Enroll-ment	Number of Schools	Number of Teachers	1985-86 Total Enroll-ment	Number of Schools	Number of Teachers
Anambra	838,470	2,084	34,267	928,738	2,071	27,074	n.a.	2,071	n.a.
Bauchi	326,472	1,830	8,542	284,120	1,830	14,526	308,267	1,798	6,256
Bendel	927,708	1,736	36,860	660,751	1,743	21,446	758,572	1,772	17,903
Benue	953,568	2,700	28,943	441,641	2,018	n.a.	n.a.	n.a.	n.a.
Borno	445,999	2,090	8,137	444,360	1,858	10,009	470,200	1,858	10,009
Cross River	872,370	1,660	24,833	845,745	1,524	24,354	616,654	1,489	15,792
Gongola	518,369	1,857	11,899	359,552	1,447	8,645	384,246	1,460	10,244
Imo	793,867	2,011	27,562	849,703	2,012	20,235	887,039	2,010	20,301
Kaduna	1,134,475	2,885	30,099	1,261,918	2,885	14,646	816,696	2,948	n.a.
Kano	752,278	3,063	18,137	762,593	3,108	16,944	765,226	3,108	n.a.
Kwara	865,972	1,305	17,944	882,8642	1,3053	n.a.	n.a.	n.a.	n.a.
Lagos	632,528	967	14,944	650,937	962	16,362	662,380	888	16,613
Niger	462,074	1,164	10,034	460,182	1,164	6,943	451,010	1,164	6,802
Ogun	445,168	1,288	12,856	359,515	1,288	11,320	369,261	1,277	11,203
Ondo	693,997	1,627	22,294	567,612	1,726	14,870	453,397	1,608	16,824
Oyo	2,070,362	1,907	32,987	1,982,525	2,740	n.a.	n.a.	n.a.	n.a.
Plateau	524,299	1,687	15,656	545,702	1,687	n.a.	511,607	1,375	15,103
Rivers	369,363	1,119	14,449	320,935	1,110	13,719	345,059	1,081	11,826
Sokoto	705,777	4,038	18,482	717,898	2,509	12,624	724,625	2,452	13,013
Federal Capital Territory (Abuja)	45,1552	198	1,865	45,1552	201	1,782	47,244	203	1,683
TOTAL	14,378,271	37,216	390,790	13,372,446	35,188	235,499	8,571,483	28,562	173,572

n.a.--not available.

[1]Akwa Ibom and Katsina did not become states until September 1987 and are therefore not included.

Source: Based on information from Nigeria, Office of Statistics, *Social Statistics in Nigeria, 1985,* Lagos, 1986, 80.

Table 3. Enrollment in Secondary Schools by State, 1980-81 to 1983-84

State[1]	1980-81 Students	Percentage	1981-82 Studen ts	Percentage	1982-83 Students	Percentage	1983-84 Students	Percentage
Anambra	153,378	7.7	250,611	9.7	180,729	6.0	117,506	3.9
Bauchi	18,007	0.9	25,989	1.0	37,330	1.2	19,792	0.7
Bendel	253,075	12.7	351,006	13.6	369,508	12.2	383,571	12.8
Benue	38,314	2.0	75,261	2.9	n.a.	n.a.	n.a.	0.0
Borno	27,164	1.4	36,275	1.4	n.a.	n.a.	n.a.	0.0
Cross River	176,940	8.9	151,182	5.9	168,816	5.6	162,999	5.4
Gongola	29,284	1.5	42,835	1.7	62,356	2.1	77,894	2.6
Imo	277,649	13.9	305,386	11.9	279,414	9.3	270,898	9.0
Kaduna	50,659	2.5	55,153	2.1	98,868	3.3	140,909	4.7
Kano	32,000	1.6	35,167	1.4	62,477	2.1	74,701	2.5
Kwara	34,333	4.2	92,536	3.6	113,129	3.7	133,937	4.5
Lagos	165,563	8.3	191,309	7.4	225,195	7.5	232,657	7.8
Niger	12,882	0.6	14,945	0.6	160,8482	5.32	66,652	2.2
Ogun	109,525	5.5	136,232	5.3	160,8482	5.32	181,654	6.1
Ondo	178,309	9.0	258,549	10.0	304,452	10.1	299,144	10.0
Oyo	244,490	12.2	373,266	14.5	557,295	18.5	571,227	19.0
Plateau	35,444	1.8	47,367	1.8	71,947	2.4	90,327	3.0
Rivers	72,916	3.7	86,502	3.4	111,475	3.7	92,627	3.1
Sokoto	32,501	1.6	44,630	1.7	45,630	1.5	74,615	2.5
Federal Capital Territory (Abuja)	0	0.0	1,767	0.1	5,460	0.2	7,978	0.3
TOTAL[3]	1,942,433	100.0	2,575,968	100.0	3,015,777	100.0	2,999,088	100.0

n.a.--not available.

[1]Akwa Ibom and Katsina did not become states until September 1987 and are therefore not included.

[2]As published.

[3]Percentages may not add to totals because of rounding.

Source: Based on information from Nigeria, Office of Statistics, *Social Statistics in Nigeria, 1985,* Lagos, 1986, 67.

Such growth was impossible without incurring a host of problems, several of which were so severe as to endanger the entire system of education. As long as the country was growing apace in terms of jobs for the educated minority through investment in expanded government agencies and services and the private sector, the growing numbers of graduates could be absorbed. But the criterion of examination results as the primary sorting device for access to schools and universities led to widespread corruption and cheating among faculty and students at all levels, but especially secondary and postsecondary. Most Nigerian universities had followed the British higher education system of "final examinations" as the basis for granting degrees, but by 1990 many were shifting to the United States system of course credits. Economic hardship among teaching staffs produced increased engagement in nonacademic moonlighting activities. Added to these difficulties were such factors as the lack of books and materials, no incentive for research and writing, the use of outdated notes and materials, and the deficiency of replacement laboratory equipment. One researcher noted that in the 1980s Nigeria had the lowest number of indigenous engineers per capita of any Third World country. Unfortunately, nothing was done to rectify the situation. The teaching of English, which was the language of instruction beyond primary school, had reached such poor levels that university faculty complained they could not understand the written work of their students. By 1990 the crisis in education was such that it was predicted that by the end of the decade, there would be insufficient personnel to run essential services of the country. It was hoped that the publication of critical works and international attention to this crisis might reverse the situation before Nigeria lost an entire generation or more of its skilled labor force.

Table 4. Enrollment in Federal Universities by State, 1980-81 to 1984-85

State[1]	1980-81	1981-82	1982- 83	1983-84	1984-85[2]
Anambra	10,290	11,838	12,139	12,193	12,200
Bauchi	0	263	512	595	700
Bendel	5,694	6,489	7,005	9,528	9,000
Benue	0	193	366	451	600
Borno	2,569	3,244	4,131	5,505	5,600
Cross River	2,798	3,687	4,816	4,816	5,000
Gongola	0	0	128	221	350
Imo	0	224	364	565	600
Kaduna	11,681	12,586	14,029	13,374	13,400
Kano	2,479	2,861	3,376	3,777	4,000
Kwara	2,010	2,784	3,512	4,622	5,000
Lagos	12,365	12,757	9,891	10,800	11,000
Niger	0	0	0	160	300
Ogun	0	0	0	236	350
Ondo	0	0	148	274	400
Oyo	17,855	21,095	22,454	24,007	24,000
Plateau	3,047	3,933	4,798	4,983	5,000
Rivers	1,754	2,428	2,916	3,302	3,500
Sokoto	883	1,366	2,063	2,534	3,000
TOTAL	73,425	85,748	92,648	101,943	104,000

[1] Akwa Ibom and Katsina did not become states until September 1987 and are therefore not included.
[2] As published.

Source: Based on information from Nigeria, Office of Statistics, *Social Statistics in Nigeria, 1985,* Lagos, 1986, 83.

Arts block, University of Ibadan
Courtesy Orlando E. Pacheco

HEALTH

Whereas traditional medicine continued to play an important role in Nigeria in 1990, the country made great strides in the provision of modern health care to its population in the years since World War II, particularly in the period after independence. Among the most notable accomplishments were the expansion of medical education, the improvement of public health care, the control of many contagious diseases and disease vectors, and the provision of primary health care in many urban and rural areas. In the late 1980s, a large increase in vaccination against major childhood diseases and a significant expansion of primary health care became the cornerstones of the government's health policies.

Nonetheless, many problems remained in 1990. Sharp disparities persisted in the availability of medical facilities among the regions, rural and urban areas, and socioeconomic classes. The severe economic stresses of the late 1980s had serious impacts throughout the country on the availability of medical supplies, drugs, equipment, and personnel. In the rapidly growing cities, inadequate sanitation and water supply increased the threat of infectious disease, while health care facilities were generally not able to keep pace with the rate of urban population growth. There were several serious outbreaks of infectious diseases during the 1980s, including cerebrospinal meningitis and yellow fever, for which, especially in rural areas, treatment or preventive immunization was often difficult to obtain. Chronic diseases, such as malaria and guinea worm, continued to resist efforts to reduce their incidence in many areas. The presence of acquired immune deficiency syndrome (AIDS) in Nigeria was confirmed by 1987 and appeared to be growing.

WELFARE

Welfare concerns in Nigeria were primarily related to its general lack of development and the effects on the society of the economic stringency of the 1980s. Given the steady population growth and the decline in urban services and incomes since 1980, it was difficult not to conclude that for the mass of the people at the lower income level, malnutrition, poor health, and overcrowded housing were perpetual problems.

Nigeria had no social security system. Less than 1 percent of the population older than sixty years received pensions. Because of the younger age of urban migrants, there were fewer older people per family unit in urban areas. Official statistics were questionable, however, because at least one survey indicated a number of elderly living alone in northern cities or homeless persons living on the streets and begging. There was some evidence that the traditional practice of caring for parents was beginning to erode under harsh conditions of scarcity in urban areas. In rural Nigeria, it was still the rule that older people were cared for by their children, grandchildren, spouses, siblings, or even ex-spouses. The ubiquity of this tradition left open, however, the possibility of real hardship for urban elderly whose families had moved away or abandoned them.

Traditionally, family problems with spouses or children were handled by extended kinship groups and local authorities. For the most part, this practice continued in the rural areas. In urban settings, social services were either absent or rare for family conflict, for abandoned or runaway children, for foster children, or for children under the care of religious instructors.

As with many other Third World nations, Nigeria had many social welfare problems that needed attention. The existence of a relatively free press combined with a history of self-criticism-- in journalism, the arts, the social sciences, and by religious and political leaders were promising indications of the awareness and public debate required for change and adaptive response to its social problems.

* * *

The literature on Nigeria is voluminous and includes several classic works on Nigeria's major ethnic groups. Among these are the chapters by M.G. Smith (Hausa), Paul and Laura Bohannan (Tiv), and Phoebe Ottenberg (Igbo) in James L. Gibbs, Jr., (ed.), *Peoples of Africa*. Urban Hausa life and its religious and political nature is explored in John N. Paden's *Religion and Political Culture in Kano*. Possibly the fullest account of a northern emirate society is S.F. Nadel's *A Black Byzantium on the Nupe*. Kanuri culture is the subject of Ronald Cohen's *The Kanuri of Bornu*, while Derrick J. Stenning's *Savannah Nomads* is the best work available on the Fulani. Simon Ottenberg's *Leadership and Authority in an African Society* and Victor C. Uchendu's brief but readable *The Igbo of Southeast Nigeria* are recommended on the Igbo. The classic work on the Yoruba is N.A. Fadipe, *The Sociology of the Yoruba*. This work, together with Robert S. Smith's *Kingdoms of the Yoruba*, is the best general work on Yoruba political society.

Understanding Islam in Nigeria still requires looking at John Spencer Trimingham's classic, *Islam in West Africa*, while Islamization is well-treated in *African Religion Meets Islam* by Dean S. Gilliland. Possibly the most important discussion on the synthesis of

Christianity and Yoruba religion is that by John D.Y. Peel in *Aladura: A Religious Movement among the Yoruba*.

Perhaps the best recent analysis of drought and climatic variation in northern Nigeria is Michael Mortimere's *Adapting to Drought*. For a general overview of population growth in Africa, including Nigeria, the World Bank study, *Population Growth and Policies in Sub-Saharan Africa*, is extremely useful, as are other standard World Bank and United National sources on current population trends.

Finally, much useful information on health and education can be found in the annual *Social Statistics in Nigeria*, published by the Nigerian Federal Office of Statistics.

Ife bronze head said to represent Olorun, god of sea and wealth

THE ECONOMY

A major feature of Nigeria's economy in the 1980s, as in the 1970s, was its dependence on petroleum, which accounted for 87 percent of export receipts and 77 percent of the federal government's current revenue in 1988. Falling oil output and prices contributed to another noteworthy aspect of the economy in the 1980s--the decline in per capita real gross national product (GNP--see Glossary), which persisted until oil prices began to rise in 1990. Indeed, GNP per capita per year decreased 4.8 percent from 1980 to 1987, which led in 1989 to Nigeria's classification by the World Bank (see Glossary) as a low-income country (based on 1987 data) for the first time since the annual *World Development Report* was instituted in 1978. In 1989 the World Bank also declared Nigeria poor enough to be eligible (along with countries such as Bangladesh, Ethiopia, Chad, and Mali) for concessional aid from an affiliate, the International Development Association (IDA).

Another relevant feature of the Nigerian economy was a series of abrupt changes in the government's share of expenditures. As a percentage of gross domestic product (GDP--see Glossary), national government expenditures rose from 9 percent in 1962 to 44 percent in 1979, but fell to 17 percent in 1988. In the aftermath of the 1967-70 civil war, Nigeria's government became more centralized. The oil boom of the 1970s provided the tax revenue to strengthen the central government further. Expansion of the government's share of the economy did little to enhance its political and administrative capacity, but did increase incomes and the number of jobs that the governing elites could distribute to their clients.

The economic collapse in the late 1970s and early 1980s contributed to substantial discontent and conflict between ethnic communities and nationalities, adding to the political pressure to expel more than 2 million illegal workers (mostly from Ghana, Niger, Cameroon, and Chad) in early 1983 and May 1985.

The lower spending of the 1980s was partly the result of the structural adjustment program (SAP) in effect from 1986 to 1990, first mooted by the International Monetary Fund (IMF--see Glossary) and carried out under the auspices of the World Bank, which emphasized privatization, market prices, and reduced government expenditures. This program was based on the principle that, as GDP per capita falls, people demand relatively fewer social goods (produced in the government sector) and relatively more private goods, which tend to be essential items such as food, clothing, and shelter.

THE COLONIAL ECONOMIC LEGACY

Early British Imperialism

The European struggle to establish forts and trading posts on the West African coast from about the mid-1600s to the mid-1700s was part of the wider competition for trade and empire in the Atlantic. The British, like other newcomers to the slave trade, found they could compete with the Dutch in West Africa only by forming national trading companies. The first such effective English enterprise was the Company of the Royal Adventurers, chartered in 1660 and succeeded in 1672 by the Royal African Company. Only a monopoly company could afford to build and maintain the forts considered essential to hold stocks of slaves and trade goods. In the early eighteenth century, Britain and France destroyed the Dutch hold on West African trade; and by the end of the French Revolution and the subsequent Napoleonic Wars (1799-1815), Britain had become the dominant commercial power in West Africa.

The slave trade was one of the major causes of the devastating internecine strife in southern Nigeria during the three centuries to the mid-1800s, when actually abolition occurred. In the nineteenth century, Britain was interested primarily in opening markets for its manufactured goods in West Africa and expanding commerce in palm oil. Securing the oil and ivory trade required that Britain usurp the power of coastal chiefs in what became Nigeria.

Formal "protection" and--eventually--colonization of Nigeria resulted not only from the desire to safeguard Britain's expanding trade interests in the Nigerian hinterland, but also from an interest in forestalling formal claims by other colonial powers, such as France and Germany. By 1850 British trading interests were concentrating in Lagos and the Niger River delta. British administration in Nigeria formally began in 1861, when Lagos became a crown colony, a step taken in response to factors such as the now-illegal activities of slave traders, the disruption of trade by the Yoruba civil wars, and fears that the French would take over Lagos. Through a series of steps designed to facilitate trade, by 1906 present-day Nigeria was under British control.

Mechanized farm in northern Nigeria Young farmers making vegetable beds at Esa-Oke agricultural settlement -- Courtesy Embassy of Nigeria, Washington

Young farmers making vegetable beds at Esa-Oke agricultural settlement
Courtesy Embassy of Nigeria, Washington

THE ROLE OF GOVERNMENT

Some of Nigeria's political leaders have advocated African socialism, an ideology that does not necessarily coincide with the Western socialist concept of the ownership of most capital and land by the state. Instead, the African variety usually has included the following: a substantial level of state ownership in modern industry, transportation, and commerce; a penchant for public control of resource allocation in key sectors; a priority on production for domestic consumption; and an emphasis on the rapid Africanization of high-level jobs. Despite the socialist rhetoric of some politicians, in practice Nigeria worked toward a mixed economy, with the directly productive sector dominated by private enterprise, the state investing in infrastructure as a foundation for private activity, and government providing programs and policies to stimulate private (especially indigenous) enterprise.

None of the major Nigerian political parties controlling national or regional governments from 1951 to 1966 (or 1979 to 1983) was a socialist party or a party strongly committed to egalitarianism. Even the Action Group, led during the first republic by the ostensibly anticapitalist Chief Obafemi Awolowo, had as its foundation the rising new class of professionals, businesspeople, and traders.

After Nigeria's 1967-70 civil war, petroleum output and prices increased rapidly. The government's control of the extraction, refining, and distribution of oil meant that, the state became the dominant source of capital. By the mid-1970s, petroleum accounted for about three-fourths of total federal revenue. To the most vigorous, resourceful, and well-connected venture capitalists (often politicians, bureaucrats, army officers, and their clients), productive economic activity lost appeal. Manipulating government spending became the means to fortune. Because of the rapid growth of the state bureaucracy and the establishment of numerous federally funded parastatals, the size of the government sector relative to the rest of the national economy hit a peak in the late 1970s.

In an effort that culminated in the 1970s, the Nigerian government gradually expanded its controls over the private sector, levying differential taxes and subsidies, increasing industrial prices relative to farm prices, favoring investment in key sectors, providing tariff and tax incentives to vital sectors, protecting favored industrial establishments from foreign competition, awarding import licenses to selected firms and industries, and providing foreign exchange to priority enterprises at below-market exchange rates. While the ostensible reasons for this policy of favoritism were to transfer resources to modern industry, expand high-priority businesses and sectors, encourage profitable enterprises, and discourage unprofitable ones, in practice the government often favored urban areas by promoting production that used socially expensive inputs of capital, foreign exchange, and high technology. Market intervention helped political and bureaucratic leaders protect their positions, expand their power, and implement their policies. Project- or enterprise-based policies (unlike reliance on the market) allowed benefits to be apportioned selectively, for maximum political advantage. Government made it in the private interest of numerous individuals to cooperate in programs that were harmful to the interests of producers as a whole. However, market-clearing prices (for farm commodities or foreign exchange), whose benefits were distributed indiscriminately, inspired little or no political support among farmers and businesspeople.

Beginning in 1979, the policy prescription of the World Bank (and IMF) was for African countries to refrain from interfering in foreign exchange and interest rates, wages, and farm prices; to privatize state-owned enterprises (especially agro-processing, farm input distribution, insurance, and retail and wholesale trade); to relax restrictions on foreign capital; and to encourage indigenous business ventures. By the early 1980s, Nigeria faced substantial international payments deficits in the midst of declining export prices and rising import prices, rising external debt payments, and negative economic growth. The government consequently undertook an its own SAP that was patterned along World Bank guidelines in 1986, with World Bank conditions including devaluation of the naira (for value of the naira-- see Glossary), reductions in real government spending, abolition of official agricultural marketing boards, the sale of public enterprises, liberalized trade, and reduced quotas and licenses.

LABOR

The size of Nigeria's labor force was difficult to calculate because of the absence of accurate census data. The labor force increased from 18.3 million in 1963 to 29.4 million in 1983. Census data apparently understated the number of self-employed peasants and farmers, but estimated that the proportion of Nigerians employed in agriculture, livestock, forestry, and fishing fell from 56.8 percent in 1963 to 33.5 percent in 1983. The percentage of the labor force employed in mining rose from 0.1 percent in 1963 to 0.4 percent in 1983. Exactly comparable data were lacking on manufacturing, but from 1965 to 1980 industry's share of the labor force rose from 10 percent to 12 percent whereas the services sector grew from 18 percent to 20 percent of the labor force (see table 5).

Table 5. Labor Force by Sector, 1983

Sector	Number (in thousands)	Percentage
Employed		
Agriculture, forestry, and fishing	9,296	33.5
Mining and quarrying	103	0.4
Manufacturing	1,343	4.8
Utilities	318	1.1
Construction	909	3.3
Trade, hotels, and restaurants	6,534	23.5
Transportation, communications, and storage	1,123	4.1
Finance, insurance, real estate, and business services	204	0.7
Community, social, and personal services	7,081	25.5
Other	865	3.1
Total employed	27,776	100.0
Unemployed	1,677	n.a.
TOTAL	29,453	n.a.

n.a.--not applicable.

Source: Based on information from Paul Hackett, "Nigeria-- Economy," in *Africa South of the Sahara, 1990*, London, 784.

Unemployment

The national unemployment rate, estimated by the Office of Statistics as 4.3 percent of the labor force in 1985, increased to 5.3 percent in 1986 and 7.0 percent in 1987, before falling to 5.1 percent in 1988 as a result of measures taken under the SAP. Most of the unemployed were city dwellers, as indicated by urban jobless rates of 8.7 percent in 1985, 9.1 percent in 1986, 9.8 percent in 1987, and 7.3 percent in 1988. Underemployed farm labor, often referred to as disguised unemployed, continued to be supported by the family or village, and therefore rural unemployment figures were less accurate than those for urban unemployment. Among the openly unemployed rural population, almost two-thirds were secondary-school graduates.

The largest proportion of the unemployed (consistently 35 to 50 percent) were secondary-school graduates. There was also a 40- percent unemployment rate among urban youth aged twenty to twenty-four, and a 31-percent rate among those aged fifteen to nineteen. Two-thirds of the urban unemployed were fifteen to twenty-four years old. Moreover, the educated unemployed tended to be young males with few dependents. There were relatively few secondary-school graduates and the lowered job expectations of primary-school graduates in the urban formal sector kept the urban unemployment rate for these groups to 3 to 6 percent in the 1980s.

MINING, PETROLEUM, AND ENERGY RESOURCES

Petroleum products accounted for two-thirds of the energy consumed in 1990, but Nigeria also had substantial resources in the form of hydroelectricity, wood, subbituminous coal, charcoal, and lignite. In the 1980s, most cooking was done with wood fuels, although in urban areas petroleum use increased. Coal, originally mined as fuel for railroads, largely had been replaced by diesel oil except in a few industrial establishments. Coal production fell from 940,000 tons in 1958 to 73,000 tons in 1986, only a fraction of 1 percent of Nigeria's commercially produced energy.

Tin and columbite output fell from the 1960s through the 1980s as high-grade ore reserves became exhausted. A fraction of the extensive deposits of iron ore began to be mined in the mid-1980s, and uranium was discovered but not exploited. Almost none of these minerals left the country, however, as petroleum continued to account for virtually all of Nigeria's mineral exports.

Mining contributed 1.0 percent of GDP in FY 1959, on the eve of independence. This sector's share (including petroleum) stood at more than 14 percent in 1988. Mining's general upward trend since 1959, as well as the fluctuations in the size of its contribution to GDP, can be attributed to the expansion and instability of the world oil market since 1973.

Table 6. Crude Petroleum Production, Selected Years, 1967-89
(in millions of barrels per day)

Year	Quantity	Year	Quantity
1967	333	1979	2,306
1969	564	1981	1,440
1971	1,628	1983	1,235
1973	2,140	1985	1,491
1975	1,861	1987	1,270
1977	2,184	1989	1,662

Source: Based on information from E. Wayne Nafziger, *The Economics of Political Instability: The Nigerian-Biafran War,* Boulder, Colorado, 1983, 150; Central Bank of Nigeria, *Economic and Financial Review* [Lagos], 23, June 1985, 80; and Economist Intelligence Unit, *Country Profile: Nigeria, 1990-91,* London, 1990, 25.

GOVERNMENT AND POLITICS

The story of Nigeria during the postcolonial era has been one of a search for the constitutional and political arrangement that, while allowing for the self-expression of its socially and culturally diverse peoples, would not hinder the construction of a nation out of this mosaic. In this search, the country has experienced cycles of military and civilian rule, civil war, and peaceful reconstruction.

If any nation typified political scientist Richard Sklar's characterization of the African continent as a "workshop of democracy," it would certainly be Nigeria. The country has experimented with different federal, state, and local government systems, learning more about its needs, resources, and constraints with each experiment. Despite the predominance of military regimes during the three postcolonial decades, Nigerian society has retained many of the fundamental building blocks of a democratic polity: vigorous entrepreneurial classes, a broad intelligentsia and numerous centers of higher education, a dynamic legal community and judiciary, diverse and often outspoken media, and, increasingly, courageous human rights organizations.

Brass statue of an oni, an Ife king of the early fourteenth or fifteenth century

Despite the differences in character and composition of the successive governments, it is still possible to identify the major threads of Nigeria's institutional evolution. As the nation finds itself once more on the threshold of transition from military to civilian rule, promised for 1992, examination of these threads is essential for understanding the Nigeria that will become the Third Republic.

Nigeria is essentially an artificial creation, which, like most other African states, is a product of colonialism. This fact is central to understanding the country's government and politics, which have been conditioned and bedeviled by the problems of accommodating several diversities: ethnic, linguistic (there are between 250 and 400 distinct languages), geopolitical, religious (there is a deepening cleavage between Christians and Muslims), and class.

Nigeria became politically independent on October 1, 1960, after about seven decades of colonial rule by the British. Prior to colonial rule, most of the groups that today make up the country were often distinguished by differences in history, culture, political development, and religion. The major differences among these precolonial groups pertained to their sociopolitical organization: anthropological and historical studies usually distinguish between societies that were centralized ("state") and those that were noncentralized ("stateless"). To the former category belonged the Sokoto Caliphate and the emirates of the north that, together with the Kanem-Bornu Empire, were advanced Islamic theocracies. Also included in this category were the Benin, Oyo, and other western kingdoms, as well as the Igala Kingdom in the middle belt (see Glossary) or lower north. In these centralized systems, there were clear divisions between the rulers and the ruled, usually based on wealth and ascribed status. Institutions of a distinctly political nature, as well as taxation systems, were already established. Of all the centralized systems, the Sokoto Caliphate with its vassal emirates had the most advanced form of state organization. Not surprisingly, it provided the model for the British colonial policy of indirect rule, i.e., the governance of indigenous peoples through their own institutions and rulers.

By contrast, in noncentralized systems such as those of the Igbo and other eastern and middle-belt groups, there was a diffusion of political, economic, and religious institutions and practices. Also to be found was a large measure of egalitarianism, democracy, and decentralized authority. Under the colonial policy of indirect rule, "traditional" rulers (known as warrant chiefs) were imposed on these stateless societies.

In the immediate precolonial period, a pronounced religious gulf separated the northern from the southern peoples. Islam had been introduced to the Hausa states and other northern parts in the fifteenth century, but it did not dominate until the jihad of 1804, which extended Islamic influence to most parts of the north and even to towns on the southern fringe, such as Oyo and Auchi. The southern peoples were devotees mainly of traditional religions who underwent increasing contact with, and exposure to, Europeans and Christianity. In some areas of the south, such as Benin and Warri, the penetration of Christianity dates to the fifteenth century. When the north experienced contact with Europeans much later, the spread of Christianity and other Western influences was slowed by the strong attachment to Islam. This fact explains in part the uneven rates of economic and educational development between the northern and southern peoples that have persisted to this day, with important consequences for government and politics.

It should not be assumed that the various population groups in precolonial Nigeria were completely separated from one another. Historians have established evidence of various forms of interaction among the peoples, the major ones being trade and superordinate-subordinate relationships. Powerful centralized systems, such as the Sokoto Caliphate and the Benin Empire, dominated several neighboring groups. Where no established group held sway over the others, as was the case among the Yoruba-speaking people in the nineteenth century, a pattern of conflicts and wars prevailed. On balance, there were pronounced differences among the people who later came to comprise Nigeria, especially when we consider the major regional groups. British rule did much to accentuate these differences and, in some cases, created new divisive sentiments. Even the nature of British conquest and the process by which its rule was established encouraged separate identities.

The conquest and colonization of the coastal area of Lagos and its hinterlands took place between 1861 and 1897. The conquest of the eastern region and the declaration of the Niger Coast Protectorate occurred in 1894. Finally, a third wave of penetration led to the declaration of a protectorate over the northern areas in 1900. In 1906 the colony of Lagos and the Protectorate of Southern Nigeria (which included the former Niger Coast Protectorate) were joined together to become the Colony and Protectorate of Southern Nigeria. Finally, in 1914 the northern and southern protectorates were amalgamated to become the Colony and Protectorate of Nigeria, although both parts continued to be administered separately.

During the period extending from amalgamation in 1914 to independence from colonial rule in 1960, Nigeria had four major constitutions, each named after the colonial governor who formulated it: the Clifford Constitution (1922), Richards Constitution (1946), Macpherson Constitution (1951), and Lyttleton Constitution (1954). Although the first two constitutions were virtually imposed on the country, the latter two involved some consultations with representatives of the people through constitutional conferences. At the Ibadan General Conference of 1950, Nigerian leaders agreed that only a federal system that allowed each of the three regions (north, west, and east as created by the Richards Constitution) to progress at its own pace would be acceptable. Until that point, the constitutions had a unitary orientation. In creating three regions and delegating some powers to them, the Richards Constitution was a forerunner of the later federal constitutions.

Although the regional leaders at the Ibadan conference had unequivocally declared their preference for federalism, the subsequent Macpherson Constitution was essentially unitary. It went farther than the Richards Constitution in devolving power to the regions but left the regions subordinate and closely tied to the central government. Because many Nigerian political leaders favored a federal system in which the regions enjoyed wide autonomy, the Macpherson Constitution engendered continuing opposition. Finally, in 1953, this constitution became unworkable.

Rather than self-government for the whole nation, the northerners wanted self-government as soon as practicable and only for any region that was ready for it. They believed that each region should progress politically at its own pace. When a constitutional conference was convened in London in 1953, a federal constitution that gave the regions significant autonomy eventually emerged. This Lyttleton Constitution was the one that remained in force, with slight amendments, until independence in 1960. It enabled the regions to become self-governing at their own pace: the two southern regions in 1956 and the northern region in 1959.

Several important developments that have continued to affect Nigeria's government and politics in the postcolonial period marked the period of colonial rule. First, British colonial rule nurtured north-south separation, which has remained the classic cleavage in the country. In particular, after Lord Frederick Lugard's pact with northern emirs to protect Islamic civilization, the north was shut off from much of the Westernizing influences to which the south was exposed. This protection gave the southern peoples a head start, especially in Western education. During the struggle for independence, northern leaders were afflicted by a constant fear of southern domination. Many of the northern responses to national politics to this day can be attributed to this fear. At the same time, with the creation of three regions that saw the northern region larger in size and population than the two southern regions, there was also a southern fear of northern domination. The image of a homogenous north, although contradicted by the cultural diversity of that region, continued in 1990 to feature prominently in most southerners' perception of national politics.

Second, in creating largely artificial regions, the British fostered the cleavage between ethnic majority and minority groups. Each region contained the nucleus of a majority group that dominated in its respective region: the Hausa/Fulani in the north, the Yoruba in the west, and the Igbo in the east. The major political parties that emerged in the regions and controlled them were based on these groups. With regional autonomy, the major groups became the major "shareholders" of the federation. Power-sharing and political calculations have consequently centered on ensuring a balance of power among these groups. The minorities, feeling oppressed and dominated, agitated for separate states in the regions. Although a panel was appointed in 1956 to inquire into the fears of the minorities and to explore ways of allaying them, their requests were not met until after independence.

Third, the uneven rates of development among the groups, which generally coincided with regional boundaries, strengthened the forces of regionalism. The creed became north for northerners, west for westerners, and east for easterners. Despite the periodic creation of more states during the postcolonial period, these regionalist feelings continued to affect national politics, especially in the distribution of national resources. One manifestation of this tendency was the ceaseless disagreements and rancor over revenue allocation.

Another consequence of these regional and ethnic divisions was the fragmentation of the national elite. Unlike a few other African countries, Nigeria had no fully national leaders at independence. Nnamdi Azikiwe, an Igbo, who had the greatest potential for becoming a national leader, was forced by regionalist pressures to become a sectional leader. The other leaders during the postindependence period--Ahmadu Bello, Abubakar Tafawa Balewa, Obafemi Awolowo, Michael Okpara, Samuel Akintola, and Aminu Kano--are best remembered as sectional leaders, even though they are usually called nationalists. This fractionalization of the political elite in turn reinforced ethnicity, regionalism, and religious conflicts, as these sentiments were often aroused in the competition for power, material resources, and privileges.

The colonial heritage, therefore, produced a country that was only weakly united. At some points, the regional leaders threatened to secede from the federation: in the early to mid-1950s northern leaders contemplated separation after their humiliation by southerners because of their refusal to support a motion for achieving self-government in 1956; in 1954 the Western Region threatened to separate itself if the colony of Lagos were not made a part of that region. There were strong countervailing factors that prevented breakup of the federation. First, British colonial rule had held the country together as one unit. Second, the regions had economic complementarity. In particular, given the export orientation of the colonial economy, the landlocked northern region depended greatly on the southern regions that had access to the sea. Third, in the final days of colonial rule, Nigerian leaders recognized the advantages conferred by the country's large size and population.

THE FIRST REPUBLIC

Nigeria became independent on October 1, 1960. The period between this date and January 15, 1966, when the first military coup d'état took place, is generally referred to as the First Republic, although the country only became a republic on October 1, 1963. After a plebiscite in February 1961, the Northern Cameroons, which before then was administered separately within Nigeria, voted to join Nigeria.

At independence Nigeria had all the trappings of a democratic state and was indeed regarded as a beacon of hope for democracy. It had a federal constitution that guaranteed a large measure of autonomy to three (later four) regions; it operated a parliamentary democracy modeled along British lines that emphasized majority rule; the constitution included an elaborate bill of rights; and, unlike other African states that adopted one-party systems immediately after independence, the country had a functional, albeit regionally based, multiparty system.

These democratic trappings were not enough to guarantee the survival of the republic because of certain fundamental and structural weaknesses. Perhaps the most significant weakness was the disproportionate power of the north in the federation. The departing colonial authority had hoped that the development of national politics would forestall any sectional domination of power, but it underestimated the effects of a regionalized party system in a country where political power depended on population. The major political parties in the republic had emerged in the late 1940s and early 1950s as regional parties whose main aim was to control power in their regions. The Northern People's Congress (NPC) and the Action Group (AG), which controlled the Northern Region and the Western Region, respectively, clearly emerged in this way. The National Council of Nigerian Citizens (NCNC), which controlled the Eastern Region and the Midwestern Region (created in 1963), began as a nationalist party but was forced by the pressures of regionalism to become primarily an eastern party, albeit with strong pockets of support elsewhere in the federation. These regional parties were based upon, and derived their main support from, the major groups in their regions: NPC (Hausa/Fulani), AG (Yoruba), and NCNC (Igbo). A notable and more ideologically-based political party that never achieved significant power was Aminu Kano's radical Northern Elements Progressive Union (NEPU), which opposed the NPC in the north from its Kano base.

There were also several political movements formed by minority groups to press their demands for separate states. These minority parties also doubled as opposition parties in the regions and usually aligned themselves with the party in power in another region that supported their demands for a separate state. Ethnic minorities therefore enabled the regional parties to extend their influence beyond their regions.

In the general election of 1959 to determine which parties would rule in the immediate postcolonial period, the major ones won a majority of seats in their regions, but none emerged powerful enough to constitute a national government. A coalition government was formed by the NPC and NCNC, the former having been greatly favored by the departing colonial authority. The coalition provided a measure of north-south consensus that would not have been the case if the NCNC and AG had formed a coalition. Nnamdi Azikiwe (NCNC) became the governor general (and president after the country became a republic in 1963), Abubakar Tafawa Balewa (NPC) was named prime minister, and Obafemi Awolowo (AG) had to settle for leader of the opposition. The regional premiers were Ahmadu Bello (Northern Region, NPC), Samuel Akintola (Western Region, AG), Michael Okpara (Eastern Region, NCNC), and Dennis Osadebey (Midwestern Region, NCNC).

Among the difficulties of the republic were efforts of the NPC, the senior partner in the coalition government, to use the federal government's increasing power in favor of the Northern Region. The balance rested on the premise that the Northern Region had the political advantage deriving from its preponderant size and population, and the two southern regions (initially the Eastern Region and the Western Region) had the economic advantage as sources of most of the exported agricultural products, in addition to their control of the federal bureaucracy. The NPC sought to redress northern economic and bureaucratic disadvantages. Under the First National Development Plan, many of the federal government's projects and military establishments were allocated to the north. There was an "affirmative action" program by the government to recruit and train northerners, resulting in the appointment of less qualified northerners to federal public service positions, many replacing more qualified southerners. Actions such as these served to estrange the NCNC from its coalition partner. The reactions to the fear of northern dominance, and especially the steps taken by the NCNC to counter the political dominance of the north, accelerated the collapse of the young republic.

The southern parties, especially the embittered NCNC, had hoped that the regional power balance could be shifted if the 1962 census favored the south. Population determined the allocation of parliamentary seats on which the power of every region was based. Because population figures were also used in allocating revenue to the regions and in determining the viability of any proposed new region, the 1962 census was approached by all regions as a key contest for control of the federation. This contest led to various illegalities: inflated figures, electoral violence, falsification of results, manipulation of population figures, and the like. Although the chief census officer found evidence of more inflated figures in the southern regions, the northern region retained its numerical superiority. As could be expected, southern leaders rejected the results, leading to a cancellation of the census and to the holding of a fresh census in 1963. This population count was finally accepted after a protracted legal battle by the NCNC and gave the Northern Region a population of 29,758,975 out of the total of 55,620,268. These figures eliminated whatever hope the southerners had of ruling the federation.

Since the 1962-63 exercise, the size and distribution of the population have remained volatile political issues. In fact, the importance and sensitivity of a census count have increased because of the expanded use of population figures for revenue allocations, constituency delineation, allocations under the quota system of admissions into schools and employment, and the siting of industries and social amenities such as schools, hospitals, and post offices. Another census in 1973 failed, even though it was conducted by a military government that was less politicized than its civilian predecessor. What made the 1973 census particularly volatile was the fact that it was part of a transition plan by the military to hand over power to civilians. The provisional figures showed an increase for the states that were carved out of the former Northern Region with a combined 51.4 million people out of a total 79.8 million people. Old fears of domination were resurrected, and the stability of the federation was again seriously threatened. The provisional results were finally canceled in 1975. As of late 1990, no other census had been undertaken, although one was scheduled for 1991 as part of the transition to civilian rule. In the interim, Nigeria has relied on population projections based on 1963 census figures.

Other events also contributed to the collapse of the First Republic. In 1962, after a split in the leadership of the AG that led to a crisis in the Western Region, a state of emergency was declared in the region, and the federal government invoked its emergency powers to administer the region directly. These actions resulted in removing the AG from regional power. Awolowo, its leader, along with other AG leaders, was convicted of treasonable felony. Awolowo's former deputy and premier of the Western Region formed a new party-- the Nigerian National Democratic Party (NNDP)--that took over the government. The federal coalition government also supported agitation of minority groups for a separate state to be excised from the Western Region. In 1963 the Midwestern Region was created.

By the time of the 1964 general elections, the first to be conducted solely by Nigerians, the country's politics had become polarized into a competition between two opposing alliances. One was the Nigerian National Alliance made up of the NPC and NNDC; the other was the United Progressive Grand Alliance (UPGA) composed of the NCNC, the AG, and their allies. Each of the regional parties openly intimidated its opponents in the campaigns. When it became clear that the neutrality of the Federal Electoral Commission could not be guaranteed, calls were made for the army to supervise the elections. The UPGA resolved to boycott the elections. When elections were finally held under conditions that were not free and were unfair to opponents of the regional parties, the NCNC was returned to power in the east and midwest, while the NPC kept control of the north and was also in a position to form a federal government on its own. The Western Region became the "theater of war" between the NNDP (and the NPC) and the AG-UPGA. The rescheduled regional elections late in 1965 were violent. The federal government refused to declare a state of emergency, and the military seized power on January 15, 1966. The First Republic had collapsed.

Scholars have made several attempts to explain the collapse. Some attribute it to the inappropriateness of the political institutions and processes and to their not being adequately entrenched under colonial rule, whereas others hold the elite responsible. Lacking a political culture to sustain democracy, politicians failed to play the political game according to established rules. The failure of the elite appears to have been a symptom rather than the cause of the problem. Because members of the elite lacked a material base for their aspirations, they resorted to control of state offices and resources. At the same time, the uneven rates of development among the various groups and regions invested the struggle for state power with a group character. These factors gave importance to group, ethnic, and regional conflicts that eventually contributed to the collapse of the republic.

The final explanation is closely related to all the foregoing. It holds that the regionalization of politics and, in particular, of party politics made the stability of the republic dependent on each party retaining control of its regional base. As long as this was so, there was a rough balance between the parties, as well as their respective regions. Once the federal government invoked its emergency powers in 1962 and removed the AG from power in the Western Region, the fragile balance on which the federation rested was disturbed. Attempts by the AG and NCNC to create a new equilibrium, or at least to return the status quo ante, only generated stronger opposition and hastened the collapse of the republic.

View of downtown Jos, a leading northern city
Courtesy Orlando E. Pacheco

Apapa, a major seaport near Lagos
Courtesy Embassy of Nigeria, Washington

MILITARY INTERVENTION AND MILITARY RULE

In most developing countries, there is a disruption of the civil-military equilibrium usually assumed in liberal democracies. In liberal tradition, the military is insulated from politics and subject to civilian control. In several developing countries, however, the military has not only intervened in the political process and overthrown the constitutional civilian authority, but it also often has established its supremacy over elected politicians. Even in those countries where the military has become almost a permanent feature of politics, military rule is still considered an aberration and symptomatic of a malfunctioning political system. In Nigeria, which typifies the scenario just presented, military rule was usually seen as a "rescue" operation necessary to save the country from civilian ineptitude. Military rule was not expected to last long; once the rescue operation was complete, the military should return to the barracks where they belonged and leave the governing to civilian politicians. The problem, however, was that although military officers accepted this rationale, military rule usually became self-sustaining.

From the onset of independent government in Nigeria in 1960 to the end of 1990, the military had ruled for twenty-one years. Altogether there were five coups d'état involving changes of government: those of January 15, 1966; July 29, 1966; July 29, 1975; December 31, 1983; and August 27, 1985. There was also an unsuccessful coup in which the head of state, General Murtala Muhammad, was killed in February 1976, and another was nipped in the bud in December 1985. An attempt to overthrow General Ibrahim Babangida was made in April 1990. Of these coups, only those of January 1966 and December 1983 were against civilian governments. Several explanations of military intervention have been added to those given by the coup plotters themselves. Whereas the latter have cited economic mismanagement and corruption, other explanations have ranged from the continuation of ethnoregional politics by military means to the personal ambitions of officers.

POLITICAL TRANSITIONS AND TRANSITION PLANNING

Political transition in Nigeria has been based not only on the military ruler's conviction that civil rule was desirable but also on the expectation of the people that, after the military performed its rescue operation, it should turn power over to civilians. Gowon and Buhari failed to meet this expectation, reducing their popular support and resulting in their overthrows. In accepting demilitarization as a necessary process, political transition has been on the agenda of every military government since Ironsi's, with the probable exception of that of Buhari. Ironsi set up a Constitution Review Committee, whose task was overtaken by the promulgation of the unitary decree; Gowon designed a transition plan, which he later aborted; the Muhammad/Obasanjo governments successfully executed a transition program and handed power over to civilians; and Babangida in 1990 was implementing a transition program, designed to culminate in civilian rule in 1992.

FEDERALISM AND INTRAGOVERNMENTAL RELATIONS

Given the territorially delineated cleavages abounding in Nigeria and the historical legacy of divisions among ethnic groups, regions, and sections, the federal imperative was so fundamental that even military governments--characteristically unitarian, hierarchical, and centralist--attached importance to the continuation of a federal system of government. The federation began as a unitarian colonial state but disaggregated into three and later four regions. In 1967 the regions were abrogated and twelve states created in their place. The number of states increased to nineteen in 1976, and to twenty-one in 1987 (see fig. 4). In addition, in 1990 there were 449 local government areas that had functioned as a third tier of government since the late 1980s.

In 1990 the Federal Military Government (FMG) included the president, the AFRC, the Federal Executive Council, the civil service, and a federal judiciary made up of federal high courts, courts of appeal, and the Supreme Court. The locus of power was the president and the AFRC, which possessed all law-making powers that could not normally be challenged in any court of law. The Federal Executive Council was an enlarged instrument of the president. The federal judiciary had appellate jurisdiction in appeals emanating from the state judiciaries. It did not have much independence because the government was directly involved in the appointment of judges and in the finances of the federal Judicial Service Commission. The integrity of the judiciary was constantly weakened by the setting up of special tribunals. Some of these tribunals were responsible for conducting trials of politicians of the Second Republic, while a few tried "miscellaneous" cases involving drug, smuggling, or foreign exchange offenses.

The state governments consisted of the military governor, a cabinet, the civil service, and the state judiciary. In most policy matters and in matters of finance, the state governments had to abide by federal directives and were subject to coordination by the National Council of States. The local governments had elected management councils comprising a chairman and councillors until June 1989, when these councils were dissolved. They were replaced by sole administrators, state civil servants appointed by the state governors. New local government elections were held in December 1989. In spite of the increasing powers of local governments, they remained subordinate to the state and federal governments and could be described as administrative agencies of these two higher levels of government.

"Civilian federalism" and "military federalism" corresponded to civilian government and to military government, respectively. According to federal theory, civilian federalism was the true form of federalism. It entailed government based on a constitutional sharing of power between the federal and state governments (and local government as well), using the principle of decentralization of powers. It was marked by party politics, which determined the nature of the federation, the configuration of powers, and the prevalence of the rule of law. The major elements of military federalism included the suspension and modification of the constitution; the omnipotence of the Supreme Military Council (SMC) at the center, and therefore the existence of only one decision-making level of government; and the ban on all (civilian) political activities. Because military federalism had been more common than civilian federalism, this model made the federal government the "master" in relation to the "dependent" state governments.

At independence largely autonomous regions possessed the residual powers in the federation and functioned almost independently. Even before the First Republic collapsed, the federal government was asserting greater powers. In particular, it controlled the national economy and possessed emergency powers to intervene in any region where law and order had broken down, as it did in the Western Region in 1962. Relative to the powers of the states in 1990, however, the regions were very powerful; they had separate constitutions, foreign missions, and independent revenue bases. All this changed under military rule.

The FMG expanded its control over the economy to the extent that in 1990 the states depended on it for up to 90 percent of their revenues. The federal government also took over such matters as education, which formerly belonged to the states. Because state governors were appointed on military assignment by the president, the states had little autonomy, except in deciding how to implement policies formulated by the federal government. Attempts by state governments to reassert their autonomy during the Second Republic were aborted by the return of military rule. Some state governments that were controlled by parties other than the NPN took the NPN-controlled federal government to court on many occasions over matters of jurisdictional competence. This trend was likely to recur during the Third Republic, when the states would seek to regain powers lost under military rule.

Another area in which successive military governments had changed intragovernmental relations was in the bolstering of local governments as a third tier of government. This process began with the 1976 local government reforms, which introduced a uniform local government system; gave local governments jurisdictional competence in matters such as markets, automobile parks, and collection of local taxes; and made it statutory for both the federal and state governments to give specified percentages of their revenues to local governments. Although these reforms were embodied in the 1979 constitution, state governments in the Second Republic refused to allow local governments any measure of autonomy, partly because they were themselves struggling to reclaim their autonomy. With the return of military rule, and as part of the transition toward the Third Republic, local governments were further strengthened.

Because the federal government accepted the recommendation of the Political Bureau that local governments should be made an effective tier of government, efforts had been made to reduce their control by state governments. In 1988 state ministries of local government, the major instrument of control, were replaced by directorates of local government in the governors' offices. All local government funds were paid directly to the local governments by the federal government rather than through the state governments. The functions and jurisdiction of local governments were streamlined, and state governments were asked to stay out of local affairs.

These measures increased the importance of local governments and infused in their civilian-elected functionaries a certain stubbornness that led to open conflicts with state governments over matters of jurisdiction. In several cases, these conflicts became the subject of litigation. State governments resisted the loss of jurisdiction, and many underscored the subordinate status of local governments at every opportunity. It would be a mistake, however, to conclude that local governments were sufficiently autonomous to be an effective tier of government.

The allocation of federal revenues was a problematic aspect of fiscal federalism because the states were unequally endowed and were virtually dependent on allocations from the federal government. Several revenue allocation commissions were set up, among them the

National Revenue Mobilization, Allocation, and Fiscal Commission established during the 1980s. The major problem arose from disagreements over the criteria that should be used in allocations--derivation, population, need, equality, or minimum government responsibility.

The federal-character principle emerged as a balancing formula in the 1979 constitution to forestall the domination of the government or any of its agenciesor resources by persons from one or a few states, ethnic groups, or sections. The uneven rates of development among the states and sections was largely responsible for the tension and controversy associated with the application of this principle, complicated by the pattern of distribution of the major ethnic groups.

The issue of state creation derived from the very nature of the federation. From three regions in 1960, the number of constituent units had increased to the present twenty-one states and the Federal Capital Territory. It was likely that a few more would be created (see Introduction.) The increasing number of states was a direct response to the demands and agitations of groups that were not satisfied with their positions in the federation. Initially, it was the minorities who agitated for more states, but in 1990 the need for states had changed. They were no longer needed to protect group identity and autonomy. Any group that sought a share of the "national cake" or that wanted to maximize its share of the cake demanded more states, although states were not designed to have an ethnic basis. An example of the latter was the Igbo, who constituted the majority in only two states, Anambra and Imo; the other major groups, the Hausa/Fulani and the Yoruba, represented majorities in about five states each. The Igbo had persistently pressed for equality with other major groups by demanding new states. Realizing that the creation of states could go on endlessly, the federal government tried to bolster local governments as another way of meeting the demands. The subordinate status of local governments, however, coupled with the continued use of the states as units for distributing national resources, made demands for more states a recurrent theme in Nigerian federalism.

According to the 1989 constitution, representation in the legislative branch was based both on population (the House of Representatives, with 453 members) and on states (the Senate with 64 members, 3 from each of the 21 states and 1 from the Federal Capital Territory), which together composed the National Assembly (see fig. 5). These figures were subject to change to reflect a possible increase in the number of states and the redistribution of population. The judicial branch consisted of the Federal High Court, the Court of Appeal, and, at the top, the Supreme Court with a chief justice and up to fifteen other justices.

THE CIVIL SERVICE

The civil service in 1990 consisted of the federal civil service, the twenty-one autonomous state civil services, the unified local government service, and several federal and state government agencies, including parastatals and corporations. The federal and state civil services were organized around government departments, or ministries, and extraministerial departments headed by ministers (federal) and commissioners (state), who were appointed by the president and governors, respectively. These political heads were responsible for policy matters. The administrative heads of the ministry were the directors general, formerly called permanent secretaries. The "chief" director general was the secretary to the government and until the Second Republic also doubled as head of the civil service. As chief adviser to the government, the secretary conducted liaison between the government and the civil service.

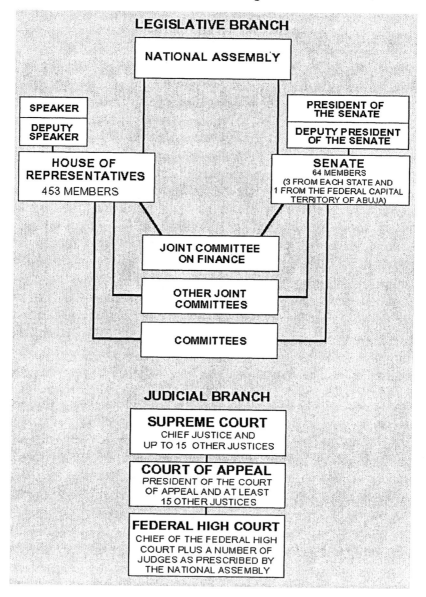

Figure 5. Legislative and Judicial Branches, According to 1989 Constitution
Source: Based on information from Constitution of Nigeria, 1989, Abuja, 1989.

The major function of the director general, as of all senior civil servants, was to advise the minister or the commissioner directly. In doing so, the director general was expected to be neutral. In the initial periods of military rule, these administrative heads wielded enormous powers. For some time, the military rulers refused to appoint civilian political heads. Even after political heads were appointed, it was years before the era of "superpermanent secretaries" to end. That happened in 1975 when, after Gowon's fall, the civil service was purged to increase its efficiency. Many of the superpermanent secretaries lost their jobs, and the subordinate status of permanent secretaries to their political bosses was reiterated. Another consequence of the purge, reinforced subsequently, was the destruction of the civil service tradition of security of tenure. The destruction was achieved by the retirement or dismissal of many who had not attained retirement age.

Until the 1988 reforms, the civil service was organized strictly according to British traditions: it was apolitical, civil servants were expected to serve every government in a nonpartisan way, and the norms of impersonality and hierarchical authority were well entrenched. As the needs of the society became more complex and the public sector expanded rapidly, there was a corresponding need to reform the civil service. The Adebo Commission (1970) and the Udoji Commission (1972) reviewed the structure and orientations of the civil service to make it more efficient. Although these commissions recommended ways of rationalizing the civil service, the greatest problems of the service remained inefficiency and red tape. Again in 1985, a study group headed by Dotun Phillips looked into the problems. It was believed that the 1988 reforms, the most current measures aimed at dealing with the problems of the service as of 1990, were based on this report.

Compared with the 1960s and 1970s, the civil service by 1990 had changed dramatically. It had been politicized to the extent that most top officials openly supported the government of the day. The introduction of the quota system of recruitment and promotion, adherence to the federal-character principle, and the constant interference of the government in the day-to-day operation of the civil service--especially through frequent changes in top officials and massive purges--meant that political factors rather than merit alone played a major role in the civil service.

The 1988 reforms formally recognized the politicization of the upper echelons of the civil service and brought about major changes in other areas. The main stated objective of the reforms was "to ensure a virile, dynamic and result-oriented civil service." As a result, ministers or commissioners vested with full executive powers were fully accountable for their ministries or commissions. The director general had become a political appointee whose length of tenure was dependent on that of the government of the day; in practice, this meant that directors general need not be career civil servants, thereby reducing the latter's career prospects. Each ministry had been professionalized so that every official, whether specialist or generalist, made his career entirely in one ministry, whereas previously an official could move among ministries. A new department--the Presidency--comprising top government officials was created at the federal level to coordinate the formulation of policies and monitor their execution, thus making it a clearinghouse between the president and all federal ministries and departments.

The reforms created a new style of civil service, but the structure might change under later governments with different priorities. In the past, the attempt by every government to effect changes in the civil service produced many discontinuities. Ministries have been constantly restructured, new ones created, and existing ones abolished. Nevertheless, the 1988 reforms might solve some of the problems of the civil service, because most civil servants tended to remain in their jobs despite reorganizations. Also, the move of the capital from Lagos to Abuja the early 1990s will provide new opportunities to apply the federal-character principle in replacing Lagosian civil servants unwilling to move.

INTEREST GROUPS AND NATIONAL POLITICS

Organized interest groups played a crucial role in national politics, especially under military regimes when other forms of direct political participation were prohibited.

Professional Associations

These associations were the most established interest groups in the country and included the Nigerian Bar Association (NBA), the Nigerian Medical Association (NMA), the Nigerian Society of Engineers, the Nigerian Economic Society, and the Nigerian Political Science Association. Many of these associations were mainly concerned with matters relating to the professional interests of their members. In pursuing professional concerns, however, they articulated and demanded important political actions. Between 1983 and 1985, for example, the NMA called a strike of medical doctors to demand an improvement in health care delivery. Its leaders were detained and the union banned until 1986. The NBA has been at the forefront of the movement for the observance of the rule of law and human rights in Nigeria. Most other associations held annual conferences at which positions were taken on national issues. The most distinguishing characteristics of professional associations were their elitist and urban base, and the nonviolent pursuit of their interests.

FOREIGN RELATIONS

A 1989 publication by the Federal Military Government, *Four Years of the Babangida Administration*, summarized the priority issues of Nigerian foreign policy: the abolition of apartheid in South Africa; the enhancement of Nigeria's relations with member countries of the European Economic Community (EEC), the United States, the Soviet Union, and with other major industrialized countries to increase the flow of foreign investments and capital into Nigeria; and continued support for international organizations, such as the Economic Community of West African States (ECOWAS), the Organization of African Unity (OAU), and the Non-Aligned Movement (NAM). Relations with other African states constituted the cornerstone of Nigerian foreign policy.

The Ministry of External Affairs was directly responsible for foreign policy formulation and implementation. Because matters were usually left in the hands of the minister and his officials, foreign policy positions could change radically from one minister to another, depending on the minister's orientation. In addition to the minister's immediate staff, there was a small foreign policy elite comprising other top government officials, interest group leaders, academicians, top military officers, religious leaders, and journalists. This elite exerted indirect influence through communiqués and press releases, as well as direct pressure on the government. In 1986 a conference--to which every stratum of this elite was invited-- was held to review Nigeria's foreign policy and recommend broad policy frameworks for the 1990s and beyond.

President Ibrahim Babangida, 1990
Courtesy Embassy of Nigeria, Washington

Several factors conditioned Nigeria's foreign policy positions. First, the ethnic and religious mix of the country required cautious positions on some issues, such as policy toward Israel. Nigeria found it difficult to restore diplomatic ties with Israel and had not done so as of 1990 because of Muslim opposition and sympathy with the rest of the Arab Muslim world. Second, Nigeria's legacy as an ex-British colony, combined with its energy-producing role in the global economy, predisposed Nigeria to be pro-Western on most issues despite the desire to maintain a nonaligned status to avoid neocolonialism. In 1990 this pro-Western posture was reinforced by Nigeria's "economic diplomacy," which involved negotiating trade concessions, attracting foreign investors, and rescheduling debt repayment to Western creditors. Third, the country's membership in and commitment to several international organizations, such as the United Nations and bodies mentioned earlier, also affected foreign policy positions. Fourth, and most important, as the most populous country in Africa and the entire black world, Nigeria perceived itself as the "giant" of Africa and the potential leader of the black race. Thus, Nigerian external relations have emphasized African issues, which have become the avowed cornerstone of foreign policy.

These factors have caused certain issues to dominate Nigerian foreign policy across various governments, but each government has had distinctive priorities and style. During the 1950s and early 1960s, foreign policy aimed at proper behavior in the international system, and British authorities played a major role in Nigerian foreign relations. Consequently, the Balewa government stressed world peace, respected sovereign equality, and maintained nonalignment based on friendship with any country that took a reciprocal position. After the fall of the First Republic, critics asserted that the government had been too proWestern and not strong enough on decolonization or integration, and that the low profile had been embarrassing. Nonetheless, Gowon continued to keep a low profile by operating within the consensus of the OAU and by following routes of quiet diplomacy.

The civil war marked a distinct break in Nigerian foreign policy. The actions of various countries and international bodies during the war increased awareness of the alignments within Africa and appreciation of the positive role that the OAU could play in African affairs. Whereas white-dominated African countries had supported Biafra, the OAU sided with the federation by voting for unity. The OAU stance proved helpful for Nigerian diplomacy. Nigeria first turned to the Soviet Union for support after the West refused to provide arms to the federation, and after the war, a less pro-Western stance was maintained. At the same time, Africa remained Nigeria's top priority. In the mid- to late 1970s, attention focused on the liberation of southern Africa, on the integration of ECOWAS, and on the need for complete economic independence throughout Africa. These goals were included in the 1979 constitution: promotion of African unity; political, economic, social, and cultural liberation of Africa; international cooperation; and elimination of racial discrimination.

NATIONAL SECURITY

On December 29, 1989, Nigerian president General Ibrahim Babangida, a Muslim, abruptly executed a major reshuffle of his ministers, the Armed Forces Ruling Council (AFRC), the national security organs, military state governors and important military commands, and took personal control of the Ministry of Defence and the security services. Ten days later, Lieutenant General Domkat Bali, a Christian, the erstwhile minister of defense who had been reassigned as minister of internal affairs, refused to accept his new post and resigned from the army. Nigeria's vice president since 1988 has been Admiral Augustus Aikhomu, a Christian. Babangida and Aikhomu have sought to share responsibilities so as to diffuse the "religious" factor in national politics. Despite these efforts, public protests erupted almost immediately against the president's alleged arbitrary decisions and discrimination against Christian middle belt (see Glossary) officers like Bali who lost their posts to northern Muslims. Then, on April 22, 1990, antinorthern rebel officers launched a bloody abortive coup against Babangida's regime, resulting in the arrest of 14 officers and more than 200 soldiers. After regaining control, Babangida announced his intention to overhaul the security system and to press ahead with his plan to restore civilian rule by October 1, 1992. Forty-two of the military rebels, including ten officers, were executed in July after sentencing by a special military tribunal; an additional twenty-seven were executed in September. Nine others, including three civilians, received prison terms ranging from seven years to life. Reports of army restiveness continued.

Benin bronze statue of warrior chief of the seventeenth century

This dramatic series of events underscored the instability and uncertainty that have pervaded Nigeria's politico-military system for more than a quarter of a century. It also emphasized the transience of any description of Nigeria's national security apparatus. Indeed, even if the Federal Military Government (FMG) were to achieve its goal of civilian restoration, the new government would almost certainly again restructure the armed forces and national security organs. Notwithstanding such anticipated changes, however, underlying conditions and trends continued to affect Nigeria's security environment into the 1990s.

At the onset of the 1990s, Nigeria was a regional power with a growing sense of self-assurance and a developing capability to demonstrate it. In the three decades since independence, its original Western orientation had shifted toward more neutral, autonomous, and Afrocentric strategic directions. Although still seeking a coherent vision of its role in Africa and the world, Lagos sought and played various roles as regional leader, peacekeeper, mediator, and arbiter. Domestically, the Nigerian polity had endured a civil war (1967-70); frequent political crises punctuated by military coups, attempted coups, and regime reshuffles; and the boom-and-bust cycle of an oil-based economy. As General Babangida's military government prepared to restore elected civilian rule in 1992, the armed forces were being drastically reduced in size and professionalized. External and internal security thus were closely linked.

Nigeria's size, demography, economic strength, and military capabilities set it apart as the dominant regional power. It was surrounded by smaller and weaker states, whose vulnerability to external influence and pressure could adversely affect Nigeria's security. The lack of regional rivals made large-scale conflicts unlikely but did not spare Nigeria border clashes with neighboring Cameroon and Chad, peacekeeping deployments to Chad and Liberia, a leadership role in the Economic Community of West African States (ECOWAS) peacekeeping force in Liberia, or strategic maneuvering against France and South Africa in Equatorial Guinea.

Nigeria's armed forces, estimated to be at least 94,500 in 1990, and among the largest in Africa, were modest in relation to the country's territory, population, and economic resources. The diversity of foreign-origin armaments reduced dependence on any single supplier but imposed significant logistical constraints; a fledgling domestic arms industry had also been established. Nigeria acquired naval, amphibious, and airlift forces and created a rapid deployment force for African contingencies, thus confirming its intention and capacity for power projection abroad. Externally, therefore, Nigeria remained basically secure and its defenses adequate.

The same could not be said, however, about internal security. A political formula for stability continued to elude successive Nigerian governments, economic and social conditions worsened during the 1980s, and the military became entrenched as the ultimate arbiter of power. Indeed, the future role of the military and the fear of coups, resulting especially from radicalization of frustrated junior officers and soldiers, haunted Babangida's regime as it attempted to create a durable constitutional government in a highly uncertain political environment. Ethnic, sectional, and religious cleavages marked the underlying political fault lines, from which the military itself was not immune, and organized labor and students continued to be the agents of public discontent. These internal sources of instability could be incited or intensified by an array of external forces, such as foreign subversion, oil prices, and foreign debt. To make matters worse, the national police and criminal justice system were strained beyond capacity. Crime was increasing, prisons were grossly overpopulated, and military rule by decree bred human rights abuses that were the object of public and international reproach.

On balance, one could find grounds for either optimism or pessimism about Nigeria's national security prospects. Indeed, there was an essential ambivalence among Nigerians and observers alike about the state's increasing autonomy and capability amidst countervailing threat perceptions. An increasing sense of national "manifest destiny" was thus tempered by limited capacity, and Nigeria's international power remained more potential than actual. Whether Nigeria would become more activist, interventionist, or assert overweening regional hegemony remained contingent on many external factors, such as its threat perceptions, the degree of regional stability, and the regional distribution of military capabilities. Much also depended on how well Nigeria coped with its social and economic crises, on the process and outcome of restoration of civilian rule, and ultimately, on the political disposition and competence of the military.

NATIONAL SECURITY ISSUES AND PERCEPTIONS

Safeguarding the sovereign, independence and territorial integrity of the state was the central pillar of Nigerian national security policy. Other guiding principles were African unity and independence, nonintervention in the internal affairs of other states, and regional economic development and security cooperation. Subordinate goals included military self-sufficiency and regional leadership. In pursuing these goals, Nigeria was diplomatic and flexible, but it employed coercive methods or measured force when necessary. Nigeria was an active participant in the United Nations (UN), the Organization of African Unity (OAU), and ECOWAS. In 1990 the leadership seemed intent on retrenchment, according priority to domestic political and economic problems, and displayed a mature and conciliatory approach to foreign policy.

Nigeria's location on the Gulf of Guinea, straddling western and equatorial Africa, its long land and coastal boundaries, and its offshore oil deposits defined the country's regional geostrategic situation. A British colonial background set it apart from its francophone neighbors, an historical anomaly that affected the local security milieu. Nigeria's relations with the major powers were shaped, in the case of Britain and France, largely by this postcolonial heritage. A short-lived defense pact with Britain after independence was terminated in 1962. In the case of the superpowers, whose interests in the region until the late 1980s were functions of their global rivalry and resource needs, Lagos deliberately balanced its relations with Washington and Moscow.

Nigeria's security concerns and threat perceptions emanated from many quarters. The country's dependence on the production and export of oil was aggravated by naval deployments of the major powers along the maritime transit routes of the South Atlantic and the Gulf of Guinea. Its experience of incursions by neighbors, coupled with fears of foreign influence or of subversion of neighbors by such potential adversaries as France, Libya, and South Africa, heightened Lagos's sensitivities about border security. Regional conditions also produced a sense of isolation and uncertainty, particularly shifts in the balance of power across northern Africa, political instability in West Africa, and encirclement by relatively weak francophone states with residual or formal defense ties to their former colonial power. More generally, conflicts throughout Africa and the related propensity for great power intervention (for example, in Chad, Zaire, Angola, and Ethiopia) and occasional eruptions of radicalization or militant pan-Africanism were inimical to Nigeria's interest. Finally, South Africa's apartheid policy, regional dominance in the continent, and nuclear capability constituted threats to Nigeria's national security goals throughout the 1980s. Broadly speaking, therefore, Nigeria's security conditions and concerns could be grouped into three separate but related categories: local and bilateral, African and regional, and global.

ARMED FORCES

Although the military history of the West African region extends back a millennium or more, Nigeria's present-day armed forces, like those of most African states, are the direct descendants of colonial military units. The officer corps was made fully indigenous by the mid-1960s, and in 1990 the Nigerian armed forces were among the largest and most professional in Africa. The military and political functions and international peacekeeping roles of the armed forces have expanded significantly but remained subject to several constraints. Nigeria was still heavily dependent on foreign arms but had embarked on a program of military industrialization. Voluntary military service and a large demographic base made recruitment easy, and training was highly professional. Nigeria's long-term challenge was to define its strategic interests and military missions more precisely and to achieve an appropriate modernized force structure to meet them.

ARMED FORCES AND SOCIETY

The military has been the dominant institution of the Nigerian polity since the mid-1960s when it became professional. The armed forces cannot rule the country indefinitely. However, no civilian successor regime can ignore the military's institutional demands and ultimate power to remove civilian authority. Long periods of military rule, concomitant claims on national resources, and the proliferation of linkages between the military and the economy have expanded military roles and evoked pronounced public responses.

INTERNAL SECURITY

Threats to internal security in Nigeria have been persistent and chronic. They stemmed from endemic divisions that were aggravated by rapid socioeconomic changes and by deteriorating economic trends. Political and civil disorder, extended periods of military rule, human rights violations, rampant crime, and inadequate security forces and penal institutions defined the internal security environment at the beginning of the 1990s.

Domestic Security

Nigeria has experienced substantial internal insecurity. Mass violence erupted frequently. During the five years immediately preceding the civil war, 124 riots were reported. The civil war between 1967 and 1970 produced about 2 million deaths. Regime instability also came to characterize political life, which was punctuated by a members of coups between 1966 and 1985; several attempted coups, often accompanied or followed by violent retribution; and periodic government reorganizations and leadership changes. Primary sources to potential dissent and opposition were illegal aliens, sectional-ethnic cleavages, religious sectarianism, the labor force and labor unions, and intellectuals. Although none of these groups was capable of overthrowing the government or of offering an alternative political formula, recurring and sometimes widespread violence involving one or more of these interests precipitated major security crises.

Nigeria's relative wealth, particularly during the oil-fueled boom of the 1970s, was a magnet for alien migrant laborers, many of whom entered illegally. Relations with these workers were tense and marked by two large-scale expulsions. In early 1983, Nigeria ordered all foreigners illegally residing and working in the country to leave within a matter of weeks; most had entered under the ECOWAS protocol on free movement of people and goods but had overstayed. At least 1.3 million West Africans--mainly from Ghana, Niger, Chad, and Cameroon--were expelled despite international protests. A second campaign to expel 700,000 illegal aliens took place in May 1985, but it was not clear how many were actually repatriated.

Nigeria's ethnic and religious heterogeneity was the most persistent source of violent conflicts. Although the issue of secession based on regional ethnic nationalism was settled by the unsuccessful Biafran experience and later muted politically by the abolition of the regions in favor of twenty-one states, the assertion or reassertion of the country's primordial "nations" remained a latent threat to national unity.

Internal Security Forces and Organizations

Between 1976 and 1986, internal security responsibilities in Nigeria were divided among the NSO, a central state security organ reporting to the president; the Ministry of Internal Affairs; the national police force; and the Ministry of Defence. As noted, the army was called upon to suppress domestic disorders on several occasions.

Intelligence Services

The NSO was the sole intelligence service for both domestic and international security during its ten-year existence. It was charged with the detection and prevention of any crime against the security of the state, with the protection of classified materials, and with carrying out any other security missions assigned by the president. Under the Buhari administration, the NSO engaged in widespread abuses of due process, including detention without charge and trial, arrests without pretext, and wiretapping.

The NSO's performance was bluntly criticized after the 1980 uprisings by the Maitatsine movement. It had penetrated the movement but failed to prevent it from instigating bloody riots.

Fulfilling one of the promises made in his first national address as president, Babangida in June 1986 issued Decree Number 19, dissolving the NSO and restructuring Nigeria's security services into three separate organizations under the Office of the Co-ordinator of National Security. The new State Security Service (SSS) was responsible for intelligence within Nigeria, the National Intelligence Agency (NIA) for foreign intelligence and counterintelligence, and the Defence Intelligence Agency (DIA) for military-related intelligence outside and inside the country. This reorganization followed a formal investigation of the NSO by former director Umaru Shinkafi.

Notwithstanding this rationalization and depoliticization of the national security services, they remained deficient in intelligence collection and analysis capabilities; they also were poorly equipped to counter security threats, such as covert foreign operations, dissident movements, coup plots, and border violations. The integrity of the new agencies also eroded after the prosecution in 1988 of the director of the DIA and the deputy director of the SSS, for the 1986 murder of *Newswatch* publisher Dele Giwa.

In the government reshuffle of December 29, 1989, Vice Admiral Patrick S. Koshoni, chief of naval staff since October 1986, became head of the National Commission for the Reorganisation of Internal Security; the Office of the Coordinator of National Security was abolished; and the SSS and NIA remained independent agencies directly responsible to the president.

Incidence and Trends in Crime

In the 1980s, serious crime grew to nearly epidemic proportions, particularly in Lagos and other urbanized areas characterized by rapid growth and change, by stark economic inequality and deprivation, by social disorganization, and by inadequate government service and law enforcement capabilities. Published crime statistics were probably grossly understated, because most of the country was virtually unpoliced--the police were concentrated in urban areas where only about 25 percent of the population lived--and public distrust of the police contributed to underreporting of crimes.

Annual crime rates fluctuated around 200 per 100,000 population until the early 1960s and then steadily increased to more than 300 per 100,000 by the mid-1970s. Available data from the 1980s indicated a continuing increase. Total reported crimes rose from almost 211,000 in 1981 to between 330,000 and 355,000 during 1984-85. Although serious crime usually constituted the larger category, minor crimes and offenses accounted for most of the increase. Crimes against property generally accounted for more than half the offenses, with thefts, burglary, and breaking and entering covering 80 to 90 percent in most years. Assaults constituted 70 to 75 percent of all offenses against persons. The British High Commission in Lagos cited more than 3,000 cases of forgeries annually.

In the late 1980s, the crime wave was exacerbated by worsening economic conditions and by the ineffectiveness, inefficiency, and corruption of police, military, and customs personnel who colluded and conspired with criminals or actually engaged in criminal conduct. In 1987 the minister of internal affairs dismissed the director and 23 other senior officials of the customs service and "retired" about 250 other customs officers for connivance in or toleration of smuggling. In October 1988, Babangida threatened to execute publicly any police or military personnel caught selling guns to criminals. Indeed, one criminologist argued that the combination of discriminatory law enforcement and official corruption served to manage rather than reduce crime, by selectively punishing petty offenders while failing to prosecute vigorously major criminals and those guilty of white collar crime.

The public response to official misconduct was to take matters into its own hands. In July 1987, butchers, traders, and unemployed persons in Minna vented their wrath over police harassment, intimidation, and extortion in a six-hour rampage against police and soldiers that was quelled by military units. In November 1989, when a police team raided suspect stores in

Katsina market, the merchants feared it was a police robbery and sounded the alarm, attracting a mob that was then dispersed by riot police. As loss of confidence in law enforcement agencies and public insecurity increased, so also did public resort to vigilante action. Onitsha vigilantes killed several suspected criminals in 1979. In July 1989, after a gang of about thirty armed men terrorized and looted a neighborhood in Onitsha without police intervention, residents vented their rage on known and suspected criminals and lynched four before riot police eventually restored order.

Drug-related crime emerged as a major problem in the 1980s. At least 328 cocaine seizures were made between 1986 and 1989, and the number of hard drug convictions surged from 8 in 1986 to 149 in 1989, with women accounting for 27 percent of the 275 total convictions during this period. Drug-induced psychoses accounted for 15 percent of admissions to four psychiatric hospitals in 1988. In a related development, the federal Ministry of Health reported in 1989 that about one-half of the drugs available in Nigeria were imitations, leading to a series of counterfeit and fake drugs decrees imposing increasingly higher penalties for violations.

Nigerians also participated heavily in international drug trafficking. One study found that 65 percent of the heroin seizures of 50 grams or more in British airports came from Nigeria, which was the transit point for 20 percent of all heroin from Southwest Asia. Another study disclosed that 20 percent of the hard drug cases in Britain involved ships of the Nigerian National Shipping Line. By the late 1980s, Nigerians were arrested almost daily in foreign countries, and hundreds languished in foreign jails for drug trafficking.

Security and Anticrime Measures

The Buhari and Babangida military administrations relied heavily on decrees and special tribunals to regulate public life and punish offenders. Soon after his takeover on December 31, 1983, Buhari issued a decree imposing life imprisonment on anyone found guilty of corruption, and he set up four tribunals consisting of three senior officers and a judge to try almost 500 political leaders detained since the coup. State Security (Detention of Persons) Decree Number 2 of 1984 suspended constitutional freedoms, empowered the chief of staff, Supreme Headquarters, to detain indefinitely (subject to review every three months) anyone suspected of "acts prejudicial to state security or . . . [contributing] to the economic adversity of the nation." The decree also authorized any police officer or member of the armed forces to arrest and imprison such persons. Likewise, the Recovery of Public Property (Special Military Tribunals) Decree Number 3 of 1984 set up tribunals to try former officials suspected of embezzlement and of other forms of misappropriation, also without right of appeal. The Exchange Control and Anti-Sabotage Tribunal dealt with certain economic crimes; a new press control law, Decree Number 4 of April 1984 (received August 1985), was enforced by a similar special tribunal, without appeal rights. The Special Tribunal (Miscellaneous Offences) Decree covered a wide range of offenses, including forgery, arson, destruction of public property, unlawful vegetable cultivation, postal matters, and cheating on examinations. By July 1984, Buhari had issued twenty-two decrees, including two retroactive to December 31, 1983, prescribing the death penalty for arson, drug trafficking, oil smuggling, and currency counterfeiting. In a related attempt to combat public indiscipline, Buhari's chief of staff,

Brigadier General Tunde Idiagbon, launched a largely symbolic and ineffective nationwide War Against Indiscipline (WAI) campaign in spring 1984.

Babangida's AFRC allowed the WAI campaign to lapse and took several other measures to mitigate Buhari's draconian rule, including abolition in July 1986 of the death sentence under Decree Number 20 of l984 for illegal ship bunkering and drug trafficking, and setting up an appeal tribunal for persons convicted under decrees 2 and 3 of 1984. However, the Babangida regime continued the Armed Robbery and Firearms Tribunals under which most of the death sentences were carried out without appeal. By early 1987, more than 300 people had been executed after conviction by these tribunals, and in 1988 another 85 executions were known to have been carried out under their sentences. The Treason and Other Offences (Special Military Tribunal) Decree of l986 empowered the AFRC to constitute another special tribunal to try military and civilian personnel for any offenses connected with rebellion. Special tribunals were also set up to hear cases arising out of civil disorders, such as the religious riots in Zaria in March 1987.

The most controversial decree remained Decree Number 2. In 1986 Babangida extended the initial detention period from three to six months but rescinded the extension after a public outcry. However, he extended detention authority to the Ministry of Internal Affairs in addition to the police and military authorities. In mid-1989 seventy to ninety persons were being held under its provisions, and in October the Civil Liberties Organisation appealed to the government to abrogate the decree and to release all those detained under it. In January 1990, the FMG amended the decree to shorten the precharge detention period to six weeks from six months, but in March the minister of justice stated that the decree would continue until the inauguration of the Third Republic.

Babangida's regime took additional legal and enforcement measures to combat illegal drug smuggling, including setting up special drug tribunals that meted out long prison terms and heavy fines; under these tribunals 120 convictions were attained by late 1987. Air transport laws were also toughened to deal with drug trafficking, and in November 1989 the minister of justice announced that a special tribunal would be set up to try air transport crimes. In October 1988, the minister of defense announced the establishment of a special "drug squad" to apprehend drug traffickers at home and abroad. Decree Number 48 of January l990 established a National Drug Law Enforcement Agency to eliminate the growing, processing, manufacturing, selling, exporting, and trafficking of hard drugs, and the decree prescribed stiffer penalties for convicted offenders. Although Babangida had abolished the death penalty for convicted drug dealers, by the end of the decade there were public calls to restore it. Stricter security measures were introduced at Lagos International Airport in 1989 to curb a crime wave there, and a plan was instituted in August 1989 to control black market activities.

The worldwide scope of crime demanded international cooperation to combat it. In l982 Nigeria and Cameroon decided to conclude extradition agreements. Nigeria also signed a regional security, law enforcement, and extradition treaty with Benin, Ghana, and Togo in December 1984; the treaty covered criminal investigation, dissident activities, currency and drug trafficking, and other criminal and security matters. In 1987 Nigeria and the United States concluded a mutual law enforcement agreement covering narcotics trafficking and expanded cooperation in other key areas. A related antidrug memorandum of understanding with the United States in March 1990 provided for a joint task force on narcotics and assistance to the new National Drug Law Enforcement Agency. A similar legal assistance pact with Britain to combat crime and drug trafficking was signed in September 1989. Nigeria also concluded an antidrug trafficking accord with Saudi Arabia in October 1990.

In the final analysis, domestic conditions will likely determine the fate of the Babangida regime and its successors for the foreseeable future. Although externally secure, Nigeria's internal problems were legion and daunting. The most salient were political fragility and instability; a military determined to be the final arbiter of political life; endemic domestic discord deeply rooted in ethnic and religious cleavages; overtaxed, ineffective, corrupt, and politicized internal security forces and penal institutions; and anticrime measures hopelessly inadequate to the task. Under such conditions, Nigeria faced major challenges in its political transition to the Third Republic.

* * *

There is voluminous literature on Nigerian military history and national security affairs. Much relevant material is published in Nigeria but is not readily accessible abroad.

Nigeria's regional strategic situation and outlook are evaluated by John M. Ostheimer and Gary J. Buckley's chapter, "Nigeria," in *Security Policies of Developing Countries*; and by Pauline H. Baker's "A Giant Staggers: Nigeria as an Emerging Regional Power" in *African Security Issues* and "Nigeria: The Sub-Saharan Pivot" in *Emerging Power: Defense and Security in the Third World*. Its participation in the ECOWAS defense pact is examined in Michael J. Sheehan's "Nigeria and the ECOWAS Defence Pact"; its maritime interests and strategy are discussed in Sheehan's "Nigeria: A Maritime Power?" and in Olutunde A. Oladimeji's "Nigeria on Becoming a Sea Power." Bassey Eyo Ate's "The Presence of France in West-Central Africa as a Fundamental Problem to Nigeria" and Ekido J.A. MacAnigboro and Aja Akpuru Aja's "France's Military Policy in Sub-Saharan Francophone States: A Threat to Nigeria's National Security" have analyzed the Franco-Nigerian security dilemma. Julius Emeka Okolo's "Nuclearization of Nigeria" and Oye Ogunbadejo's "Nuclear Capability and Nigeria's Foreign Policy" discuss Nigeria's nuclear policy options.

Data on military forces and order of battle are available in such annual publications as *The Military Balance*, published by the International Institute for Strategic Studies in London, and the various Jane's yearbooks. Supplementary information is available in John Keegan's *World Armies* and in the annual *Defense and Foreign Affairs Handbook*. Statistics and other information on arms transfers, military spending, and armed forces are contained in the United States Arms Control and Disarmament Agency's annual *World Military Expenditures and Arms Transfers* and in the Stockholm International Peace Research Institute's annual *World Armaments and Disarmament*.

Internal security and human rights conditions are evaluated annually in the *Amnesty International Report* and in the United States Department of State's *Country Reports on Human Rights Practices*. *The International Law of Human Rights in Africa*, compiled by M. Hamalengwa et al., is a useful reference for African states.

Country briefs on police forces are found in John M. Andrade's *World Police and Paramilitary Forces* and in Harold K. and Donna Lee Becker's *Handbook of the World's Police*. Alan Milner's now-dated *The Nigerian Penal System* provides essential historical background that is supplemented by Oluyemi Kayode's chapter, "Nigeria," in *International Handbook of Contemporary Developments in Criminology*.

Finally, specialized current news sources and surveys are indispensable for research on contemporary national security affairs. The most useful and accessible include the annual *Africa Contemporary Record*, and such periodicals as *Africa Research Bulletin*, *Africa Confidential*, *Defense and Foreign Affairs Weekly*, *Jane's Defence Weekly*, *International Defense Review*, and the most useful single source, *African Defence/Afrique Defense*. (For further information and complete citations, see Bibliography.)

GLOSSARY

fiscal year (FY)
An annual period established for accounting purposes. Through FY 1979-80 the Nigerian government's fiscal year ran from April 1 to the following March 31. The latter fiscal year was succeeded by a nine-month FY 1980 that ended December 31, 1980. From January 1, 1981, the fiscal year was made coterminous with the calendar year.

GDP (gross domestic product)
A value measure of the flow of domestic goods and services produced by an economy over a period of time, such as a year. Only output values of goods for final consumption and for intermediate production are assumed to be included in final prices. GDP is sometimes aggregated and shown at market prices, meaning that indirect taxes and subsidies are included; when these have been eliminated, the result is GDP at factor cost. The word *gross* indicates that deductions for depreciation of physical assets have not been made.

GNP (gross national product)
GDP (*q.v.*) plus the net income or loss stemming from transactions with foreign counties. GNP is the broadest measurement of the output of goods and services by an economy. It can be calculated at market prices, which include indirect taxes and subsidies. Because indirect taxes and subsidies are only transfer payments, GNP is often calculated at a factor cost, removing indirect taxes and subsidies.

International Monetary Fund (IMF)
Established along with the World Bank (*q.v.*) in 1945, the IMF is a specialized agency affiliated with the United Nations and is responsible for stabilizing international exchange rates and payments. The main business of the IMF is the provision of loans to its members (including industrialized and developing countries) when they experience balance of payments difficulties. These loans frequently carry conditions that require substantial internal economic adjustments by the recipients, most of which are developing countries.

Lomé Convention
A series of agreements between the European Economic Community (EEC) and a group of African, Caribbean, and Pacific (ACP) states, mainly former Euopean colonies, that

provide duty- free or preferential access to the EEC maket for almost all ACP exports. The Stabilization of Export Earnings (Stabex) scheme, a mechanism set up by the Lomé Convention; provides for compensation for ACP export lost thorugh fluctuations in the world prices of agricultural commodities. The Lomé Convention also provides for limited EEC development aid and investment funds to be disbursed to ACP recipients thourgh the European Development Fund and the European Investment Bank. The Lomé Convention is updated about every five years. Lomé I, took effect on April 1, 1976; Lomé II, on January 1, 1981; Lomé III, on March 1, 1985; and Lomé IV, on December 15, 1989.

middle belt

Traditionally an ethnic and political zone stretching from east to west across the central section of Nigeria and inhabited by many minor ethnic groups who had been unable to obtain significant political influence because of long-term dominance by the Hausa-Fulani and Kanuri emirates. As used by economists and geographers, the term does not always coincide with ethnic and political divisions but usually designates the area between the characteristic northern and southern economies; in this context the area extends roughly from 7°30'N to 11°N. Since the civil war of 1967-70 and the replacement of the former administrative regions by states, use of the term has diminished among Nigerians who wish to downplay the regional connotation formerly attached to it.

naira (N)

Nigeria's basic currency unit. It is subdivided into 100 kobo (k). The naira was introduced on January 1, 1973, replacing the Nigerian pound (q.v.) at the rate of two naira for one pound. At that time N1 equaled US$1.52. The naira subsequently lost value against the dollar; average exchange rate in 1990: N8.04 per US$1.00.

Nigerian pound (N£)

Basic currency unit until January 1, 1973, when it was replaced by the naira (q.v.). N£1 was valued at US$2.80 until December 1971; thereafter N£1 equaled US$3.04.

Paris Club

The informal name for a consortium of Western creditor countries that have made loans or have guaranteed export credits to developing nations and that meet in Paris to discuss borrowers' ability to repay debts. The organizaiton has no formal or institutional existence and no fixed membership. Its secretariat is run by the French treasury, and it has a close relationship with the World Bank (q.v.), the International Monetary Fund (q.v.), and the United Nations Conference on Trade and Development (UNCTAD).

Sahel

A narrow band of land bordering the southern Sahara, stretching across Africa, and including northern Nigeria. It is characterized by an average annual rainfall of between 150 and 500 millimeters and is mainly suited to pastoralism.

Special Drawing Right(s)
A monetary unit of the International Monetary Fund (IMF) (*q.v.*) based on a basket of
   international currencies consisting of the United States dollar, the German deutschmark,
   the Japanese yen, the British pound sterling, and the French franc.

Sudan
Geographical region (northern reaches now more commonly referred to as the Sahel)
   stretching across Africa from Cape Verde on the Atlantic Coast to the Red Sea between
   8° and 16° north latitude, just south of the Sahara Desert, characterized by savanna and
   semiarid steppe. Term derived from Arabic *bilad as sudan* (literally "land of the blacks").
   Not to be confused with Sudan, the country.

World Bank
Informal name used to designate a group of three affiliated international institutions: the
   International Bank for Reconstruction and Development (IBRD), the International
   Development Association (IDA), and the International Finance Corporation (IFC). The
   IBRD, established in 1945, has the primary purpose of providing loans to developing
   countries for productive projects. The IDA, a legally separate loan fund but administered
   by the staff of the IBRD, was set up in 1960 to furnish credits to the poorest developing
   countries on much easier terms than those of conventional IBRD loans. The IFC, founded
   in 1956, supplements the activities of the IBRD through loans and assistance specifically
   designed to encourage the growth of productive private enterprises in the less developed
   countries. The president and certain senior officers of the IBRD hold the same positions
   in the IFC. The three institutions are owned by the governments of the countries that
   subscribe their capital. To participate in the World Bank group, member states must first
   belong to the International Monetary Fund (IMF--*q.v.*).

BIBLIOGRAPHY

Acharya, Shankar N. "Perspectives and Problems of Development in Sub-Saharan Africa," *World Development*, 9, February 1981, 109-47.

Achebe, Chinua. *Anthills of the Savannah*. New York: Doubleday, 1987.

Achike, Okay. *Groundwork of Military Law and Military Rule in Nigeria*. Enugu, Nigeria: Fourth Dimension, 1978.

Adamolekun, Ladipo. (ed.). *Nigerian Public Administration, 1960-1980*. Ibadan: Spectrum Books, 1985.

Adamolekun, Ladipo. *Politics and Administration in Nigeria*. Ibadan: Spectrum Books, 1986.

Adamu, Haroun, and Alaba Ogunsanwo. *Nigeria: The Making of the Presidential System-- 1979 General Elections*. Kano, Nigeria: Triumph, 1983.

Adamu, Mahdi. *The Hausa Factor in West Africa*. Zaria, Nigeria: Ahmadu Bello University Press, 1978.

Adejuyigbe, Omolade, Leo Dare, and Adevanti Adepoju (eds.). *Creation of States in Nigeria: A Review of Rationale, Demands, and Problems*. (Papers presented at National Conference on Creation of States in Nigeria, February 24-28, 1982, University of Ife.) Lagos: Federal Government Printer, 1982.

Adekson, J. Bayo. *Nigeria in Search of a Stable Civil-Military System*. Boulder, Colorado: Westview Press, 1981.

Adenubi, A. (ed.). *Timeless Tai: A Collection of the Writings of T. Solarin*. Lagos: F and A, 1985.

Afigbo, A. *Ropes of Sand: Studies in Igbo History and Culture*. Ibadan: Oxford University Press, 1981.

Afonja, Simi, and Tola Olu Pearce (eds.). *Social Change in Nigeria*. London: Longman, 1986.

Africa Contemporary Record: Annual Survey and Documents, 1987-88. (Eds., Colin Legun and Marion E. Doro.) New York: Africana, 1989.

Africa South of the Sahara, 1990. London: Europa, 1989.

Agbakoba, Olisa. "In Defence of National Security: An Appraisal of the Nigerian Intelligence System," *Afrika- Spectrum* [Hamburg], January-February 1984, 51-58.

Agboola, S.A. *An Agricultural Atlas of Nigeria*. Oxford: Oxford University Press, 1979.

------. "Some Factors of Population Distribution in the Middle Belt of Nigeria." Pages 291-97 in John Charles Caldwell and Chukuka Okonjo (eds.), *The Population of Tropical Africa*. London: Longman, 1968.

Aguda, T. Akinola. *The Judiciary in the Government of Nigeria*. Ibadan: New Horn Press, 1983.

Ajayi, J.F. Ade, and Bashir Ikara (eds.). *Evolution of Political Culture in Nigeria*. Ibadan: Ibadan University Press for Kaduna State Council for Arts and Culture, 1985.

Ajayi, J.F. Ade, and Michael Crowder (eds.). *History of West Africa*. (3d ed.) (2 vols.) London: Longman, 1988.

Ake, Claude (ed.). *The Political Economy of Nigeria*. London: Longman, 1985.

Akindele, R.A. "Nigeria's External Economic Relations, 1960- 1985," Pt. 1. *Afrika Spectrum* [Hamburg], 1, 1986, 5-34.

------. "Nigeria's External Economic Relations, 1960-1985," Pt. 2. *Afrika Spectrum* [Hamburg], 2, 1986, 143-61.

Akindele, R.A., and Bassey E. Ate. "Nigeria's Foreign Policy, 1986-2000 A.D.: Background and Reflections on the Views from Kuru," *Afrika Spectrum* [Hamburg], 3, 21, 1986, 363-70.

Akintola, J.O. *Rainfall Distribution in Nigeria, 1892- 1983*. Ibadan: Impact, 1986.

Akpan, Ntieyang Udo. *The Struggle for Secession, 1966- 70*. London: Cass, 1972.

Alhaji, Alhaji Abubakar. "Amplification of the 1990 Budget," *Management in Nigeria* [Lagos], 26, January-February 1990, 13-23.

Alubo, S. Ogoh. "Doctoring as Business: A Study of Entrepreneurial Medicine in Nigeria," *Medical Anthropology*, 12, 1990, 305-24.

Alubo, S.Ogoh. "Human Rights and Militarism in Nigeria." Pages 197-207 in George W. Shepherd, Jr. and Mark O.C. Aniko (eds.), *Emerging Human Rights*. Westport, Connecticut: Greenwood Press, 1990.

------. "Power and Privilege in Medical Care: An Analysis of Medical Services in Post-Colonial Nigeria," *Social Science and Medicine*, 24, No. 5, 1987, 453-62.

------. "The Political Economy of Doctors' Strikes in Nigeria: A Marxist Interpretation," *Social Science and Medicine*, 22, No. 4, 1986, 467-77.

Aluko, Olajide (ed.). *Essays on Nigerian Foreign Policy*. London: Allen and Unwin, 1981.

Amnesty International Report, 1989. London: Amnesty International, 1989.

Andrade, John M. "Nigeria." Page 149 in John M. Andrade (ed.), *World Police and Paramilitary Forces*. New York: Stockton Press, 1985.

Andreski, I. *Old Wives' Tales: Life-Stories from Ibibioland*. New York: Schocken, 1970.

Anifowose, Rem. *Violence and Politics in Nigeria: The Tiv and Yoruba Experience*. New York: Nok, 1982.

Arlinghans, Bruce E. (ed.). *Africa Security Issues*. Boulder, Colorado: Westview Press, 1984.

Arnold, Guy. *Modern Nigeria*. London: Longman, 1977.

Aronson, I. *The City Is Our Farm*. Boston: G.K. Hall, 1978.

Asobie, H.A. "Bureaucratic Politics and Foreign Policy: The Nigerian Experience, 1960-1975," *Civilisations* [Brussels], 30, Nos. 3-4, 1980, 253-70.

Ate, Bassey Eyo. "The Presence of France in West-Central Africa as a Fundamental Problem to Nigeria," *Millennium* [London], 12, No. 2, Summer 1983, 110-26.

Awa, Eme O. *Federal Government in Nigeria*. Berkeley: University of California Press, 1964.

Awolowo, Obafemi. *Awo: Autobiography of Chief Obafemi Awolowo*. Ibadan: 1960.

------. *The People's Republic*. Ibadan: Oxford University Press, 1968.

------. *Thoughts on Nigerian Constitution*. Ibadan: Oxford University Press, 1968.

Ayandele, E.A. *The Missionary Impact on Modern Nigeria, 1842-1914*. London: Longman, 1966.

Ayeni, Victor, and Kayode Soremekun (eds.). *Nigeria's Second Republic*. Lagos: Daily Times, 1988.

Ayoade, John A.A. "Ethnic Management in the 1979 Nigerian Constitution," *Publius*, 16, No. 2, Spring 1986, 73- 90.

Azikiwe, Nnamdi. *My Odyssey: An Autobiography*. London: Hurst, 1970.

Babangida, Ibrahim Badamasi. "The March Towards a New Sustainable Political and Economic Order in Nigeria," *Management in Nigeria* [Lagos], 26, January-February 1990, 7-12.

Baker, Pauline H. "A Giant Staggers: Nigeria as an Emerging Regional Power." Pages 76-97 in Bruce E. Arlinghaus (ed.), *African Security Issues*. Boulder, Colorado: Westview Press, 1984.

------. "Nigeria: The Sub-Saharan Pivot." Pages 267-303 in Rodney W. Jones and Steven A. Hildreth (eds.), *Emerging Powers: Defense and Security in the Third World*. New York: Praeger, 1986.

------. *Urbanization and Political Change: The Politics of Lagos, 1917-1967*. Berkeley: University of California Press, 1974.

Barbour, Kenneth Michael, et al. *Nigeria in Maps*. New York: Africana, 1982.

Bascom, William Russell. *The Yoruba of Southwestern Nigeria*. New York: Holt, Rinehart, and Winston, 1969.

Beaver, Paul. *World Naval Aviation*. Coulsdon, Surrey, United Kingdom: Jane's Information Group, 1989.

Becker, Harold K., and Donna Lee Becker. *Handbook of the World's Police*. Metuchen, New Jersey: Scarecrow Press, 1986.

Beckett, Paul. *Education and Power in Nigeria*. London: Hodder and Stoughton, 1977.

Bello, Ahmadu. *My Life: An Autobiography*. London: 1962.

Berry, Sara. *Fathers Work for Their Sons: Accumulation, Mobility, and Class Formation in an Extended Yoruba Community*. Berkeley: University of California Press, 1985.

Bienen, Henry, and V.P. Diejomaoh (eds.). *The Political Economy of Income Distribution in Nigeria*. New York: Holmes and Meier, 1981.

Bienen, Henry, and V.P. Diejomaoh (eds.). *The Political Economy of Income Distribution in Nigeria*. New York: Holmes and Meier, 1981.

Bienen, Henry. *Political Conflict and Economic Change in Nigeria*. London: Cass, 1985.

Biersteker, Thomas J. *Multinationals, the State, and Control of the Nigerian Economy*. Princeton: Princeton University Press, 1987.

Boam, T.A. "Nigeria's Staff College," *Army Quarterly and Defence Journal* [Tavistock, Devon, United Kingdom], 108, No. 3, July 1978, 269-77.

Bohannan, Paul J. *Tiv Economy*. Evanston, Illinois: Northwestern University Press, 1968.

------. "The Tiv of Nigeria." Pages 513-46 in James L. Gibbs, Jr. (ed.), *Peoples of Africa*. New York: Holt, Rinehart, and Winston, 1965.

Bohannan, Paul, and Laura Bohannan. *A Source Notebook on Tiv Religion*. New Haven: Human Relations Area Files, 1969.

Bradbury, R.E. "The Kingdom of Benin." Pages 1-35 in Daryll Forde and Phyllis Mary Kaberry (eds.), *West African Kingdoms in the Nineteenth Century*. London: Oxford University Press, 1967.

Bulow, Jeremy, and Kenneth Rogoff. "Cleaning up Third World Debt Without Getting Taken to the Cleaners," *Journal of Economic Perspectives*, 4, Winter 1990, 31-42.

Caldwell, John Charles, and Chukuka Okonjo (eds.). *The Population of Tropical Africa*. London: Longman, 1968.

Caldwell, John Charles, and Pat Caldwell. "The Cultural Context of High Fertility in Sub-Saharan Africa," *Population and Development Review*, 13, 1987, 409-37.

Caldwell, John Charles, and Pat Caldwell.------. "Fertility Control as Innovation: A Report on In-depth Interviews in Ibadan, Nigeria." Pages 233-51 in E. van de Walle (ed.), *The Cultural Roots of African Fertility Regimes: Proceedings of the Ife Conference, February 25- March 1, 1987*. Ile-Ife, Nigeria: Department of Demography and Social Statistics, Awolowo University, and Population Studies Center, University of Pennsylvania, 1987.

Caldwell, John Charles, and Pat Caldwell.------. "The Limitation of Family Size in Ibadan City, Nigeria." Pages 347-63 in E. van de Walle (ed.), *The Cultural Roots of African Fertility Regimes: Proceedings of the Ife Conference, February 25-March 1, 1987*. Ile-Ife, Nigeria: Department of Demography and Social Statistics, Awolowo University, and Population Studies Center, University of Pennsylvania, 1987.

Callaghy, Thomas M. "Toward State Capability and Embedded Liberalism in the Third World: Lessons for Adjustment." Pages 115-38 in John Waterbury et al., *Fragile Coalitions: The Politics of Economic Adjustment*. New Brunswick, New Jersey: Transaction Books, 1989.

Callaway, Barbara. *Muslim Hausa Women in Nigeria*. Syracuse: Syracuse University Press, 1981.

Carter, H. Marshall, and Otwin Marenin. "Students and Police in Nigeria: The Power of Stereotypes," *Africa Today*, 27, No. 4, 1980, 21-34.

Central Bank of Nigeria. *Annual Report and Statement of Accounts, 1987*. Lagos: 1988.

Central Bank of Nigeria. ------. *Annual Report and Statement of Accounts, 1988*. Lagos: 1989.

Central Bank of Nigeria. ------. *Annual Report and Statement of Accounts, 1989*. Lagos: 1990.

Central Bank of Nigeria. ------. *Economic and Financial Review* [Lagos], 23, June 1985, 80.

Chubb, L.T. *Ibo Land Tenure*. (2d ed.) Ibadan: Ibadan University Press, 1961.

Church, Ronald James Harrison. *West Africa*. (8th ed.) London: Longman, 1980.

Claessens, Stijn, and Ishac Diwan. "Liquidity, Debt Relief, and Conditionality." Pages 213-25 in Ishrat Husain and Ishac Diwan (eds.), *Dealing with the Debt Crisis*. Washington: World Bank, 1989.

Clarke, John I., and Leszek A. Kosinski. *Redistribution of Population in Africa*. London: Heinemann, 1982.

Clayton, Anthony, and David Killingray. *Khaki and Blue: Military and Police in British Colonial Africa*. Athens: Ohio University Center for International Affairs, 1989.

Cline-Cole, J.A. Falola, H.A.C. Main, M.J. Mortimore, J.E. Nichol, and F.D. O'Reilly. *Wood Fuel in Kano*. Tokyo: United Nations University Press, 1990.

Cohen, Abner. *Custom and Politics in Urban Africa*. Berkeley: University of California Press, 1969.

Cohen, Ronald. *Dominance and Defiance: A Study of Marital Instability in an Islamic African Society*. Washington: American Anthropological Association, 1971.

------. *The Kanuri of Bornu*. New York: Holt, Rinehart, and Winston, 1967.

Coleman, James Smoot. *Nigeria: Background to Nationalism*. Berkeley: University of California Press, 1958.

Coleman, James Smoot. *Nigeria: Background to Nationalism*. Berkeley: University of California Press, 1958.

Collier, Paul. "Oil and Inequality in Rural Nigeria." Pages 191- 217 in Dharan Ghai and Samir Radwan (eds.), *Agraria Policies and Rural Poverty in Africa*. Geneva: International Labour Organisation, 1983.

Collins, Paul. *Administration for Development in Nigeria: Introduction and Readings*. Lagos: African Education Press, 1980.

Crowder, Michael. *The Story of Nigeria*. London: Faber and Faber, 1962.

Dada, Ayorinde. *National Conference on Mass Failure in Public Examinations*. Ibadan: Heinemann, 1987.

de St. Jorre, John. *The Nigerian Civil War*, London: Hodder and Stoughton, 1972.

Defense and Foreign Affairs Handbook, 1989. Alexandria, Virginia: International Media, 1989.

Denholm-Young, C.P.S. "R.W.A.F.F.," *Army Quarterly and Defence Journal* [Tavistock, Devon, United Kingdom], 105, No. 1, January 1975, 60-66.

Diamond, Larry, Juan J. Linz, and Seymour Martin Lipset (eds.). *Democracy in Developing Countries: Comparing Experience with Democracy*. Boulder, Colorado: Lynne Rienner, 1990.

Diamond, Larry. "Nigeria Update," *Foreign Affairs*, 64, No. 2, Winter 1985-86, 326-36.

Diamond, Larry. *Class, Ethnicity, and Democracy in Nigeria: The Failure of the First Republic*. New York: Syracuse University Press, 1988.

Dudley, Billy J. *Instability and Political Order: Politics and Crisis in Nigeria*. Ibadan: Ibadan University Press, 1973.

------. *An Introduction to Nigerian Government and Politics*. Bloomington: Indiana University Press, 1982.

------. *Parties and Politics in Northern Nigeria*. London: Cass, 1968.

Duru, R.D. "Problems of Data Collection for Population Studies in Nigeria with Particular Reference to the 1952/53 Census and the Western Region." Pages 71-77 in John Charles Caldwell and Chukuka Okonjo (eds.), *The Population of Tropical Africa*. London: Longman, 1968.

Dusgate, Richard H. *The Conquest of Northern Nigeria*. London: Cass, 1985.

Eades, Jeremy Seymour. *The Yoruba Today*. New York: Cambridge University Press, 1980.

Economic Commission for Africa. *The Abuja Statement*. (Proceedings of Conference, Abuja, June 15-19, 1987.) Abuja, Nigeria: 1987.

------. *African Alternative Framework to Structural Adjustment Programmes for Socio-Economic Recovery and Transformation (AAF-SAP)*. (E/ECA/CM.15/6/Rev. 3.) Addis Ababa: 1989.

------. *ECA and Africa's Development, 1958-1983*. (E/ECA/CM. 9/20.) Addis Ababa: 1983.

------. *Survey of Economic and Social Conditions in Africa, 1983-1984*. (E/ECA/CM 11/16.) Addis Ababa: 1985.

Economist Intelligence Unit. *Country Profile: Nigeria, 1989- 90*. London: 1989.

------. *Country Report: Nigeria* [London], No. 1, 1990.

------. *Country Profile: Nigeria, 1990-91*. London: 1990.

------. *Country Report: Nigeria*. Nos. 1-4. London, 1990.

Eicher, Carl K. and Carl Liedholm (eds.). *Growth and Development of the Nigerian Economy*. East Lansing: Michigan State University, 1970.

Ejiofor, Lambert U. *The Dynamics of Igbo Democracy*. New York: Oxford University Press, 1981.

Ekong, Ekong E. *Sociology of the Ibibio: A Study of Social Organization and Change*. Calabar, Nigeria: Scholars Press, 1983.

El Samhouri, Mohammed. "Flexible Exchange Rates and Export Instability: The Impact of the Post-1973 International Monetary System on the Developing Countries." (Ph.D dissertation, Kansas State University, 1989.)

Elaigwu, J. Isawa. *Gowon: The Biography of a Soldier- Statesman*. Ibadan: West Books, 1986.

Eleazu, Uma O. *Nigeria: The First 25 Years*. Ibadan: Heinemann, 1985.

Encyclopedia of the World's Air Forces. New York: Facts on File, 1988.

Erbe, Susanne. "The Flight of Capital from Developing Countries," *Intereconomics*, 20, November-December 1985, 268-75.

Fadipe, N.A. *The Sociology of the Yoruba*. Ibadan: Ibadan University Press, 1970.

Fafunwa, A. Babs. *History of Education in Nigeria*. London: Allen and Unwin, 1974.

Fage, J.D. *A History of West Africa: An Introductory Survey*. Cambridge: Cambridge University Press, 1969.

Falola, Toyin (ed.). *Britain and Nigeria: Exploitation or Development?* London: Zed Books, 1987.

Falola, Toyin, and Julius Omozuanvbo Ihonvbere. *The Rise and Fall of Nigeria's Second Republic, 1979-1983*. London: Zed Books, 1985.

Falola, Toyin, and Julius Omozuanvbo Ihonvbere. *The Rise and Fall of Nigeria's Second Republic, 1979-83*. London: Zed Books, 1985.

Faulkner, O.T., and J.R. Mackie. *West African Agriculture*. London: Cambridge University Press, 1933.

Fika, Adamu. *The Kano Civil War and British Over-Rule*. London: Oxford University Press, 1978.

Flint, John. *Sir George Goldie and the Making of Nigeria*. London: Oxford University Press, 1960.

Floyd, Barry. *Eastern Nigeria: A Geographical Review*. London: Macmillan, 1969.

Forde, Daryll, and G.I. Jones. *The Ibo and Ibibio-Speaking Peoples of South-Eastern Nigeria*. (Ethnographic Survey of Africa, Western Africa, Pt. 3.) London: Oxford University Press for the International African Institute, 1950.

Forde, Daryll, and Phyllis Mary Kaberry (eds.). *West African Kingdoms in the Nineteenth Century*. London: Oxford University Press, 1967.

Forde, Daryll, and Richenda Scott. *The Native Economies of Nigeria*. London: Faber and Faber, 1946.

Forrest, Thomas. *Politics, Policy, and Capitalist Development in Nigeria, 1970-1990*. Boulder, Colorado: Westview Press, 1992.

Gambari, Ibrahim Agboola. *Party Politics and Foreign Policy: Nigeria During the First Republic*. Zaria, Nigeria: Ahmadu Bello University Press, 1980.

Garba, Joseph Nanven. *Diplomatic Soldiering: Nigerian Foreign Policy, 1975-1979*. Ibadan: Spectrum Books, 1987.

Gastil, Raymond D. *Freedom in the World: Political Rights and Civil Liberties, 1987-88*. Westport, Connecticut: Greenwood Press, 1988.

Gboyega, Alex. *Political Values and Local Government in Nigeria*. Lagos: Malthouse Press, 1987.

Ghai, Dharan, and Samir Radwan (eds.). *Agrarian Policies and Rural Poverty in Africa*. Geneva: International Labour Organisation, 1983.

Gibbs, James L., Jr. (ed.). *Peoples of Africa*. New York: Holt, Rinehart, and Winston, 1965.

Gilliland, Dean S. *African Religion Meets Islam: Religious Change in Northern Nigeria*. Lanham, Maryland: University Press of America, 1986.

Graf, William. "Issues and Substance in the Prescription of Liberal-Democratic Forms for Nigeria's Third Republic," *African Affairs* [London], 88, No. 350, January 1989, 91-100.

------. *The Nigerian State*. London: Currey, 1989.

Green, Margaret Mackeson. *Land Tenure in an Ibo Village in South-Eastern Nigeria*. (Monographs on Social Anthropology, No. 6.) London: Lund, Humphries for London School of Economics and Political Science, 1941.

Grove, Alfred Thomas. *The Changing Geography of Africa*. Oxford: Oxford University Press, 1989.

Hackett, Paul. "Nigeria--Economy." Pages 775-89 in *Africa South of the Sahara, 1990*. London: Europa, 1989.

Hamalengwa, M., C. Flinterman, and E.V.O. Dankum (eds.). *The International Law of Human Rights in Africa: Basic Documents and Annotated Bibliography*. Boston: Nijhoff, 1988.

Hanning, Hugh (ed.). *The Peaceful Uses of Military Forces*. New York: Praeger, 1967.

Hansen, Art, and Della E. McMillan (eds.). *Saharan Africa*. Boulder, Colorado: Lynne Rienner, 1987.

Harbeson, John (ed.). *The Military in African Politics*. New York: Praeger, 1987.

Hill, Polly. *Rural Hausa*. Cambridge: Cambridge University Press, 1972.

Hopkins, Anthony G. *An Economic History of West Africa*. London: Longman, 1973.

Humana, Charles (ed.). *The Economist World Human Rights Guide*. New York: Facts on File, 1986.

Husain, Ishrat, and Ishac Diwan (eds.). *Dealing with the Debt Crisis*. Washington: World Bank, 1989.

Huth, W.P. *Traditional Institutions and Land Tenure as Related to Agricultural Development among the Ibo of Eastern Nigeria*. Madison, Wisconsin: Land Tenure Center, 1969.

Ibrahim, Jibrin. "The Political Debate and the Struggle for Democracy in Nigeria," *Review of African Political Economy* [Sevenoaks, Kent, United Kingdom], No. 37, December 1986, 38-48.

Idachaba, Francis Sulemanu, et al. *Rural Infrastructures in Nigeria*. (7 vols.) Ibadan: Ibadan University Press, 1985.

Ihonvbere, Julius Omozuanvbo. "Economic Contraction and Foreign Policy in the Periphery: A Study of Nigeria's Foreign Policy Towards Africa in the Second Republic," *Afrika Spectrum* [Hamburg], 3, 22, 1987, 267-84.

Ikime, Obaro (ed.). *Groundwork of Nigerian History*. Ibadan: Heinemann Educational Books for Historical Society of Nigeria, 1980.

Ikime, Obaro. *The Fall of Nigeria*. London: Heinemann, 1977.

Ikporukpo, C.O. "Politics and Regional Policies: The Issue of State Creation in Nigeria," *Political Geography Quarterly* [London], 5, No. 2, 1986, 127-39.

International Labour Organisation. "Jobs and Skills Programme for Africa." *First Things First: Meeting the Basic Needs of the People of Africa.* Addis Ababa: 1981.

Isichei, Elizabeth. *A History of the Igbo People.* London: Macmillan, 1976.

Ityavyar, Dennis. "Background to the Development of Health Services in Nigeria," *Social Science and Medicine,* 24, No. 6, 1987, 487-99.

------. "Health Services Inequalities in Nigeria," *Social Science and Medicine,* 27, No. 11, 1988, 1223-35.

Jane's Fighting Ships, 1989-90. (Ed., Richard Sharpe.) London: Jane's Information Group, 1989.

Jane's Weapon Systems, 1988-89. (Ed., Bernard H.L. Blake.) London: Jane's Information Group, 1988.

Jane's World Railways, 1989-90. (Ed., Geoffrey Freeman Allen.) Coulsdon, Surrey, United Kingdom: Jane's Information Group, 1989.

John de St. Jorre. *The Nigerian Civil War.* London: Hodder and Stoughton, 1972.

Johnson, Elmer H. (ed.). *International Handbook of Contemporary Developments in Criminology,* 2. Westport, Connecticut: Greenwood Press, 1983.

Jones, Rodney W., and Steven A. Hildreth (eds.) *Emerging Powers: Defense and Security in the Third World.* New York: Praeger, 1986.

Joseph, Richard A. *Democracy and Prebendal Politics in Nigeria: The Rise and Fall of the Second Republic.* New York: Cambridge University Press, 1987.

------. "Principles and Practices of Nigeria's Military Government." Pages 67-91 in John Harbeson (ed.), *The Military in African Politics.* New York: Praeger, 1987.

Kastfelt, Niels. "Rumours of Maitatsine: A Note on Political Culture in Northern Nigeria," *African Affairs* [London], 88, No. 350, January 1989, 83-90.

Kayode, Oluyemi. "Nigeria." Pages 473-93 in Elmer H. Johnson (ed.), *International Handbook of Contemporary Developments in Criminology,* 2. Westport, Connecticut: Greenwood Press, 1983.

Keegan, John (ed.). *World Armies.* (2d ed.) Detroit: Gale Research, 1983.

Kirk-Greene, Anthony Hamilton Millard (ed.). "A Sense of Belonging: The Nigerian Constitution of 1979 and the Promotion of National Loyalty," *Journal of Commonwealth and Comparative Politics* [London], 26, No. 2, July 1988, 158-72.

Kirk-Greene, Anthony Hamilton Millard (ed.). ------. *Crisis and Conflict in Nigeria: A Documentary Sourcebook.* (2 vols.) London: Oxford University Press, 1971.

Kirk-Greene, Anthony Hamilton Millard, and D. Rimmer. *Nigeria since 1970: A Political and Economic Outline.* New York: Africana, 1981.

Kolodziej, Edward A., and Robert E. Harkary (eds.) *Security Policies of Developing Countries.* Lexington, Massachusetts: Lexington Books, 1982.

Kowal, Jan M., and A.H. Kassam. *Agricultural Ecology of Savanna: A Study of West Africa.* Oxford: Clarendon Press, 1978.

Kowal, Jan M., and Donata T. Knabe. *An Agroclimatological Atlas of the Northern States of Nigeria.* Zaria, Nigeria: Ahmadu Bello University Press, 1972.

Labayle Couhat, Jean, and Bernard Prezelin (eds.). *Combat Fleets of the World, 1988-89.* Annapolis: Naval Institute Press, 1988.

Lagemann, Johannes. *Traditional African Farming Systems in Eastern Nigeria.* Munich: Weltforum, 1977.

Lessard, Donald, and John Williamson (eds.). *Capital Flight and Debt*. Washington: Institute for International Economics, 1987.

Lewis, Flora. "Oil Crisis of '73 Wreaking Economic Havoc," *Kansas City Times*, November 22, 1988, 7.

Lewis, W. Arthur. *Reflections on Nigeria's Economic Growth*. Paris: Organisation for Economic Co-operation and Development, 1967.

Lovejoy, Paul E. *Transformations in Slavery: A History of Slavery in Africa*. Cambridge: Cambridge University Press, 1983.

Lovejoy, Paul E., and Jan S. Hogendorn. *Slavery in Muslim Nigeria. The Abolition of Slavery under British Rule*. Cambridge: Cambridge University Press, forthcoming 1992.

Luckham, Robin. *The Nigerian Military: A Sociological Analysis of Authority and Revolt: 1960-67*. Cambridge: Cambridge University Press, 1971.

Mabogunje, Akin L. *Urbanization in Nigeria*. New York: Africana, 1962.

MacAnigboro, Ekido J.A., and Aja Akpuru Aja. "France's Military Policy in Sub-Saharan Francophone States: A Threat to Nigeria's National Security," *Strategic Analysis* [New Delhi], April 1989, 107-19.

Mackintosh, John P. (ed.). *Nigerian Government and Politics*. London: Allen and Unwin, 1966.

Madunagu, Edwin. *Problems of Socialism: The Nigerian Challenge*. London: Zed Books, 1982.

Marris, Peter. *Family and Social Change in an African City: A Study of Re-Housing in Lagos*. Routledge and Kegan Paul, 1962.

Martin, Susan. *Palm Oil and Protest: An Economic History of the Ngwa Region, South-Eastern Nigeria, 1800-1980*. Cambridge: Cambridge University Press, 1988.

Mason, Michael. "Population Density and `Slave Raiding': The Case of the Middle Belt in Nigeria," *Journal of African History*, 10, 1969, 551-64.

Mba, Nina. "Kaba and Khaki: Women and the Militarized State in Nigeria." Pages 69-90 in Jane L. Parpart and Kathleen A. Staudt (eds.), *Women and the State in Africa*. Boulder, Colorado: Lynne Rienner, 1989.

Meier, Gerald M. (ed.). *Leading Issues in Economic Development*. New York: Oxford University Press, 1976.

Meier, Gerald M., and William F. Steel (eds.). *Industrial Adjustment in Sub-Saharan Africa*. New York: Oxford University Press, 1989.

Melson, Robert, and Howard Wolpe (eds.). *Nigeria: Modernization and the Politics of Communalism*. East Lansing: Michigan State University Press, 1971.

Miles, William F.S. *Elections in Nigeria: A Grassroots Perspective*. Boulder, Colorado: Lynne Rienner, 1988.

Milner, Alan. *The Nigerian Penal System*. London: Sweet and Maxwell, 1972.

Morgan, William Basil, and John Charles Pugh. *West Africa*. London: Methuen, 1969.

Morgan, William Thomas Wilson. *Nigeria*, London: Longman, 1983.

Mortimore, Michael J. *Adapting to Drought: Farmers, Famines, and Desertification in West Africa*. Cambridge: Cambridge University Press, 1989.

Morton-Williams, Peter. "The Yoruba Kingdom of Oyo." Pages 36-69 in Daryll Forde and Phyllis Mary Kaberry (eds.), *West African Kingdoms of the Nineteenth Century*. London: Oxford University Press, 1967.

Nadel, Siegfried Frederick. *A Black Byzantium: The Kingdom of Nupe in Nigeria*. London: Oxford University Press for International Institute of African Languages and Culture, 1942.

Nafziger, E. Wayne. *The Economics of Developing Countries*. Englewood Cliffs, New Jersey: Prentice Hall, 1990.

------. *The Economics of Political Instability: The Nigerian- Biafran War*. Boulder, Colorado: Westview Press, 1983.

Nelson, Joan M., et al. *Fragile Coalitions: The Politics of Economic Adjustment*. New Brunswick, New Jersey: Transaction Books, 1989.

------. *Inequality in Africa: Political Elites, Proletariat, Peasants, and the Poor*. New York: Cambridge University Press, 1988.

Netting, Robert M. *Hill Farmers of Nigeria: Cultural Ecology of the Kofyar of the Jos Plateau*. Seattle: University of Washington Press, 1968.

Nicholson, Sharon. "Climate, Drought, and Famine in Africa." Pages 107-28 in Art Hansen and Della E. McMillan (eds.), *Saharan Africa*. Boulder, Colorado: Lynne Rienner, 1987.

Nicolson, I.F. *The Administration of Nigeria, 1900-1960: Men, Methods, and Myths*. Oxford: Clarendon Press, 1969.

Nicolson, I.F. *The Administration of Nigeria, 1900-1960: Men, Methods, and Myths*. Oxford: Clarendon Press, 1969.

Nigeria Year Book, 1987. Apapa, Nigeria: Times Press, 1987.

Nigeria. Executive Office of the President. Department of Information. *Nigeria 1982: Official Handbook*. Lagos: Academy Press, n.d.

------. Ministry of Economic Development. *Third National Development Plan, 1975-1980*. (2 vols.) Lagos: 1975.

------. Office of Statistics. *Social Statistics in Nigeria, 1985*. Lagos: 1986.

------. Ministry of Information. *Second National Development Plan, 1970-74*. Lagos: Federal Government Printer, 1970.

------. Ministry of National Planning. *Fifth National Development Plan, 1981-85*. Lagos: 1980.

------. National Assembly. *Government of the Federal Republic of Nigeria: Approved Budget, 1983 Fiscal Year*. Lagos: Federal Government Press, 1983.

------. Office of Statistics. *Annual Abstract of Statistics, 1986*. Lagos: n.d.

------. Office of Statistics. *Social Statistics in Nigeria, 1986*. Lagos: 1987.

------. Office of Statistics. *Social Statistics in Nigeria, 1987*. Lagos: 1988.

------. Office of Statistics. *Social Statistics in Nigeria, 1988*. Lagos: 1989.

------. Office of Statistics. *Social Statistics in Nigeria, 1989*. Lagos: 1990.

------. Office of Statistics. *Social Statistics in Nigeria*. Lagos: 1985.

"Nigeria." In *DMS Market Intelligence Report: Middle East and Africa*. Coulsdon, Surrey, United Kingdom: Jane's Information Group, October 1989.

"Nigeria." Pages 147-52 in Hugh Hanning (ed.), *The Peaceful Uses of Military Forces*. New York: Praeger, 1967.

"Nigeria: The Army's Role," *Army Quarterly and Defence Journal* [Tavistock, Devon, United Kingdom], 115, No. 2, April 1985, 135-40.

Nigerian Economic Society. *Poverty in Nigeria: Proceedings of the 1975 Annual Conference of the Nigerian Economic Society*. Ibadan: Ibadan University Press, 1975.

Nigeria's New Government: A Confidential Report on the Structure, Policies, and Personalities of the Babangida Administration. Washington: Defense and Foreign Affairs, October 1985.

Njaka, Elechukwu Nnadibuagha. *Igbo Political Culture.* Evanston: Northwestern University Press, 1974.

Norman, David W., Emmy B. Simmons, and Henry M. Hays. *Farming Systems in the Nigerian Savanna: Research and Strategies for Development.* Boulder, Colorado: Westview Press, 1982.

Nwabueze, Benjamin Obi. ------. *Nigeria's Presidential Constitution: The Second Experiment in Constitutional Democracy.* London: Longman, 1984.

Nwabueze, Benjamin Obi. *A Constitutional History of Nigeria.* Essex, New York: Longman, 1982.

Nwankwo, G.O. *The Nigerian Financial System.* London: Macmillan, 1980.

Nwokedi, Emeka. "Sub-Regional Security and Nigerian Foreign Policy," *African Affairs* [London], 84, No. 335, April 1985, 195-209.

Nye, Peter Hague, and David J. Greenland. *The Soil under Shifting Cultivation.* (Technical Communication No. 51.) Harpenden, Hertfordshire, United Kingdom: Commonwealth Bureau of Soils, 1960.

Nzimiro, Ikenna. "Militarization in Nigeria: Its Economic and Social Consequences," *International Social Science Journal* [Oxford], 35, 1 (No. 95), 1983, 125-39.

Ogunbadejo, Oye. "Nuclear Capability and Nigeria's Foreign Policy." Pages A136-A151 in Colin Legum (ed.), *Africa Contemporary Record,* 16. New York: Africana, 1985.

------. "Nuclear Nonproliferation in Africa: The Challenges Ahead," *Arms Control,* 10, No. 1, May 1989, 68-86.

Okigbo, Pius N.C. "Interpersonal Income Distribution in Nigeria." Pages 313-29 in Nigerian Economic Society, *Poverty in Nigeria: Proceedings of the 1975 Annual Conference of the Nigerian Economic Society.* Ibadan: Ibadan University Press, 1975.

------. *National Development Planning in Nigeria, 1900- 92.* London: Currey, 1989.

Okolo, Julius Emeka. "Nuclearization of Nigeria," *Comparative Strategy,* 5, No. 2, 1985, 135-57.

------. "Securing West Africa: The ECOWAS Defence Pact," *World Today* [London], 39, No. 5, May 1983, 177-84.

Okonjo, Chukuka. "A Preliminary Medium Estimate of the 1952 Mid- Year Population of Nigeria." Pages 78-95 in John Charle Caldwell and Chukuka Okonjo (eds.), *The Population of Tropical Africa.* London: Longman, 1968.

Okonjo. I.M. *British Administration in Nigeria, 1900-1950: A Nigerian View.* New York: Nok, 1974.

Okotie-Eboh, Festus Sam. *The Rededication Budget: Budget Speech, 31st March 1965.* Lagos: Ministry of Information, 1965.

Oladimeji, Olutunde A. "Nigeria on Becoming a Sea Power," *Proceedings of the United States Naval Institute,* 115, 3, March 1989, 69-74.

Olowu, Dele. "Bureaucratic Corruption and Public Accountability in Nigeria: An Assessment of Recent Developments," *International Review of Administrative Sciences* [Brussels], 51, No. 1, 1985, 7-12.

Oluleye, James J. *Military Leadership in Nigeria, 1966-1979.* Ibadan: Ibadan University Press, 1985.

Omu, Paul Ufuoma. "The Nigerian Command and Staff College, Jaji: Ten Years of Development and Success," *Army Quarterly and Defence Journal* [Tavistock, Devon, United Kingdom], 117, No. 2, April 1987, 166-70.

Ostheimer, John M., and Gary J. Buckley. "Nigeria." Pages 285-303 in Edward A. Kolodziej and Robert E. Harkavy (eds.), *Security Policies of Developing Countries*. Lexington, Massachusetts: Lexington Books, 1982.

Othman, Shehu. "Classes, Crises, and Coup: The Demise of Shagari's Regime," *African Affairs* [London], 83, No. 333, October 1984, 441-61.

Otite, Onigu. *Autonomy and Independence: The Urhobo Kingdom of Okpe in Modern Nigeria*. Evanston: Northwestern University Press, 1973.

Ottenberg, Phoebe. "The Afikpo Ibo of Eastern Nigeria." Pages 1- 39 in James L. Gibbs, Jr. (ed.), *Peoples of Africa*. New York: Holt, Rinehart, and Winston, 1965.

Ottenberg, Simon. *Leadership and Authority in an African Society: The Afikpo Village Group*. Seattle: University of Washington Press, 1971.

Oyediran, Oye (ed.). *Essays on Local Government and Administration in Nigeria*. Lagos: 1988.

------. *Nigerian Government and Politics under Military Rule, 1966-79*. New York: St. Martin's Press, 1979.

Oyewole, A. *Historical Dictionary of Nigeria*. (African Historical Dictionaries, No. 40.) Metuchen, New Jersey: Scarecrow Press, 1987.

Oyovbaire, Sam Egite (ed.). *Federalism in Nigeria: A Study in the Development of the Nigerian State*. New York: St. Martin's Press, 1984.

Ozigi, A.O. *Education in Nigeria*. London: Allen and Unwin, 1981.

Paden, John N. *Ahmadu Bello, Sardauna of Sokoto: Values and Leadership in Nigeria*. London: Hodder and Stoughton, 1986.

-------. *Religion and Political Culture in Kano*. Berkeley: University of California Press, 1973.

Panter-Brick, S.K. (ed.). *Nigerian Politics and Military Rule: Prelude to the Civil War*. London: Athlone Press, 1970.

------. *Soldiers and Oil: The Political Transformation of Nigeria*. London: Cass, 1978.

Parpart, Jane L., Kathleen A. Staudt (eds.). *Women and the State in Africa*. Boulder, Colorado: Lynne Rienner, 1989.

Peel, John David Yeadon. *Aladura: A Religious Movement among the Yoruba*. London: Oxford University Press for International African Institute, 1968.

Peshkin, Alan. *Kanuri School Children*. New York: Holt, Rinehart, and Winston, 1972.

Phillips, Anne. *The Enigma of Colonialism: British Policy in West Africa*. Bloomington: Indiana University Press, 1989.

Population Reference Bureau. *1990 World Population Data Sheet*. Washington: 1990.

Post, Ken. W.J. *The Nigerian Federal Election of 1959*. Ibadan: 1963.

Pullan, Robert Alan. "The Concept of the Middle Belt: A Climatic Definition," *Nigerian Geographic Journal* [Lagos], 5, 1962, 39-52.

Rake, Alan. "And Now the Struggle for Real Development," *African Development*, Nos. 10-12, December 1976, 1263-64.

Rimmer, Douglas. "Alternatives to Structural Adjustment and the Future of the Nigerian Economy." Paper for Conference on Democratic Transition and Structural Adjustment in Nigeria, Hoover Institution, Stanford, California, August 25-29, 1990.

Rogoff, Kenneth. "Symposium on New Institutions for Developing Country Debt," *Journal of Economic Perspectives*, 4, Winter 1990, 3-6.

Sada, Pius O., and F.O. Odemerho. *Environmental Issues and Management in Nigerian Development*. Ibadan: Evans Brothers, 1988.

Sanda, A.O., Olusola Ojo, and Victor Aveni (eds.). *The Impact of Military Rule on Nigeria's Administration*. Ile-Ife, Nigeria: Faculty of Administration, University of Ife, ca. 1987.

Schatz, Sayre P. *Nigerian Capitalism*. Berkeley: University of California Press, 1978.

------. "Pirate Capitalism and Inert Economy of Nigeria," *Journal of Modern African Studies*, 22, March 1984, 45-57.

Schenk, Herbert H., and Leo Waldrick. *1984 World's Submarine Telephone Cable Systems*. Washington: GPO for National Telecommunications and Information Administration, Department of Commerce, 1984.

Schram, Ralph. *A History of the Nigerian Health Services*. Ibadan: Ibadan University Press, 1971.

Schwarz, F. *Nigeria: The Tribes, the Nation, or the Race--The Politics of Independence*. Westport, Connecticut: Westview Press, 1965.

Shaw, Timothy M., and Julius Omozuanvbo Ihonvbere. *Towards a Political Economy of Nigeria: Petroleum and Politics at the (Semi)-Periphery*. Brookfield, Vermont: Avebury, 1988.

Sheehan, Michael J. "Nigeria: A Maritime Power?" Pages 395-407 in Jeffrey C. Stone (ed.), *Africa and the Sea*. Aberdeen: Aberdeen University African Studies Group, 1985.

------. "Nigeria and the ECOWAS Defence Pact?," *Army Quarterly and Defence Journal* [Tavistock, Devon, United Kingdom], 117, No. 1, January 1986, 9-15.

Shepherd, George W., and Mark O.C. Aniko (eds.). *Emerging Human Rights*. Westport, Connecticut: Greenwood Press, 1990.

Sklar, Richard L. *Nigerian Political Parties: Power in an Emergent African Nation*. Princeton: Princeton University Press, 1963.

Sklar, Richard L. *Nigerian Political Parties: Power in an Emergent African Nation*. Princeton: Princeton University Press, 1963.

Smith, M.G. "The Hausa of Northern Nigeria." Pages 119-55 in James L. Gibbs, Jr. (ed.), *Peoples of Africa*. New York: Holt, Rinehart, and Winston, 1965.

Smith, Mary F. *Baba of Karo: A Woman of the Muslim Hausa*. London: Faber and Faber, 1954.

Smith, Robert S. *Kingdoms of the Yoruba*. (3d ed.) Madison: University of Wisconsin Press, 1988.

Soyinka, Wole. *Ake: The Years of Childhood*. London: Collings, 1981.

------. *Isara: A Voyage Around `Essay'*. New York: Random House, 1989.

------. *The Man Died: Prison Notes of Wole Soyinka*. New York: Harper and Row, 1982.

Stenning, Derrick J. *Savannah Nomads*. London: Oxford University Press, 1959.

Stolper, Wolfgang F. *Planning Without Facts: Lessons in Resource Allocation for Nigeria's Development*. Cambridge: Harvard University Press, 1966.

------. "Problems of Development Planning." Pages 819-23 in Gerald M. Meier (ed.), *Leading Issues in Economic Development*. New York: Oxford University Press, 1976.

------. "Social Factors in Economic Planning with Special Reference to Nigeria." Pages 225-30 in Carl K. Eicher and Carl Liedholm (eds.), *Growth and Development of the Nigerian Economy*. East Lansing: Michigan State University, 1970.

Stone, Jeffrey C. (ed.). *Africa and the Sea*. Aberdeen: Aberdeen University African Studies Group, 1985.

Stremlau, John J. *The International Politics of the Nigerian Civil War, 1967-1970*. Princeton: Princeton University Press, 1977.

Stremlau, John J. *The International Politics of the Nigerian Civil War, 1967-1970*. Princeton: Princeton University Press, 1977.

Suberu, Rotimi Timothy. "Federalism and Nigeria's Political Future: A Comment," *African Affairs* [London], 87, No. 348, July 1988, 431-39.

Taylor, Michael J.H. "Nigeria." Page 112 in *Encyclopedia of the World's Air Forces*. New York: Facts on File, 1988.

Teal, Francis. "Domestic Policies, External Constraints, and Economic Development in Nigeria since 1950," *African Affairs* [London], 87, No. 346, January 1988, 69-81.

The Military Balance, 1989-1990. London: Brassey's for International Institute for Strategic Studies, 1989.

Thomas, M.F., and G.W. Whittington. *Environment and Land Use in Africa*. London: Methuen, 1969.

Trimingham, John Spencer. *Islam in West Africa*. London: Oxford University Press, 1959.

Tukur, Mahmud, and Tunji Olagunju (eds.). *Nigeria in Search of a Viable Polity*. (Papers presented at Conference on Institutional and Administrative Perspectives for National Development.) Zaria, Nigeria: Baraka Press, 1972.

Tumano, Tekena N. *The Evolution of the Nigerian State: The Southern Phase, 1898-1914*. London: Longman, 1972.

------. *Nigeria and Elected Representation, 1923-1947*. London: Heinemann, 1966.

Uchendu, Victor Chikezie. *The Igbo of Southeast Nigeria*. New York: Holt, Rinehart, and Winston, 1965.

Udo, Reuben K. *Geographical Regions of Nigeria*. London: Heinemann, 1970.

Ukwu I. Ukwu (ed.). *Federal Character and National Integration in Nigeria*. Kuru, Nigeria: National Institute for Policy and Strategic Studies, 1987.

United Nations Development Programme and the World Bank. *African Economic and Financial Data*. Washington: 1989.

United Nations Fund for Population Activities. "Nigeria: Background Report Needs Assessment for Population Assistance." (Working paper prepared for Population Council, UNFPA Workshop.) New York: October 1979.

United Nations. Centre for Development Planning, Projections, and Policies. "Implementation of Development Plans: The Experience of Developing Countries in the First Half of the 1970s," *Journal of Development Planning*, No. 12, 1977, 1-69.

------. Food and Agriculture Organization. *Atlas of African Agriculture*. Rome: 1986.

------. Department of International Economic and Social Affairs. *World Economic Survey, 1990*. New York: 1990.

United States. Arms Control and Disarmament Agency. *World Military Expenditures and Arms Transfers, 1972-1982*. Washington: GPO, 1984.

------. Arms Control and Disarmament Agency. *World Military Expenditives and Arms Transfers, 1988*. Washington: GPO, 1989.

------. Arms Control and Disarmament Agency. *World Military Expenditures and Arms Transfers, 1989*. Washington: GPO, 1990.

------. Department of State. *Country Reports on Human Rights Practices for 1989*. (Report submitted to United States Congress, 101st, 2d Session, Senate, Committee on Foreign Relations, and House of Representatives, Committee on Foreign Affairs.) Washington: GPO, 1990.

Usman, Yusufu Bala (ed.). *Studies in the History of the Sokoto Caliphate*. Zaria, Nigeria: Ahmadu Bello University Press, 1979.

Van de Walle, E. (ed.). *The Cultural Roots of African Fertility Regimes: Proceedings of the Ife Conference, February 25-March 1, 1987*. Ile-Ile, Nigeria: Department of Demography and Social Statistics, Awolo University, and Population Studies Center, University of Pennsylvania, 1987.

Vivekananda, F., and B.E. Aigbokhian. "Militarization and Economic Development in Nigeria," *Scandinavian Journal of Development Alternatives* [Stockholm], 6, Nos. 2-3, 1987, 106-21.

Waterbury, John, et al. *Fragile Coalitions: The Politics of Economic Adjustment*. New Brunswick, New Jersey: Transaction Books, 1989.

Watts, Michael. *Silent Violence: Food, Famine, and Peasantry in Northern Nigeria*. Berkeley: University of California Press, 1983.

Watts, Michael. *Silent Violence: Food, Famine, and Peasantry in Northern Nigeria*. Berkeley: University of California Press, 1983.

Wente-Lukas, Renate. *Handbook of Ethnic Units in Nigeria*. Stuttgart: Steiner, 1974.

Whitaker, C. Sylvester. *The Politics of Tradition: Continuity and Change in Northern Nigeria, 1946-66*. Princeton: Princeton University Press, 1970.

Williams, Gavin (ed.). *Nigeria: Economy and Society*. London: Collings, 1976.

World Armaments and Disarmament: Stockholm International Peace Research Institute Yearbook, 1989. Oxford: Oxford University Press, 1989.

World Bank and International Finance Corporation. *Social Indicators and Development*. Washington: 1987.

------. "Impact of Adjustment Policies on Manufacturing in Nigeria." Pages 139-42 in Gerald M. Meier and William F. Steel (eds.), *Industrial Adjustment in Sub-Saharan Africa*. New York: Oxford University Press, 1989.

------. *Nigeria: Medium-Term Development Prospects*. Washington: 1989.

------. *Sub-Saharan Africa. From Crisis to Sustainable Growth: A Long-Term Perspective Study*. Washington: 1989.

World Bank. *Accelerated Development in Sub-Saharan Africa: An Agenda for Action*. Washington, 1981.

------. *Population Growth and Policies in Sub-Saharan Africa*. Washington: 1986.

------. *The World Bank Atlas, 1988*. Washington: 1988.

------. *World Debt Tables, 1990-1991: External Debt of Developing Countries, Country Tables*, 2. Washington: 1990.

------. *World Development Report, 1982*. New York: Oxford University Press, 1982.

------. *World Development Report, 1985*. New York: Oxford University Press, 1985.

------. *World Development Report, 1986*. New York: Oxford University Press, 1986.

------. *World Development Report, 1989*. New York: Oxford University Press, 1989.

------. *World Development Report, 1990*. New York: Oxford University Press, 1990.

World Defense Almanac (Special Issue: *Military Technology*), January 1989.

World Radio TV Handbook, 1990. (Ed., Andrew G. Sennitt.) Hvidovre, Denmark: Billboard, 1990.

Zartman, I. William (ed.). *The Political Economy of Nigeria.* New York: Praeger, 1983.

(Various issues of the following periodicals were also used in the preparation of this paper: *African Business* [London]; *Africa Report*; *Africa Research Bulletin* [Exeter, United Kingdom]; *Economist* [London]; *Financial Times* [London]; Nigeria, Office of Statistics, *Digest of Statistics* [Lagos] and *West Africa* [London].)

INDEX

#

1989 constitution, 89, 165
1993 presidential election, 1, 40, 41, 44, 46

A

Abacha, General Sani, 1, 4, 6-9, 11-13, 29, 41-43, 46-48, 51, 52
Abiola, Moshood, 1, 6, 12, 33
Abubakar, General Abdulsalam, 1, 7, 8, 14, 46, 47, 52
Aburi Agreement, 112
Action Group, 18, 19, 34, 102-04, 107, 109-111, 118, 119, 150, 158
African Development Bank, 12
agriculture, 55, 65, 72, 88, 94, 95, 116, 142, 151
AIDS, 1, 4, 5, 15, 55, 82, 87, 145
Akintola, 18, 19, 22-24, 103, 109-111, 157, 159, 186
Aladura movement, 87, 136
Albright, Madeline, 3, 14
All People's Party (APP), 1, 9, 10
Alliance for Democracy (AD), 1, 9, 10
Angola, 5, 15, 31, 96, 173
Annan, Kofi, 4, 7
anti-terrorism campaign, 2, 5
Arafat, Yasser, 91
Armed Forces Ruling Council (AFRC), 163, 170, 178
armed forces, 29, 38, 49, 50, 54, 84, 92, 114, 123, 171, 172, 174, 177, 179
assassination, 20, 23, 24, 28, 29, 35, 38, 86
autonomy, 30, 34, 48, 53, 85, 94, 105, 107, 156-158, 164, 165, 172
Awolowo, Chief Obafemi, 18, 23, 25, 27, 34, 35, 38, 39, 45, 62, 101-103, 107, 109-112, 117-119, 150, 157, 158, 160, 186, 188

Azikiwe, Dr. Nnamdi, 18, 32, 35, 38, 42, 102, 103, 107, 110, 119, 157, 158, 187

B

Babangida, General Ibrahim, 6, 7, 40, 41, 42, 44, 46, 86-89, 91, 92, 122, 123, 162, 168-170, 172, 175-179, 187, 195
Balewa, Abubakar Tafawa, 18, 23, 24, 104, 108, 157, 158
banking system, 54
Benin, 17, 63, 81, 95-98, 136, 142, 155, 171, 178, 187
Berlin Conference, 85, 99
Biafran secession, 6
Bight of Biafra, 112
Britain, 6, 18, 20, 40, 83-85, 88, 96, 98, 99, 101, 108, 110, 113, 118, 149, 173, 177, 179, 190
British Commonwealth of Nations, 91, 102
British rule, 72, 85, 155
Buhari, General Muhammadu, 6, 86, 121
bureaucracy, 74, 151, 159
Burundi, 43, 44, 49
Bush Administration, 2, 13
Bush, President George, 1, 4, 5, 15

C

Cameroon, 37, 81, 85, 91, 93, 108, 125, 126, 129, 135, 148, 172, 175, 178
Canada, 64, 83, 102
Central Bank of Nigeria, 4, 120, 153, 188
Chad, 81, 91, 125, 126, 148, 172, 173, 175
chemical, 64, 82
China, 17, 37
Christianity, 85, 94, 101, 129, 132, 136, 147, 155
Christians, 5, 32, 82, 91, 122, 132, 133, 136, 137, 155

civil service, 25-27, 39, 85, 86, 102, 112, 115, 121, 131, 163, 165-167
civilian government, 1, 2, 6-8, 14, 42, 44, 50, 86, 92-94, 115, 118, 121, 162, 163
civilian rule, 1, 6, 8, 13, 14, 38, 42, 46, 83, 86, 111, 117, 118, 122, 123, 153, 154, 159, 162, 170, 172, 173
Clifford Constitution, 156
climate, 34, 67, 126, 127
Clinton Administration, 12-14
Clinton, President William, 1, 3, 4, 12-15
coalition government, 86, 107, 158, 159, 160
collective bargaining, 75, 76, 79
colleges, 57, 58, 60, 63-65, 67, 82, 141, 142
colonial era, 72, 94, 137, 140
colonial rule, 5, 18, 44, 93, 101, 131, 155-157, 160
colonization, 149, 156
Commonwealth of Nations, 84, 91, 102
communities, 20, 35, 60, 61, 68, 94, 97, 130, 148
compensation, 61, 63, 182
computer training, 64
Congo, 5, 15, 17
constitution, 8, 9, 13, 18, 30, 36, 38, 47, 53, 83-86, 89, 102, 103, 105-08, 110, 111, 117-119, 122, 131, 156, 158, 163-165, 170
corruption, 2-4, 9, 11, 13-15, 23, 24, 46, 48, 54, 58, 86, 89, 111, 116, 117, 120-122, 143, 162, 176, 177
coups d'état, 92, 162
crime rates, 176
criminal justice system, 172
curriculum, 57, 60, 64

D

Dahomey, 17
de Klerk, Frederick W., 91
decentralization of the military, 48, 50
democracy, 2, 4, 7, 8, 12-15, 38, 40, 41, 50, 52, 83, 92, 93, 111, 153, 155, 158, 160
democratic government, 89
democratic process, 52, 89, 90, 93, 117
Democratic Republic of Congo, 5, 15
democratic system, 3, 14
democratically elected president, 33, 42, 47
democratization, 4, 15
dictatorship, 40, 41, 59
discrimination, 61, 128, 130, 170
domestic discontent, 89
drug trafficking, 12, 13, 177, 178

E

early history of Nigeria, 94
Eastern Nigeria, 18-22, 26, 30, 31, 34, 36-38, 190-193, 196
Eastern Region, 19, 23-25, 30, 35, 104, 106, 109, 111-115, 158, 159
Economic Community of West African States (ECOWAS), 3, 84, 91, 168, 170, 172, 173, 175, 179, 195, 197
economic crisis, 2, 5, 122
economic development, 53, 75, 85, 86, 88, 106, 118, 120, 173
economic growth, 54, 94, 151
economic interdependence, 55
economic planning, 88
education, 4, 11, 15, 26, 27, 29, 35, 53, 55, 57-69, 82, 87, 102, 103, 106, 107, 129, 131, 132, 135, 138-141, 143, 145, 147, 154, 156, 164
Egypt, 17, 127
elected government, 14, 40, 49
elite, 7, 43, 49, 53, 101, 129, 137, 140, 157, 160, 168
Enahoro, Chief, 27, 31
energy resources, 153
entrepreneurship, 26, 74
Equatorial Guinea, 172
Ethiopia, 17, 20, 22, 23, 49, 95, 148, 173
ethnic bonds, 33
ethnic cleansing, 27
ethnic diversity, 17, 31, 51, 129
ethnic relations, 102, 130
ethnic representation, 91
ethnic rivalries, 14
ethnic violence, 2, 4
ethnicity, 61, 102, 128, 129, 131, 132, 157
Europe, 10, 64, 74, 84, 98, 99
Europe, Eastern, 74
European colonial activities, 85
European Economic Community (EEC), 83, 88, 91, 168, 181
European Union, 1, 2, 10, 11
exploitation, 61, 99, 106
extrajudicial killings, 4, 12

F

family, 4, 11, 12, 14, 23, 33, 61, 72, 134, 135, 137, 146, 152
federal constitution, 18, 38, 107, 156, 158
Federal Executive Council, 25, 107, 118, 163

federal government, 18, 19, 21-25, 91, 105, 106, 109-111, 113, 114, 116, 117, 119, 120, 130, 131, 148, 159, 160, 163-165

Federal Military Government, 25, 28, 86, 115, 163, 168, 171

federalism, 37, 156, 163, 164, 165

feudalism, 72

financial resources, 63, 69

financial stability, 68

financial support, 69

First Republic, 39, 86, 89, 118, 119, 158, 160, 164, 170, 189, 190

fiscal year, 2, 15, 88, 181

flexibility, 65, 121

food imports, 82, 88

forced migrations, 40

foreign debt, 54, 55, 92, 120, 122, 172

foreign loans, 88

foreign policy, 52, 55, 84, 168-170, 173

France, 99, 100, 113, 149, 172, 173, 179, 186, 193

Freedom Charter, 35

freedom of the press, 8, 56

fuel shortage, 11, 54

G

Gabon, 113

general elections, 160

genocide, 22, 112, 113, 114

geographical regions, 49

geography, 66

Germany, 84, 99, 100, 149

Ghana, 31, 37, 40, 95, 107, 109, 110, 112, 120, 148, 175, 178

government reforms, 164

government spending, 55, 120, 151

government, 7, 9, 12, 14, 16, 18, 20, 21, 23-25, 28, 31-33, 36, 37, 60, 63, 68, 74, 76, 79, 83, 86, 91, 97, 115, 150, 151, 153, 163, 168, 171, 185, 186, 189, 191-196

Gowon, Lieutenant Colonel Yakubu, 23, 27, 28, 32, 36, 38, 42, 86, 112-114, 116-118, 162, 166, 170, 190

grants, 15, 68

gross domestic product (GDP), 7, 11, 55, 82, 88, 106, 148, 153, 181

growth, 3, 17, 53, 54, 61, 81, 88, 96, 102, 115, 117, 119, 132, 137, 138, 140, 141, 143, 145-147, 151, 176, 183

Guinea-Bissau, 48

H

Hausa-Fulani, 6, 17-21, 29, 30, 32, 33, 35, 43, 45, 49, 130, 137, 182

health care, 55, 75, 145, 168

health problems, 87

HIV/AIDS crisis, 1

human immunodeficiency virus, 55

human resources, 58, 62, 69

human rights, 4, 9, 12, 13, 52, 154, 168, 172, 174, 179

I

Ibo, 6, 17-21, 23-28, 30- 34, 39, 44, 188, 190, 191, 196

Igbo, 48, 82, 85- 87, 93, 94, 96, 97, 101- 104, 106, 111-116, 118, 128, 130- 132, 137, 146, 155, 157, 158, 165, 185, 190, 192, 195, 198

illegal immigration, 91, 120

imprisonment, 11, 12, 19, 54, 177

independence, 5, 6, 18, 20, 22, 23, 29-32, 35, 37-39, 41, 42, 44, 48-50, 52, 53, 73, 83, 86, 89, 91, 92, 94, 105-107, 109, 112, 113, 131, 136, 138, 140, 141, 145, 153, 156-158, 163, 164, 170, 171, 173

independent electoral commission, 1

Independent National Electoral Commission (INEC), 9

industrial relations, 75-77

infectious disease, 145

information technology, 57, 60, 64

institutionalization, 53

interest groups, 39, 89, 168

internal security, 47, 118, 172, 174, 175, 179

International Monetary Fund (IMF), 9, 122, 123, 148, 151, 181, 182, 183

Internet, 15, 16, 60

intervention, 40, 54, 59, 74, 75, 85, 98, 151, 162, 173, 177

intimidation, 19, 66, 111, 176

investment, 3, 4, 13, 14, 15, 54, 61, 66, 72, 74, 88, 110, 116, 120, 123, 143, 151, 182

Ironsi, Major General Johnson Aguiyi, 21, 23-30, 35, 42, 86, 162

Islam, 31, 82, 85, 93, 94, 119, 132-135, 146, 155, 191, 198

Ivory Coast, 113, 114

J

Japan, 78, 83, 88

jihad, 85, 93, 133, 135, 155

Jos Plateau, 85, 95, 125, 126, 194

K

Kenya, 49
knowledge, 57, 59, 64, 78, 95, 134, 135

L

labor force, 144, 151, 152, 174
law enforcement agencies, 12, 177
law enforcement, 3, 12, 14, 54, 65, 176-178
leadership, 9, 10, 15, 18, 22, 25, 29, 34, 47, 50, 51, 52, 54-56, 58, 69, 91, 97, 101, 109, 113, 119, 133, 136, 140, 160, 172-174
legislation, 13, 58, 61
Legislative Council, 85, 102, 105
Liberia, 48, 91, 172
Libya, 173
local government, 59, 60, 82, 89, 104, 131, 153, 163-165
Lomé Convention, 88, 89, 181, 182
Lyttleton Constitution, 105, 156

M

Macpherson Constitution, 105, 156
Mali, 31, 148
manufactured goods, 58, 73, 83, 149
manufacturing, 64, 88, 151, 178
market economy, 75
militancy, 32
military aid, 4
military coup, 6, 17, 20, 23, 25, 26, 35, 39, 41, 42, 47, 49, 50, 94, 131, 158, 172
military government, 4, 38, 41, 47, 74, 84, 93, 112, 115, 117, 159, 162, 163, 164, 172
military governors, 23, 92
military junta, 6, 11, 12, 13, 40
military personnel, 54, 176
military rule, 6, 25, 33, 34, 38, 40-44, 47, 83, 89, 162, 164, 166, 172, 174
military tribunals, 40, 92
money, 4, 11, 32, 61, 63, 88
Morocco, 95, 102
Mozambique, 37
Muhammad, Brigadier General Murtala, 86
Muhammad, General Murtala, 86, 162
murder, 66
Muslims, 3, 5, 32, 82, 104, 129, 130, 132, 134, 135, 137, 139, 155, 170

N

naira, 55, 83, 88, 120, 123, 151, 182
national agenda, 22, 55
national army, 50
National Council of Nigeria and the Cameroons, 35, 102
National Council of Nigerian Citizens (NCNC), 18, 19, 35, 102-104, 107, 109-111, 119, 158-160
National Democratic Coalition of Nigeria (NADECO), 8
National Economic Emergency, 86, 123
National Electoral Commission of Nigeria (NECON), 6
National Party of Nigeria (NPN), 38, 39, 118, 119, 120, 121, 164
national police, 4, 84, 172, 175
national politics, 156-158, 168, 170
National Science Foundation (NSF), 68
national security, 11, 84, 121, 130, 170-173, 175, 176, 179, 180, 185, 193
national unity, 8, 41, 102, 115, 175
nationalism, 85, 100, 102, 121, 122, 175
nationhood, 56, 131
natural resources, 46, 68
natural, 8, 41, 46, 58, 68, 89, 97, 109
New York, iii, iv, 14, 16, 17, 29, 34, 41, 43, 44, 46, 47, 52, 79, 185-200
Niger Basin, 98, 99, 125, 126
Niger, 3, 11, 18, 31, 46, 81, 83, 85, 89, 91, 93, 95, 96, 98-100, 106, 113, 116, 119, 120, 122, 125, 126, 128, 133, 136, 142-144, 148, 149, 156, 175
Nigerian civil war, 20
Nigerian economy, 11, 51, 73, 74, 76, 79, 148
Nigerian Federation, 19, 29, 33-38, 42
Nigerian Medical Association (NAM), 168
Nigerian National Alliance, 18, 19, 22, 160
Nigerian National Democratic Party (NNDP), 18, 19, 22, 102, 111, 160
Nigerian People's Party (NPP), 38, 39, 119
Nkrumah, Kwame, 109
Non-Aligned Movement, 168
northern domination, 23, 26, 33, 37, 43, 44, 47, 49, 112, 157
Northern Elements Progressive Union (NEPU), 104, 119, 158
Northern Nigeria, 18-22, 26-28, 30-38, 85, 140, 189, 191, 192, 197, 199
Northern People's Congress (NPC), 18, 19, 22, 23, 102, 104, 106, 107, 109-111, 118, 119, 158, 159, 160

Nyerere, President Julius, 38

O

Obasanjo, General Olusegun, 1-7, 10, 14, 15, 29, 38, 42-47, 49, 51, 52, 86, 122, 162
oil boom, 86, 94, 119, 121, 131, 148
oil companies, 11, 116
oil exports, 11
oil fields, 112
oil imports, 11
oil prices, 87, 92, 116, 120, 123, 148, 172
oil production, 89
oil revenues, 11, 39, 40, 46, 117
opposition parties, 119, 158
Organization of African Unity (OAU), 20, 22, 23, 38, 49, 84, 91, 108, 118, 168, 170, 173
Organization of the Islamic Conference, 91, 122
Organization of the Petroleum Exporting Countries (OPEC), 40, 86, 91, 116
organized crime, 13

P

pan-Africanism, 34, 46, 100, 173
Paris Club, 3, 15, 88, 182
peacekeeping, 1, 4, 15, 91, 172, 174
People's Democratic Party (PDP), 1, 9, 10, 44, 45
police, 4, 40, 54, 65, 84, 110, 112, 113, 117-119, 122, 172, 175-179
policy initiatives, 53
political parties, 6, 8-10, 18, 19, 31, 84, 85, 89, 105, 120, 123, 130, 132, 150, 157, 158
political prisoners, 1, 7, 9, 13
political process, 13, 52, 162
political stability, 59, 111
political transition, 162, 179
Portugal, 95, 96, 113
postcolonial period, 156-158
poverty, 58
presidential elections, 6, 10, 13, 93
Primary Health Care, 82, 87
private sector, 39, 58, 62, 72-74, 138, 140, 143, 151
privatization, 9, 11, 88, 123, 148
professional training, 65

R

racial discrimination, 170
radical, 54, 58, 69, 98, 109, 110, 119, 158
recession, 86, 87, 120-123, 132
regionalism, 34, 102, 103, 105, 157, 158

rehabilitation, 54, 114
religious clashes, 2, 4
religious organizations, 66
Republic of Biafra, 20, 21, 38, 112
Retardation, 66
Richards Constitution, 105, 156
Roman Catholic Church, 136
Rwanda, 44, 49

S

Sahel, 116, 127, 182, 183
savanna, 85, 94, 95, 97, 98, 125-127, 183
Second Republic, 86, 89, 118-120, 123, 131, 163, 164, 166, 187, 190-192
Senegal, 48
separatism, 32, 34
separatist movements, 48, 104
sexual harassment, 61
Shagari, President Shehu, 118
sharia, 2, 3, 84, 91, 134
Sierra Leone, 3, 5, 15, 48, 107
slave trade, 85, 93, 95-98, 148, 149
slavery, 72, 93, 94, 98
small business, 54
social justice, 52
social life, 41, 66, 131, 133
social reforms, 1
social security, 53, 146
social services, 55, 75, 106, 146
socialism, 72, 109, 117, 150
Sokoto Caliphate, 85, 93, 98, 99, 135, 155, 199
South Africa, 4, 17, 37, 91, 113, 168, 172, 173
Soviet Union, 113, 168, 170
Soyinka, Wole, 8, 33, 34, 41, 47, 197
Special Drawing Right, 183
special education, 66
stability, 31, 41, 43, 48, 54, 58, 59, 68, 109, 111, 159, 160, 172
standard of living, 86, 91
steel industry, 120
structural adjustment program (SAP), 86, 88, 89, 93, 122, 123, 131, 148, 151, 152, 189
sub-Saharan Africa, 11, 87, 127, 137
Sudan, 49, 95, 127, 183
Supreme Military Council, 25-28, 30, 122, 163

T

Tanzania, 17, 31, 37, 113
tax incentives, 68, 151
tax system, 54
taxation, 53, 155

taxes, 54, 68, 74, 106, 151, 164, 181
technology, 61-64, 66, 142, 199
telecommunications, 75, 83, 88
terrorism, 2, 5
Third Republic, 71, 74, 76, 84, 92, 93, 154, 164, 178, 179, 191
Togo, 49, 178
trade and investment, 3, 4, 14, 15
trade unions, 72, 74, 89, 117, 131
transportation, 53, 83, 88, 91, 114, 150
tribalism, 21, 24, 25, 34, 39, 43, 48, 128
tyranny, 51

U

U.S. and Nigeria Trade and Investment Council, 3
U.S.-Nigerian relations, 12
Uganda, 118
unemployment, 2, 54, 58, 86, 87, 109, 116, 121, 123, 152
United Nations, 9, 84, 91, 108, 113, 169, 173, 181, 182, 188, 198
United Nigeria Congress Party (UNCP), 6
United Party of Nigeria (UPN), 38, 39, 118, 119
United People's Party, 110
United Progressive Grand Alliance, 19, 160
United States, iv, 1-5, 11-17, 59, 64, 67, 68, 83, 84, 88, 89, 94, 102, 113, 143, 168, 178, 179, 183, 195, 198, 199

universities, 15, 57, 58, 60, 62-67, 82, 117, 122, 129-131, 137, 141-143
urbanization, 87, 106, 137

W

welfare, 52, 53, 58, 146
Western Europe, 74, 113
Western Nigeria, 18-21, 30, 31, 34-37, 49
workers, 65, 68, 72, 86, 91, 92, 102, 116, 119, 131, 132, 136, 148, 175
World Bank, 9, 12, 81, 86-88, 115, 123, 147, 148, 151, 181-183, 188, 191, 198, 199
World War I, 5, 85, 87, 101, 102, 136, 140, 145
World War II, 85, 87, 102, 106, 140, 145
World Wide Web, 60

Y

Yoruba, 6, 10, 17-19, 21-25, 29-31, 33, 34, 39, 41, 44-46, 48, 56, 82, 85, 87, 93, 94, 96, 98, 101-104, 106, 109, 115, 119, 130, 132, 133, 136, 137, 140, 146, 147, 149, 155, 157, 158, 165, 186, 187, 189, 190, 193, 196, 197

Z

Zambia, 113